IMPERIAL BODIES

FROM THE LIBRARY OF

IMPERIAL BODIES

*The Physical Experience of the Raj,
c.1800–1947*

E. M. Collingham

Polity

First published in 2001 by Polity Press in association with Blackwell Publishers Ltd

Editorial office:
Polity Press
65 Bridge Street
Cambridge CB2 1UR, UK

Marketing and production:
Blackwell Publishers Ltd
108 Cowley Road
Oxford OX4 1JF, UK

Published in the USA by
Blackwell Publishers Inc.
350 Main Street
Malden, MA 02148, USA

A catalogue record for this book is available from the British Library.

Library of Congress Cataloging-in-Publication Data

Collingham, E. M. (Elizabeth M.)
  The physical experience of the Raj, *c.*1800–1947/E. M. Collingham.
    p. cm.
  Includes bibliographical references and index.
  ISBN 0–7456–2369–7 (hb: acid-free paper) — ISBN 0–7456–2370–0 (pbk. acid-free paper)
    1. British—India—Social life and customs   2. India—History—British occupation, 1765–1947.   3. Body, Human—Social aspects—India.   I. Title.

  DS428 .C65 2001
  954.03—dc21   00–012194

Typeset in 10.5 on 12pt Sabon by Kolam Information Services Pvt. Ltd, Pondicherry, India
Printed in Great Britain by MPG Books Ltd, Bodmin, Cornwall
This book is printed on acid-free paper.

Contents

Plates

Acknowledgements

I have incurred many debts while writing this book and it is my pleasure now to acknowledge them.

The research for my Ph.D, out of which this book grew, was financed by the Economic and Social Research Council, the Prince Consort and Thirlwall Fund, and the Holland Rose Fund. For their assistance I am indebted to the staff of the Bodleian Library, Oxford; the University Library, Cambridge, where Terri Barringer enthusiastically hunted out interesting material in the Royal Commonwealth Society Collection; and the Oriental and India Office Collections, London.

In particular I would like to thank Louise Houghton and Kevin Greenbank at the Centre for South Asian Studies, Cambridge, for making the photographic and archival collection fully available to me.

The late Master, David Crighton, and the Fellows who make up the Society of Jesus College, Cambridge, made me very welcome and provided me with a congenial working atmosphere in which to finish writing, for which I am very grateful.

Intellectually I am indebted to Partha Mitter and Carol Dyhouse, whose inspirational teaching encouraged me to go into research. Chris Bayly was a fine supervisor and has continued to give me unflagging support. He patiently read the many drafts which transformed the thesis into a book and never failed to give generously of his time and ideas. His criticism has always been constructive and I cannot thank him enough.

Many friends and colleagues have given me helpful suggestions and comments. I would like to thank Bridie Andrews, Susan Bayly, Maxine Berg, Peter Burke, William Dalrymple, Clive Dewey,

Rebecca Earle, Manuel Frey, Will Gould, Colin Jones, Polly O'Han-lon, Roy Porter, Rajit Ray, Anil Sethi, Robert Travers, Carey Watt and Phil Withington. For their assistance and hospitality in London and in India I am grateful to Aidan and Francesca Bunting, Rupert and Emma Featherstone, John and Susan Gnanasundaram and their family, Sue Lascelles, Matt Belfrage, Andrea and David Lowe and Siva and Vatsala Sivasubramanian. For support and encouragement I would like to thank John Cornwell, John Eaton, Peter and Irmgard Seidel and Mary Burwood; for sustaining tea parties I thank Will Gould, Geoff Harcourt and the other tea-party comrades, and Jude and Jessie Sargent, without whom Haworth would have been very lonely; for numerous dinners and light relief Rebecca Earle, David, Gabriel and Isaac Mond, Brechtje Post, Maarten van Casteren, Shai-laja, Stephen and Edwin Fennell, Silke Secco-Grütz and Terry Roop-naraine. My god–daughter Thea Fennell has brightened many an afternoon and weekend. Thomas Seidel has enriched both my intel-lectual and my emotional life. Without him this book would never have been written and it is dedicated to him.

The author and publishers would like to thank the following for permission to use the illustrations: Plates 1, 2, 3, 4, 5, 6, 7, 13, 14, 15, 17 and 20 are reproduced by permission of the British Library. Plates 10, 11, 12 and 16 are reproduced by permission of the Centre for South Asian Studies, Cambridge. Plate 19 is reproduced by kind permission of Colonel W. A. Salmon and the Centre for South Asian Studies, Cambridge. Plates 8 and 18 are reproduced by permission of the Syndics of Cambridge University Library. Plate 9 is reproduced by kind permission of Michael Luck.

Glossary

abdar	Servant responsible for cooling and serving drinks
alkaluk	A long coat with an embroidered bib
ayah	A lady's maid or nursemaid
baba logue	Children
babu	A respectable Bengali gentleman (although the term took on a pejorative tone when it was used to refer to Bengali clerks)
banyan	Trader or undershirt of Muslim
basun	Chick-pea flour
bhistee	Water-carrier
box-wallah	Itinerant salesman when applied to Indians (it was also used pejoratively to refer to Anglo-Indians in trade)
burra khana	Big dinner
burra sahib	Great master
chattah	Umbrella, traditionally signifying royalty
chilumchee	A brass or copper basin for washing the hands and feet
chobdar	Stick bearer, attendant on Indian nobles and Anglo-Indian officials of rank
chota haziri	Early breakfast
conjee cap	Starched nightcap
cutcherry	Administrative office or courthouse
dak bungalow	Rest-house for travellers
dak runner	Post runner
dandy	Boatman
darshan	A viewing of an august or holy person
dastûr	Custom

dhaye	Wet-nurse
dhobi	Washerman
dhoti	Man's waistcloth, worn folded, tucked and draped
durbar	An Indian ceremony involving the formal reception of guests and the exchange of gifts
griffin	Newcomer
har-carrier	Garland carrier
hookah	Indian hubble-bubble pipe
jama	Surcoat with a full skirt and a fitted cross-over bodice
khadi	Handwoven cloth
khansaman	Head servant
khelat	Gift of cloth in a durbar ceremony, symbolizing the incorporation of the recipient's body into that of the donor
khichri	Meal of rice, lentils and spices often eaten by the poor
khidmutgar	Head waiter
khurta pyjama	Knee-length tunic and baggy trousers
kittesan **bearer**	Umbrella bearer
laudal	Probably a sweet-smelling liquid, similar to rose water
mate bearer	Assistant bearer
mofussil	The provinces, country stations and districts
moorah	Footstool
munshi	A teacher of Indian languages, or secretary
mussack	Goatskin water container
nautch	Dance performed by dancing girls
nawab	Title given to Muslim gentlemen of distinction, originally a title given to a governor serving under the Emperor
palanquin	A covered litter for travelling in, carried by either four or six carriers on poles across their shoulders
peishwaz	Indian robe or gown
peon	Footman
poshteen	A skin coat worn over an *alkaluk*
pugri	A turban, often with a piece of cloth hanging down at the back to protect the neck from the sun
puja	A religious ceremony or rite
pundit	A learned man, usually learned in Sanskrit
satyagraha	Passive resistance, as advocated by Gandhi
setringee	Probably a low bench
shampooing	Massage, particularly of the head and feet

shikar	Sport, in the sense of hunting and shooting
sirdar **bearer**	Head bearer
sowar	Indian cavalry soldier
suttee	Hindu custom whereby a widow immolates herself on her husband's funeral pyre
terai hat	A soft felt hat to protect the head from the sun
thugee	The robbery of travellers by a specialized gang of thieves
tonjon	A sedan or portable chair
zenana	Part of the house reserved for the women of the family

Introduction

The British experience of India was intensely physical. From the wretchedness of seasickness on the voyage out, to, on arrival, the 'itching, unsightly bumps' caused by the 'incessant bites of innumerable mosquitoes'; the torture of prickly heat which made Ellen Drummond feel as though 'a-hundred needles' were running into her; the pain of the 'boils which break out when... [prickly heat] gets very bad'; the dry heat of northern India which 'developed finally into an obsessive torture dominating thought and talk and action' or the steamy heat of Bengal which 'takes all the strength and the succour out of you like a vapour-bath', India proved a torment to the British body.[1] All the senses were assaulted by the heat, dust, dirt, noise and smells, which could be 'Vile, foul, penetrating, body- and soul-destroying'.[2] Even worse than 'the petty annoyances of the insect race, the destructive moisture, the obtrusive reptiles... [was] the slow, midnight, wasting fever, and the quick, mysterious pestilence that walks in the noon day, and defies the power of science'.[3] The agonies of disease and the threat of a rapid death were spectres which hung over every British colonist in India. Lucretia West, after hearing of the death of a Mrs Newnham, who had taken 'Tiffen here last Thursday, had an attack of fever that night, expired last evening', was shocked to find that 'Here people die one day, and are buried the next. Their furniture sold the third, and they are forgotten the fourth.'[4] Herbert Maynard concluded 'Possibly there never was so strange and painful and wonderful and uninviting an existence lived since the world began to spin.'[5]

All Europeans, even if they escaped serious disease or death, were believed to undergo a subtle constitutional transformation.

Throughout the nineteenth century the medical orthodoxy stated that the heat of the Indian climate over-stimulated the organs of the body resulting in sluggishness and congestion. The altered state of the colonist's metabolism was made physically manifest in a sallow skin and general lassitude, in the decline in fertility among European women, and in the sickly, querulous natures of children born and raised in India. The British body's physical deterioration was complemented by an idiosyncratic appearance. The loose trousers and white waistcoats which made conspicuous those who returned to Britain from India in the early nineteenth century were replaced in the later imperial era by the equally distinctive white flannels of the sahib. Besides an altered appearance, the colonist was said to acquire an 'Asiatic' arrogant manner, the consequence of the fact that 'He has been so long accustomed to measure his own humanity by the standard of a conquered and degraded race.'[6] The experience of India was thus perceived to be written on the Anglo-Indian[7] physique, from the boils, mosquito bites and the altered composition of the fibres and tissues of the body, to the colonist's characteristic clothing and confident demeanour.

It is clear, then, that the body was central to the colonial experience, but the body, as the site where social structures are experienced, transmuted and projected back on to society, is ill-defined as a historical object. It is Pierre Bourdieu's concept of 'habitus' which has most influenced the conceptualization of the body, which is to be found in this book.[8] The habitus can be understood as a set of schemas or dispositions, acquired through the processes of socialization, which act as principles by which the individual organizes his or her behaviour.[9] Through the habitus the structures of the class-specific social world in which the individual finds him or herself are transferred into the individual.

> Adapting a phrase of Proust's, one might say that arms and legs are full of numb imperatives. One could endlessly enumerate the values given body, *made* body, by the hidden persuasion of an implicit pedagogy which can instil a whole cosmology, through injunctions as insignificant as 'sit up straight' or 'don't hold your knife in your left hand', and inscribe the most fundamental principles of the arbitrary content of a culture in seemingly innocuous details of bearing or physical and verbal manners, so putting them beyond the reach of consciousness and explicit statement.[10]

In this way social structures are transformed into patterns of behaviour, or lifestyles, shared by the other members of society with a similar habitus. Thus the habitus acts as a bridge between personality structure and social structure.

Bourdieu's concept of habitus demonstrates that the values, attitudes and ideologies of a society are literally embodied. 'Body size, volume, demeanour, ways of eating and drinking, walking and sitting, speaking, making gestures etc.' all reveal, consciously and unconsciously, the social structures as they are embedded in the body.[11] The body as an object of historical inquiry can therefore be approached through the everyday practices surrounding it. In his innovatory essay 'Body Techniques', Marcel Mauss, following the biography of an individual, mapped out a set of spheres of bodily practice from birth and the bodily techniques of infancy (e.g. suckling and weaning), through adolescence to the activities of adult life (e.g. sleep, rest, gait, posture and gesture, exercise), to reproduction (e.g. sexuality), care and adornment of the body (e.g. medical practices, washing, clothing), consumption (e.g. eating and drinking), the regulation of physical contact (e.g. touching, physical violence), followed by illness and death.[12] Mauss's spheres are neither exclusive nor comprehensive but they provide a ground plan for the investigation of the British body in India, widened by setting the body within the spatial context of urban and domestic space. The wide range of spheres brought together by an investigation into the body opens up the possibility of identifying a coherence between these different spheres on the level of cultural structures.

The study of the British body in India traces the transformation of the early nineteenth-century nabob from the flamboyant, effeminate and wealthy East India Company servant, open to Indian influence and into whose self-identity India was incorporated, to the sahib, a sober, bureaucratic representative of the Crown. This shift from an open to a closed and regimented body appears to reflect the emergence, between 1650 and 1900, of what might be termed a modern European bourgeois body. Work on early modern Europe shows that the body in this period was conceptualized as open and in flux with its environment.[13] Rather than acting as an enveloping shell, separating the internal and external worlds, the skin was thought of as open and porous.[14] Gradually this conceptualization of the body altered until by the nineteenth century the body was visualized as a closed entity which needed to be preserved intact, separate from the environment. Among the bourgeoisie the body was bounded off from the environment in line with a withdrawal of many bodily practices into the private sphere. Rituals of cleanliness were re-sited in the private space of the bathroom, the black suit and the corset restrained and disciplined men's and women's bodies,[15] and complex regimes of diet and exercise were developed which sought to train and improve the physique.[16] The result of this process of emotional regulation and discipline was the transformation of the open unaffected body of the Georgian middle ranks into a tightly regulated Victorian bourgeois body.

Michel Foucault and Norbert Elias explain this process as the consequence of the changing configuration of modern society. Setting out to overthrow the idea that since the seventeenth century European society had progressed towards an enlightened humanitarianism, Foucault argued in *Madness and Civilization* and *The Birth of the Clinic* that the medical gaze became increasingly intrusive and oppressive, defining the body through the medium of the clinical gaze as a passive object, the reality of which was prescribed by medical discourse. In *Discipline and Punish* he charted the effects on individuals of the intrusion of the gaze of the state into their lives. As the power of the monarch faded during the seventeenth century the state shifted from using the body of an offender, during the ritual of public execution, as a symbol of its authority, to imposing discipline or technologies of power, 'general formulas of domination', on all individuals.[17] Discipline was enforced through the regimentation of space and time. Space was subdivided into factories, schools and prisons, and within these institutions space was partitioned by allotting each individual a particular area correspondent to the rank he or she occupied within the hierarchy of the institution. Time was meted out in hours, minutes and seconds. The more the actions of the body were regimented within these time spans, the more exhaustively the body could be exploited. Discipline was founded on minute detail: it treated the body like a machine and moulded it into a state of aptitude or docility.[18] The disciplining of the body as a machine was combined with the regimentation of the body as a biological organism through the construction of sexuality. The control of populations combined with the disciplining of individual bodies – anatomo-politics – to produce bio-politics.[19] Thus, Foucault redefined the body as the site where political power is exercised and announced the death of the subject.

A Foucauldian approach to the body tends to conceptualize it as the passive object of discourses of power. Foucault's neglect of the body as the site where experience is felt and interpreted means that he tends to ignore the self-consciousness of the individual. This leads to the treatment of the body as an unchanging entity throughout history, always 'available as a site which receives meaning from, and is constituted by external forces'.[20] The limits of Foucault's thinking on the body can be escaped by adopting a view of discourse as the product of particular social groups with specific ends in mind. In this way 'competing regimens and images of the body' can be integrated into the discussion.[21] It can then be acknowledged that discourse does not always have the desired – or a homogenous – effect, and that individuals negotiate and draw upon a variety of discourses in the construction of their bodies.[22]

While Foucault approaches the relationship of society and the body during the period of European modernization from above, Norbert Elias approaches the relationship from a different direction. In his major work, *The Civilizing Process*, Elias argues that the monopolization of power by developing nation states, and the consequent complexity of the relatedness, and intertwining, of the effects of individual acts, was linked to changes in the personality structure of individuals. The increasing complexity of society required the individual to act in a more differentiated way. Although social control was imposed less and less by external powers, in order to succeed in a complex society the individual had to exercise self-restraint.[23] The by-product of self-restraint was the construction of an 'affective wall' between oneself and the bodies of others, as well as a distancing of oneself from one's own body, which was manifested in the refinement of many forms of behaviour, such as table manners.[24] This display of regulated behaviour functioned as a means of social differentiation.

There are many areas of difficulty in Elias's argument: the reliance on etiquette books which specify behaviour but do not tell us how people actually behaved; the emphasis on state formation, and the small amount of space which he gives to the discussion of the role of religion, the family, urbanization, the division of labour, population growth, disease, and groups within society which attempted to impose certain norms of behaviour on 'lower orders'.[25] However, the essential aspect of his work is that he links social and economic change to changes in personality structure through the concept of 'figurations'. 'Elias's hypothesis is that firstly, there are non-intentional interconnections between intentional acts, and secondly, that (at least up to now in history) these non-intentional interconnections have prevailed over the intentional meanings fabricated by people.'[26] The behaviour of individuals takes place within a structure which is created by the actions of individuals but which has implications and effects which are greater than those individual acts. Elias argues that these 'blind' structures have a dynamic of their own and that patterns and directions can be detected within this unplanned process, although it is necessary to be careful not to view the process as linear and inevitable.

On first reading, Foucault and Elias appear to be incompatible: Foucault argues that the body is defined and controlled by external forces, while Elias argues that the configuration of modern society encourages the internalization of restraints which gradually become a part of the individual's psyche.[27] Both theorists were, however, concerned with the same problem – the increasing regulation of the individual as a result of the process of modernization. Their conceptualization of the body as the locus of power struggles brings their arguments together. In fact Foucault's argument that bodies become increasingly disciplined is perhaps more convincing if we view his discourses of power as akin to the blind structures which Elias links to changes in personality structure.[28] Elias's conceptualization of figurations allows the balance of power to be seen as in a state of fluctuation, shifting and differentiated in its effect, rather than as a monolithic force.

Despite the complexity of the theoretical literature on the body, and the quantity of research it has generated, there remains no study of the European body within the colonial context.[29] This study of the British body in India sets out to explore the impact of colonialism on the bodies of its protagonists and the way in which power impacted on the bodies of those wielding it rather than its intended subjects. Members of the civil service form the core community under investigation as it was their bodies which formed the main focus of official and medical discourses about how the British should rule in India. The term 'Anglo-Indian' is used as a shorthand to refer to this official community in India. Evidence from other sections of the British community such as the military, planters and businessmen has not been ignored, but the lower orders of British society play a lesser part in the analysis due to their more shadowy role in the expression of British power.[30]

Confronted by their physical transformation in India, as well as the manifestly different bodies the Indian climate and culture shaped, the Anglo-Indians engaged in a process of defining what made a body British. Britishness in the colonial context was, then, conceptualized through a dialogue with difference.[31] The Anglo-Indians were profoundly affected by the processes of change within society in the metropole, or home country, but the transformation from nabob to sahib in India was more complex than the playing out of European developments in an exotic setting. The following chapters demonstrate that the Anglo-Indian body developed both its own distinctive signifiers and its own momentum of change.

Chapter 1 looks at the way in which the body of the nabob (and 'nabobess') was formed at the centre of debates surrounding the questions of how to rule India and how to survive in the tropics. In the early nineteenth century the British in India were able to draw upon a wide variety of sometimes conflicting discourses about suitable conduct in India. As a consequence the bodily norms of the early Company servants remained fluid, able to incorporate tensions and the existence of competing sets of beliefs and attitudes. During this period the British were open to Indian influences, and aspects of Indian practice were incorporated into the display of British power and authority as the Company servants set about projecting an image of themselves as the new Indian ruling aristocracy. Traces of India can be found in Anglo-Indian ceremonial display, in their personal habits of eating, clothing, hookah-smoking and cleanliness, and in the Anglo-Indian household, which incorporated large numbers of Indian servants and frequently an Indian mistress. Thus the British body in India developed a set of distinctive norms which marked it out as different from the British body in the metropole. Some Anglo-Indian norms such as those relating to cleanliness were even transferred back to the metropole and incorporated into the cultural fabric of Britain.

The transformation from nabob to sahib involved a process of bodily closure which forms the main focus of chapter 2. The early history of British rule in India is fundamentally the history of the interaction of structures of power as the British vied with the French, minor Indian princes, and the Emperor in Delhi in the process of establishing their dominion. As the British consolidated their hold on India the Anglo-Indian body lay at the centre of a process of what might be termed 'state formation'. Elias's theory would suggest that the increasing restraint which characterizes the transformation of nabob into sahib can be linked to the concentration of power in India in the hands of the British. Lengthening chains of interdependence stimulated the internalization of external restraints and the creation of an 'affective wall' which distanced the British body from India, as well as from itself. The political shift towards utilitarianism, changing ideas about disease and health, and the increasing commercialization of Anglo-Indian society, created a dialogue between the state, the economy and the body which resulted in a process of anglicization. In line with the political shift towards rule in a British idiom, India was edged out of the bodily practices of eating and clothing. Metropolitan signifiers of respectability were subtly transformed within the colonial context and reformulated as distinctively Anglo-Indian signifiers of Britishness. A British environment for the body was sought in hill stations such as Simla, and medicine struggled to preserve the Britishness of the

Anglo-Indian body. The Indian mistress gradually disappeared from Anglo-Indian households while relations between the British and the Indians deteriorated.

The specific conditions in India placed limits on the process of anglicization, and these limits are explored in chapter 3. Cultural change was patchy, and within the domestic sphere India continued to influence childcare practices, the layout and use of domestic space and the relationship between master and mistress and the household servants. Here the dissonance between political shifts and cultural change can be observed. This is highlighted by the impact of the Mutiny on the process of anglicization. Although it brought about important political changes, it had surprisingly little impact on the openness of Anglo-Indian domestic life to India and its influences.

In the latter half of the nineteenth century racial theory, the body and the ideology of prestige worked in dialogue together to produce the sahib. Chapter 4 examines the importance of the sahib as an instrument of British rule. While the British were still in the process of establishing their dominion, they demonstrated their authority with the partially indianized figure of the nabob. Once power was firmly in their hands with the transferral of Indian government from the Company to the Crown, they legitimized their rule by re-casting themselves as the embodiment of racial superiority, pre-ordained to rule over the Indians, trapped as they were within their racially inferior bodies. Thus, the British grounded their authority in the bodily difference between ruler and ruled, thereby ensuring that the body became the central site where racial difference was understood and reaffirmed in British India. The ruling style was re-worked and the flamboyance of the nabob was concentrated into imperial ceremonial where the relationship between ruler and ruled was symbolically enacted. The real work of government was separated off into the bureaucratic world of the office, where the civil servant stoically laboured away doing the real work of running the country.

The nineteenth-century figure of the sahib was carried forward into the twentieth century. Here, though, he became an increasingly outdated and fragile figure. The civil servant was so overburdened by paperwork that the ability of the government to make decisions was hampered. The power of the body as a symbol of prestige was gradually eroded by Indian nationalism and the Indian refusal to respond to the British with deference. British ceremony was increasingly met with hostility, culminating in the riots which broke out during the Prince of Wales's visit in 1920–1. Finally, the symbolic resonance of the Anglo-Indian official's body was fatally undermined by the violence which marked inter-racial relations and which came to a head with the massacre at Amritsar in 1919. It was revealed that prestige rested not upon physical superiority but upon physical force.

Solidified around the idea of prestige, a distinctive Anglo-Indian culture was in place by the last decades of the nineteenth century. Foucault's conceptualization of power as the driving force impacting on the body takes on a new edge in the colonial situation where the medical discourse in particular extended its power to define the body due to the threat of fatal and untreatable tropical disease. The position of the British civil servants in India as government employees also intensified the power of the official discourse of prestige to shape the British body, even within the domestic sphere. Chapter 5 explores the way in which the medical and official discourses were re-worked on the site of the body and manifested in increasingly regimented eating, clothing, bathing and sexual practices. The ability of the regimes of work, leisure, health and sexuality to regulate the body gained a sharpened significance outside Europe where they were vital in the demonstration of racial difference. After the First World War, viewed against the background of the rapidly changing political scene in India and the metropole, the social life of Anglo-India began to seem archaic. Political concerns began to break down the barriers between the races. The British were increasingly forced to work and socialize with Indians. This eroded the construction of bodily difference which prestige relied upon.

Between 1800 and 1857 changes in bodily practice kept pace with the traditional periodization of Indian history. After 1857 an alternative chronology is revealed, with changes in bodily practice shifting at different times in different spheres and, most importantly, failing to keep pace with the political changes of the twentieth century. By 1939 the Anglo-Indians found themselves culturally and bodily out of step and inadequate in the face of the political and social demands of the twentieth century. In particular they were faced with the fact that their disregard for the Indian response to the British body had severely undermined their position. Indeed, Indian responses play only a small part in this history, reflecting the curious lack of attention paid to them by the British. For the Anglo-Indians the strategies they adopted were a self-fulfilling rhetoric. As long as the majority of the Indians they came into contact with conformed to their expectations, the Indian response impacted very little upon the construction of their bodies. Aunt Fenny, in Paul Scott's *The Day of the Scorpion*, sums up the Anglo-Indian attitude: 'We have responsibilities that let us out of trying to see ourselves as they see us. In any case it would be a waste of time. To establish a relationship with Indians you can only afford to be yourself and let them like it or lump it.'[32] This arrogant assumption that they could take their impact on the Indian population for granted contributed to the downfall of the British in India in the twentieth century. Caught in bodies which represented an aristocratic concept of rule, outmoded in a newly democratic Britain as well as the India of the independence movement, the legitimacy of British rule in India was brought into question to the extent that the British themselves lost confidence in the values which they thought of themselves as embodying. As confidence in imperialism and empire dissolved, so too did confidence in the emblem of the British body. This was reflected in the ultimate Indian rejection of the British body. Under the influence of Gandhi, Indian nationalists discarded westernized dress in favour of the *dhoti* or *khurta pyjama* made from *khadi* (handwoven cloth), thus presenting the British with the challenge of a reinvented and proudly Indian body.[33]

PART I

The Nabob c.1800–1857

1

The Indianized Body

He was as lonely here as in his jungle at Boggley Wollah. He scarcely knew a single soul in the metropolis; and were it not for his doctor, and the society of his blue pill, and his liver complaint, he must have died of loneliness. ... Now and then he would make a desperate attempt to get rid of his superabundant fat; but his indolence and love of good living speedily got the better of these endeavours at reform, and he found himself again at his three meals a day. He never was well dressed; but he took the hugest pains to adorn his big person, and passed many hours daily in that occupation.[1]

Jos Sedley, William Thackeray's fat, vain, cowardly and foolish creation, is typical of fictional representations of the nabob, a term derived from the Muslim title for the governor of a district, which was applied to East India Company servants who returned to Britain with large personal fortunes.[2] By the turn of the century the persona of the nabob was firmly fixed in the public mind. He made his appearance throughout the eighteenth century in magazines, periodicals, newspapers, cartoons, fiction and plays such as Samuel Foote's *The Nabob*, performed at the Haymarket in 1772, as a figure of fun and the target of lampooners of new wealth.[3] Neither British nor Indian but a particular blend of the two, he was identifiable by his dry yellow skin; his liver complaint and consequent biliousness; his propensity to drink large quantities of wine and eat copious dinners; his extravagant attire, which generally included a white waistcoat; his fondness for smoking a hookah and, when in India, his enjoyment of *nautches* which he would attend wearing the loose clothing of the natives. He was reputed to inhabit certain areas of London – 'such is the nabobery into which Harley-street, Wimpole-street and

Gloucester-place, daily empty their precious stores of bilious human-ity', as well as spa towns where he struggled to reclaim his health, ruined by the harsh Indian climate.[4]

The nabob was to a large extent a fictional figure whose creation in Britain was stimulated by a number of Company servants who returned from India with large fortunes and social aspirations, and by the trial of Warren Hastings (1788–95) during which the behav-iour of the East India Company's government came under public scrutiny. However, the nabob was not simply a fictional character. The caricature of the Briton in India was based on the reality of Anglo-Indian life. In the late eighteenth century the British in India were faced with two vital questions. Firstly, how were they to rule India? Secondly, how were they to survive the hostile Indian environ-ment now that their role as rulers rather than merchants required long-term residence in the country? This chapter examines the way in which the dialogues which arose out of the need to solve these problems generated a range of possible codes of behaviour which the Anglo-Indians drew upon in the construction of their bodies. Firstly, the British ceremonial ruling style of magnificence and the way in which this constructed the Anglo-Indian officials as a new Indian aristocracy is investigated. In the second section the construc-tion by the medical discourse of a different, more ascetic, indianized British body is examined. Both rule and survival in an Indian idiom drew attention to the problem of bodily corruption in the Indian environment, and the implications of these anxieties for the nabob are then explored. Even greater anxiety was felt with regard to the indianization of women's bodies, and the fourth section looks at the limits placed on their assimilation of India. Finally, cleanliness is used as a case study through which to explore the depth of the indianiza-tion of the British body in India.

Rule in an 'Indian idiom'[5]

With the acquisition of Bengal in 1765, Company officials gradually replaced Indians in administrative positions and took over many of the functions of their Mughal predecessors, including the adminis-tration of law and order, the collection of revenue and the super-vision of temples and shrines. By replacing the Mughals without dismantling the Mughal structure of government the British put themselves in the position of men whom they had previously described as degenerate and despotic, whose rule they claimed had led to the decay of large regions of India. On the other hand practicality as well as the British belief in the essential conservatism of the Indian people made them wary of instigating radical change.[6] Their dilemma was solved by orientalist scholarship which, encouraged by Warren Hastings and led by the principal orientalist scholar, William Jones, uncovered a sophisticated ancient Indian culture. On the basis of this oriental scholarship, the British argued that their role as governors of India was to rediscover India's ancient laws and traditions, which had fallen into decay under Mughal rule, and to reimpose them upon India in a process which Nigel Leask terms 'reverse acculturation'.[7] In this way India's natural form of government would be restored and British rule could be cast as a benevolent form of despotism. The British likened their return of India to an ideal classical past to the actions of the ancient Romans in Greece.[8] Thus the acquisition of Indian territory by the British was legitimized by administration in an 'Indian idiom', which at the same time recalled the splendid classical past of Europe.[9] This had far-reaching implications for the British administrators, who saw themselves as a new Indian nobility and extended the legitimization of rule in an Indian idiom to the individual by adopting a range of Indian practices.

An important aspect of rule in an Indian idiom was the use of magnificent ceremony by the British. As a ruling power in India, the East India Company nominally recognized the authority of the Mughal emperor in Delhi although in reality the Company considered itself to be equal to him and other regional Indian rulers. These regional rulers were at the same time attempting to assert their own independent political legitimacy through flamboyant displays of wealth and power. This occurred most dramatically in Awadh, which actually broke with the Mughal emperor in 1819 and marked its independence by staging an elaborate coronation ceremony which combined Mughal and European symbols of power.[10] The British concluded that ceremony was as important in India as it was in Britain, where one reaction to the French Revolution had been an increase in public ceremonial by George III in order to impress the prestige of the monarchy upon the minds of the lower orders.[11] They therefore responded by creating an equally impressive backdrop of display and ceremony against which they moved across the Indian scene. With the arrival of Lord Wellesley as Governor-General in 1798 the pomp and ceremony of early British rule reached its height. The Governor-General acquired semi-royal status, surrounded by the trappings of silver-stick bearers, club bearers, fan bearers and sentries in the new setting of Government House, which Wellesley built as a more suitable residence than Fort William for the representative of

British authority in India. Lord Valentia defended the project with the argument that displays of wealth on an extravagantly Indian level were essential to the consolidation of British power.

> The sums expended upon it [Government House] have been considered as extravagant by those who carry European ideas and European economy into Asia; but they ought to remember, that India is a country of splendor, of extravagance, and of outward appearances: that the Head of a mighty empire ought to conform himself to the prejudices of the country he rules over; and that the British, in particular, ought to emulate the splendid works of the Princes of the House of Timour, lest it should be supposed that we merit the reproach which our great rivals, the French, have ever cast upon us, of being alone influenced by a sordid, mercantile spirit. In short, I wish India to be ruled from a palace, not from a counting-house; with the ideas of a Prince, not with those of a retail dealer in muslins and indigo.[12]

Display was required not only of the Governor-General but of all the representatives of the Company, especially the civilians and their families, who seeing themselves as the successors of the Mughal elite, surrounded themselves with Indian signifiers of nobility. In public they were attended by large retinues. Sophia in *Hartly House, Calcutta* felt as though she were 'a kind of state prisoner' of the climate and ceremony, fatigued by 'gaudy trappings and the pomp of retinue'. She 'sigh[s] for one delightful strole in St. James' Park, unincumbered by palanquins, kittesan-bearers, the clamour of har-carriers &c. &c.',[13] as the lady depicted in her *tonjon* in plate 1 might well have done. In the creation of a form of ceremonial appropriate to the Indian situation the British borrowed from the rituals of their own country (mace bearers and state carriages) as well as from the Mughals (elephants, stick bearers, spear-men and peacock plumes). James Campbell described how in Ceylon judges were:

> attended . . . by a band of natives, armed with lances, and are likewise surrounded by a host of tom-tom beaters, who drum away with all their might, and by a set of fellows blowing, as loudly and discordantly as possible, the most horridly squeaking pipes imaginable; thus altogether forming such a ridiculous group, that it is impossible to refrain from laughing at the kind of absurd stage effect produced. . . . but no doubt all this parade and show (so highly prized here by civilians in general), were supposed to make a strong impression upon the minds of the natives, and to increase, in their eyes, the importance of the law dignitary.[14]

Plate 1   Surrounded by pomp and ceremony. 'A lady in a *tonjon* palanquin with attendants.'

Thus the British adopted a composite mode of communication, shaped by Indian ideas of appropriate forms of display, as well as their own notions of ceremony in medieval England and the splendour of oriental magnificence.[15] This combination of oriental and occidental magnificence constructed the body of the nabob at its centre as a hybrid of East and West.

The pomp of retinue was complemented by the residences of the East India Company officials, which functioned as magnificent stage-settings imparting grandeur to the bodies of the Anglo-Indians who lived within them. Once the British moved out of the enclosure of the factories (the fortified area around the warehouses), they built themselves imposing houses in the neo-classical style in pleasant areas of the Presidency towns of Calcutta, Madras and Bombay. In contrast to simple unpretentious eighteenth-century town houses in Britain, the homes of the Anglo-Indians resembled the country seats of the English nobility.[16] J. H. Stocqueler commented that some of the buildings at Garden Reach in Calcutta were 'on a scale of much grandeur and elegance, and surrounded by extensive grounds, laid out in miniature representations of the beautiful parks of England'.[17] Although the furnishings in these palaces failed to maintain the illusion of grandeur projected by the exterior – insects and the climate did too much damage to furniture to make extravagant expenditure worthwhile – the life which the British led within their homes sustained the idea of them as a new Indian nobility. Every

Anglo-Indian household employed a large retinue of servants, indeed some Anglo-Indian households rivalled those of noblemen in Britain. Mrs Elwood observed that 'an English ménage at Bombay, . . . on the most limited scale, is far greater than those of persons of equal rank and fortune in Great Britain, and yet the Anglo-inhabitants of Bombay are as much behind those of Calcutta and Madras, in expense, and in the superfluity of servants which swell their retinues, as they exceed their countrymen at home in these particulars.'[18] Even households in the *mofussil*, where homes were much humbler, employed large numbers of servants, especially as in isolated areas small-scale farms were often attached to the house in order to provide food. Fanny Parks listed the servants required by a private family, and their pay, while she was living in Cawnpore where her husband was Acting Collector. The list is worth reproducing as it shows the possible size of an Anglo-Indian retinue and the different sorts of servants the British employed, and describes their tasks (see Appendix).[19] At the centre of such a household the body of the nabob was constructed as that of a powerful patriarch.[20]

Anglo-Indians were aware that the number of their servants would appear extravagant and unnecessary to their relatives at home. Lieutenant-Colonel Tredway-Clarke, a single soldier, who kept twenty-two servants at a cost of £17 4s. a month, excused himself thus to his sister: 'the above will appear an enormous sum to you, but I assure you it is a very reduced establishment for a Person in my situation – and there is not one Servant in the List that I could be without.'[21] Such large numbers of servants could place a burden on finances, but the British felt that they were forced to accept the situation as the caste system was understood to 'render the occupations of all perfectly distinct' so that the number and different types of tasks each servant was willing to perform were limited.[22] At the same time the British played a part in encouraging and perpetuating the complex differentiation of domestic servants. As part of their exploration of Indian society they catalogued castes and their connected occupations, including those of household servants.[23] By fixing this information through painting and the written word the British interpreted what were once fluid Indian ideas of caste and occupation as rigid sets of rules.[24] It was to the advantage of domestic servants to encourage this British perception of fixed caste restrictions as the decline of the Mughal aristocracy meant that large numbers of servants were seeking employment, and the differentiation of tasks ensured employment for the largest number possible. British influence had a similar effect in many spheres of Indian life. The British reliance on Brahmin pundits to codify Hindu law meant that brahmin concepts of Indian society were imposed on what was a less brahmin-dominated society than the British supposed. As peasant society consolidated, a more inflexible and stratified system emerged, while the employment of Brahmins in the British administration encouraged socially aspiring groups to imitate a brahminical lifestyle.[25] This colonial reconstruction of tradition, together with the Company's heavy demands for revenue from the Indian economy, brought about 'changing relations of material production and social reproduction' which altered the cultural life of India, allowing brahmins to assert and impose their notions of caste hierarchy and social privilege on Indian society as a whole.[26]

While their influence was inadvertently changing the nature of Indian society, the British were simultaneously attempting to adapt to it. The British use of ceremonial can be seen as a response to their political failings within the Indian context. Although they saw themselves as successors to the Mughals they were aware that in the eyes of the Indian population they lacked embodied legitimacy as India's rulers. The Indians knew that they were merchants and administrators, not noblemen, while from the perspective of both Hinduism and Islam they were regarded as impure.[27] In the early nineteenth century the British strove to overcome this inadequacy by constructing their bodies according to what they perceived as Indian notions of how a ruling body should look and behave. The body of the nabob was therefore a product of a dialogue between Indian and British ideas of the appropriate ruling body.[28]

The large number of servants employed by the British addressed the problem of legitimacy to some extent as they took on the character of a small, permanent durbar around the official. In the durbar, a ceremony which cemented links between ruler and ruled, the giving of *khelat* was a central element, symbolizing the incorporation of the body of the receiver into that of the donor, while at the same time signifying a bond of protection.[29] Household servants were incorporated into the body politic of their master in the same way by the cloth, liveries and badges of office which they were given. Thus a bond which had significance in the Indian context was formed between servants and their British master, and this contributed to the nabob's status within Indian society. The employment of large numbers of servants also created lines of patronage which stretched out into the surrounding community, forging a link between the Indian people and the nabob. These lines of patronage fostered economic dependence on the British, which gave a section of the Indian community a vested interest in their prosperity. This was one way in which British rule became rooted in the economic life of

India, enhancing its political legitimacy in the eyes of its subjects. At the same time British authority was limited by dependency on those Indians employed as accountants and go-betweens in commercial affairs. C. N. White, a member of the Madras Board of Revenue in 1793, was amazed that Company servants involved in revenue matters in the Madras area had neglected to learn the local languages as this would have saved them 'from the disgrace of being constantly made the dupes of intriguing servants'.[30]

While servants generated a particular form of legitimacy in the Indian context, for the British the large numbers of servants functioned more simply as impressive status symbols. As Lord Valentia's comments on Government House suggest, the British in India used the grandeur of ceremony to divert attention away from their role as 'retail dealer[s] in muslins and indigo' and the lowly social origins this implied.[31] By using display to constitute themselves as an Indian aristocracy, Company officials used India as a space where they, as men drawn from sections of British society which were no longer – or never had been – ascendant, could reconstitute themselves as persons of rank. In this way the social hierarchy which operated in the metropolis was disrupted in the colony. Studies on the social background of covenanted civilians as well as officers in the Indian army, suggest that they were drawn from the same social circle as the directors, who controlled patronage. In other words, they came from a circumscribed section of the traditional middle class (London banking and commercial families) and the landed gentry, particularly landed families from Scotland, Wales and north-western England, areas which 'must have had large numbers of redundant "gentlemen"'.[32] It would seem that, among both civilians and army officers the aristocracy, small-scale businessmen, artisans and men of the new entrepreneurial middle class, were under-represented.[33] This would suggest that, even in its earliest phase, imperialism was driven, as Joseph Schumpeter has suggested for the later nineteenth century, by declining and peripheral groups whose aspirations were anachronistic.[34] Once in India the substantial salaries of the civil servants, 'varying from £500 to £10,000 per annum, [with a]...furlough allowance and retiring annuity handsome and all sufficient',[35] allowed them to maintain a lifestyle which they could not have aspired to in Britain. This, combined with the deference with which they were met by Indians, their semi-despotic political position and the young age at which they attained positions of great responsibility, tended to encourage in them an inflated notion of their own importance.

David MacFarlan is typical of the type of man who went out to India. The son of an advocate who belonged to a Scottish landed family, he landed at Calcutta in 1816 at the age of nineteen, having spent two years at the East India College, Haileybury. Four years later he held the position of Joint Magistrate of Monghyr. Here he found himself in an extraordinary position of power over a large number of Indian subjects, and on a par with the local Indian elite. David wrote to his grandmother, 'a prince in Europe does not create half such a sensation when he moves as I do here – the landlords of estates come to meet me with offerings of valuable things... The Hindoos call me "incarnation of the deity" and Moosulmans, "your excellency".'[36] In India the usual indicators of social rank were replaced by professional position, and the civilians' position as rulers allowed them to occupy the summit of the social hierarchy, despite sharing a similar social background with the military. Unsurprisingly, their arrogance was resented by other sections of the Anglo-Indian community.

> There is a very large and excellent society at Madras, which is divided into various parties. Many of the British inhabitants affect great splendour in their mode of living, and move in a very different sphere from what they have been accustomed to in their own country. The civil servants of the Company are looked upon as the nobility of India – They assume an air of much consequence, often treat the rest of their countrymen with supercilious arrogance, and behold, with particular disdain, the profession of the sword, to which they owe all their pomp and splendour.[37]

Although the civilians styled themselves as the aristocracy of Anglo-Indian society the dominance of the official section of the community was such that the society as a whole took on an aristocratic air. The engineers and surgeons, chaplains and lawyers, who would have made up a middle-class, were so small in number that instead of forming their own social ethos they, too, adopted a grandiose manner. Even the lower orders of Anglo-Indians, the 'time-expired soldiers turned tavern-keepers,... small shop-keepers, ...European servants who had set up on their own,... sailors and craftsmen' imitated their betters to the best of their ability.[38] The aspirations of these lower sections of Anglo-Indian society, combined with the association of the Company officials with trade, did much to give the nabob the reputation of the parvenu. India was seen to invert the British social order by providing the opportunity for 'clerks' and 'pedlars' to sit on 'the thrones of Aurangzebe'.[39] This inversion of metropolitan social categories was a characteristic of colonial societies in general. At the Cape in the late eighteenth century restrictions were placed on emancipated slave women's dress as their tendency to dress as well or better than respectable women blurred social distinctions. Similar complaints were common in nineteenth-century Australia where women of all classes could afford to adopt the finery of the upper classes.[40]

One aspect of the nabob's lifestyle which marked him out as an aristocrat in India was his existence at the centre of a large number of menials employed solely for the purpose of attending to his bodily needs. On his return to Britain, a defining characteristic was said to be his swagger, which revealed him to be a man used to commanding others.[41] The Anglo-Indian did not carry his own *chattah* (an umbrella traditionally signifying royalty), this was carried by the *chattah* bearer; if he stirred more than a few yards out of doors he was relieved of the necessity of walking by the use of his palanquin; washing and dressing required little exertion on his part as he was ministered to by a bevy of attendants. One of the favourite subjects of illustrators of Anglo-Indian manners was the nabob dressing. *The young civilian's toilet*, a plate in William Tayler's *Sketches Illustrating the Manners and Customs of the Indians and Anglo-Indians* (see plate 2), shows a gentleman just out of his bath sitting in an armchair wearing a dressing gown. A servant holds up a mirror for him so that he can see whether the *sirdar* bearer is brushing his hair satisfactorily. The *mate* bearer washes the civilian's feet while a punkah boy cools him with a hand-held fan and the *khansaman* brings in his morning cup of coffee.[42] His indulged person acts as a symbol of European superiority and distinction in the same way that the French courtly aristocrat of the *ancien régime* who whiled away the hours drinking chocolate *en deshabillée* represented gentility.[43] Such pictures constructed the nabob as a person of grandeur, above the concerns of his own body, but at the same time suggested a man who was helpless without the assistance of servants. H. B. Henderson, a Lieutenant-Colonel in the Indian army, who mischievously constructed himself as a stereotypical nabob, claimed that on the voyage back to England without the benefit of his retinue of servants he could scarcely dress himself.[44] Just as the continental aristocrat was regarded with some disdain in Britain, so might the nabob be seen in his home country as a self-indulgent fop. The consumption of oriental luxuries within Britain was seen as a dangerous process which weakened and feminized the economy.[45] The Anglo-Indian morning routine of bathing and dressing which enacted the indianization of the body suggested a similar process which induced an emasculating level of indolence in its subject.[46] Realizing the unmanly image this would produce in Britain, many writers defended

Plate 2 The pampered civilian plays the part of the aristocrat. 'The young civilian's toilet.'

the habits of the nabob on the grounds of the Indian climate, which according to Thomas Williamson 'arbitrarily imposes the necessity for retaining some classes of servants, unknown in England; or at least, supposed to be exclusively attached to the convenience of ladies, and of sick persons'. Williamson justified body servants, as well as the distinctively Anglo-Indian practice of putting one's feet up on a table or *moorah* (footstool), as appropriate measures to counteract the fatigue induced by the stupefying heat. *Chattahs* and palanquins, adopted from the natives, were explained as expedient protection from the harsh sun, exposure to which could result in death. Summing up, he warned:

> We . . . must coincide with the habits of the natives, to a certain extent, if we mean to retain health, or to acquire comfort. . . . I do not mean to say that we should imitate, much less adopt, without discrimination, all we see; but it may be considered an axiom, that, by taking the general

outline of indigenous customs for our guide, if we err, it will be on the safe side. Nothing can be more preposterous than the significant sneers of gentlemen on their first arrival in India; meaning, thereby, to ridicule, or to despise, what they consider effeminacy, or luxury.[47]

Those who defended the aristocratic but dangerously effeminizing habits of the nabob on the grounds of climate were supported by the pronouncements of Company doctors. James Johnson, one of the first physicians to tackle the problem of the survival of Europeans in a tropical climate on land rather than at sea, cited the above passage by Williamson in his influential book *The Influence of Tropical Climates, More Especially the Climate of India, on European Constitutions*. He went on to defend the palanquin on medical grounds as well as that other luxurious Indian practice, *shampooing* (massage), considering them particularly agreeable to tropical residents suffering from 'languid circulation of the blood'.[48] Richard Reece, who produced *The Medical Companion for Visitors to the East and West Indies*, argued that such indulgences were necessary to keep the temperate constitution in a passive state so that the body, the functions of which would have been slowed down by the climate, would not be overtaxed.[49] Here the perceived needs of the body in the alien climate of India complemented orientalism in its construction of the nabob as an indianized aristocrat. The legitimization of rule in an Indian idiom was extended to the individual in that it justified the adoption of a range of Indian practices by Company officials. The hybrid ceremony which surrounded civilians, the retinues of servants which created ties with the Indian community while at the same time ensuring that British households were run to some extent according to Indian ideas, the reliance on body servants, the adoption of *shampooing*, palanquins and *chattahs*, all indianized the body of the Briton as part of the process of constructing the British as the legitimate ruling class within India. In this way forms of luxury and nobility which would have been seen as illicit in Europe at this time were legitimized as appropriate within the context of an Indian style of government in a tropical climate.

Survival in an 'Indian idiom'

The solution to the second question, of how to survive, was the domain of the East India Company surgeons,[50] who founded their views about tropical disease on the doctrine of environmentalism.

This approach understood the body to be in a state of constant interaction with the environment, a view summarized by Jean-Joseph de Brieude: 'The clime he inhabits, the seasons he encounters, the food he eats, the passions he indulges in, the type of work he pursues, the arts he practices, the earth he digs, finally, the air he breathes, change in different ways the humors he assimilates as well as those he exhales.'[51] The logic of this view was that different climates produced different constitutions. Climate consequently became a significant explanatory tool in the European encounter with the Orient, used to elucidate differences between occidentals and orientals. The steamy heat of Bengal was supposed to induce sloth of mind and body, while the fertility of the land provided little inducement to effort.[52] This combined with the effects of the tyranny of Mughal government resulted in a stagnant society made up of apathetic effeminate individuals.[53] Temperate climates, on the other hand, were believed to breed strong independent types, full of manly vigour.[54] Thus it was believed that the transplantation of a European constitution into a tropical environment sent it into a state of disequilibrium, leaving it vulnerable to the vicious diseases found in these areas.[55]

The debate about the preservation of the health of Europeans in the tropics therefore focused on the restoration of constitutional equilibrium. This was to be achieved through a regimen which managed what had been referred to since the days of ancient humoral pathology as the 'non-naturals' – air, food and drink, waking and sleep, motion and rest, evacuation and repletion, and the passions of the mind. Observing that indigenous peoples appeared to be more resistant to local diseases, the first East India Company surgeons reasoned that the Indian constitution was better adapted to survive in the tropical environment and that one way to preserve European health would be to try to alter, or indianize, the European frame by adjusting the management of the non-naturals. This solution had been put into practice by the Portuguese, who attempted to indianize their constitutions by adopting an exclusively Indian diet after having been heavily bled.[56] The influential James Johnson advised that the British should 'Study well the clime, [and] mould to its manners our obsequious frames.'[57] In the section of his book which dealt with regimen Johnson argued that although 'a strange medley of ludicrous and ridiculous customs' could be ignored, 'indigenous customs [were]...a useful guide to survival' and that Europeans would do well to adopt some of them.[58] Many East India Company surgeons followed Johnson's example and looked to Indian practices for inspiration. Thus, medicine reinforced the indianization of the

Anglo-Indian's body as not only did the British rule, but they also attempted to survive, in an Indian idiom.

However, the model of an indianized body which the prescriptions of the medical discourse constructed was very different from the luxurious and grandiose indianized body which the discourse of rule created. In early nineteenth-century Britain the 'underlying principle which established both the moral and the medical order' was the doctrine of temperance, while luxury and stimulation were considered to be synonymous with immorality and illness.[59] James Johnson's acceptance of luxurious and stimulating practices such as *shampooing* and the indolence of palanquins was the exception to the general rule. His chapter on prophylaxis began in the same vein as British books on regimen, with the admonition 'TEMPERANCE and COOLNESS. . . . is, in reality, the grand principle of Inter-tropical Hygiene, which must ever be kept in view, and regulate all our measures for the preservation of health.'[60] The openness of medical writers to Indian practices thus tended to be limited to those aspects of Hindu doctrine which accorded with British ideas of a moderate regimen. This highly selective British attitude to Indian practices meant that the indianization of British bodies tended to be patchy and at times contradictory. The figure created by the medical recommendations was an altogether more ascetic version of the nabob than that created by the attempt to rule in an Indian idiom.

In his discussion of a suitable diet for the European in a tropical climate, Johnson applied the principle of temperance very strictly. Having identified over-stimulation and a tendency to plethora as the greatest risk to the European newly arrived in a tropical climate he recommended a cooling vegetable diet, even though vegetarianism was beginning to be dismissed as quackery in Britain.[61] His advice was based on the eighteenth-century view of a vegetable diet as an antiseptic regimen which cleansed the bodily fluids of impurities while meat, as a stimulant, induced plethora, especially if taken in large quantities. Additional moral weight had been given to the vegetable diet by its association with Methodism.[62] In North India, as Mughal influence waned, clerical and administrative communities which had come under the influence of Mughal customs resumed more orthodox Hindu practices, and strict vegetarianism was adopted by middle-class castes attempting to raise their social position.[63] The brahminical prohibition of wine and meat, as well as the simple diet of rice and vegetables of the Hindu poor, appealed to the temperance-minded British physicians as laudable Indian customs which contributed greatly to the health of the Indian population. Johnson held up frugal Indian eating habits as an example to the

British: 'Those...who...adhere to the dictates of their religion and cast with great pertinacity, and seldom admit animal food within the circle of their repasts...are certainly exempted from numerous ills that await our and their countrymen, who transgress the rules of temperance.'[64] Thus British physicians held up Brahmins as models of suitable behaviour.

The adoption of a 'Hindu' diet was used by Thomas Medwin, who fictionalized his experience as a soldier in India, to demonstrate the extent of his fictional nabob's state of indianization. Julian 'just arrived [in Cheltenham] on furlow from Bengal', had all the characteristic features of a nabob including a tawny countenance and a weakness for 'ample potations of the juice of the grape'. He had become 'a person neither English nor Indian, Christian nor Hindu. In diet he was a rigid disciple of Brama', eating fish, rice, potatoes and other vegetables, and fruit, and looking 'upon the slaughter of a cow as only next to the murder of a human being.'[65] Suffering from a feeling of alienation in his own country, and tormented by melancholia caused by the premature death of his Indian bride, Medwin's character is a Romantic figure, recalling a Byronic hero. Shelley had also incorporated the vegetable diet into the Romantic movement in his *Vindication of a Natural Diet*, which expounded on the moral virtues of vegetarianism and condemned meat-eating due to the brutalizing effect which the slaughter of animals for food had on mankind.[66] Medwin's ascetic, Romantic model of an indianized body, comes close to the ideal nabob as constructed by the medical discourse, which regarded the brahmin dietary code as an example to the British. This ascetic brahminical code of behaviour does not seem to have been entirely confined to fictional nabobs. In her journal Mrs Fenton recorded a meeting with a version of Julian in the flesh.

> There was one circumstance which staggered my credulity; there was here an Englishman, born and educated in a Christian land, who was become the wretched and degraded partaker in this heathen worship, a General S—, who has for some years adopted the habits and religion, if religion it may be named, of these people; and he is generally believed to be in a sane mind, rather a man of ability, it makes you pause in vain attempt to account for such delusion.[67]

Most Anglo-Indians, however, took little heed of arguments in favour of the vegetable diet, and many resisted medical attempts to indianize their constitutions. David MacFarlan responded with indignation to his brother's apparent suggestion that he might adopt the frugal Hindu diet in order to preserve his health.

Man is a carnivorous animal . . . and certainly if he acquires the taste for it [mutton] in that cold climate where you live, he must much more here where the exhaustion of the substance and the spirits is so infinitely greater. . . . In short I think the conclusion is by no means, that since the Hindoos are healthy we should be so too, – give us a Hindoo constitution such as I presume they derive from their fathers and mothers, feed us upon rice all our infancy and youth up and then tell us to go on with it and not to take to flesh – but do not say to a man whose habit has been formed upon the gross food of a cold climate whose 'limbs were made in Scotland or in England either' – that he is to withdraw its customary support, you may depend upon it if he does it will all topple down and leave him but a rickety fabric with which to face again the cold blasts of the North.[68]

In fact the Anglo-Indians of the early nineteenth-century were renowned for extravagant consumption of food, especially of meat, which cost very little in India.[69] Reverend Cordiner commented disapprovingly that the arrangement of Anglo-Indian dinners was 'trusted entirely to native servants, who load them with dishes of solid meat, estimating the goodness of a dinner by the quantity which they crowd upon the board; and in most houses there is but a scanty supply of vegetables.'[70] The Anglo-Indians' eating habits betrayed their social origins, as they mirrored those of the 'country squires and parsons, doctors and attorneys' in Britain for whom 'a good dinner was still one, . . . where all the dishes were placed at once on the table – "six or seven ribs of roast beef . . . a boiled turkey . . . and an enormous ham".'[71] Cordiner went on to bemoan that the example of the natives who 'drink nothing after their meals stronger than water' was also perilously ignored as the large quantities of meat were washed down with plenty of claret and pale ale.[72] Meat-eating was, however, part of the Muslim and Rajput culture. Thus, the excessive consumption, especially of meat, which formed one of the stock images of the nabob, means that he was more commonly thought of as an Asiatic prince or a medieval baron than as an ascetic.

An Indian *burra khana* (big dinner) would have been a hot, crowded and filling affair as the crowd of diners would have been augmented by the presence of table servants. Everyone brought along his or her own *khidmutgar* to wait at table, and Williamson also recommended the attendance of the *abdar* to serve the drinks. These uncomfortable and unhealthy dining habits were endured as they served well to underline the status of the Company grandee in India, while at the same time they maintained a sense of bodily difference between the British and their Indian subjects, thus acting as a means of celebrating the nabob's Britishness despite his oriental surroundings. In particular the beefsteak clubs of India were reminiscent of the beefsteak clubs of eighteenth-century England where the members celebrated their Englishness in a hearty fashion. *The Englishman* reported on such a club's monthly meeting in Meerut in 1834: 'The members of the Club, and their guests sat down to an excellent dinner, but the beefsteaks and oyster sauce (such sauce!) claimed a greater degree of attention than any of the delicacies with which the table was covered! There was lots of singing...the party broke up at 2 o'clock.'[73]

The majority of Anglo-Indians appear to have favoured a morally reprehensible 'hot' diet based on stimulating meat, spicy Indian food, brandy, and strong wines and ale, revelling in levels of excessive consumption which would have been regarded as detrimental to the moral economy in Britain. While these food habits contributed to the image of the British in India as a wealthy elite, they also emphasized the danger of corruption inherent in the codes of behaviour current in Anglo-Indian society. The risk of effeminization as a result of the luxurious use of body servants was combined with the threat of developing an internal morbid condition brought on by over-stimulation. This association of the nabob – in his manifestation as an Indian aristocrat – with the dangers of bodily corruption, was intensified by the reputation that Anglo-Indian society acquired for vices other than that of gluttony.

The dangers of indianization

It was feared that the entertainments of the young and inexperienced writer or cadet in India were likely to lead to moral and bodily degeneration. Horses, curricles and extravagant parties meant that many young men soon fell into the trap of living beyond their means. According to Lord Valentia gambling, both at cards and on horses, was the worst source of debt: 'there are a few steady and practised gamblers, who encourage every species of play among the young servants of the Company, and make a considerable profit by their imprudence. As those are marked characters, I wonder they are not sent away.'[74] The Presidency towns were considered the worst centres of idleness and dissipation, but cadets in military cantonments faced long hours of ennui shut up in their bungalows during the heat of the day and George Spilsbury, a military surgeon, described how the resultant boredom gave 'rise to loo parties, an amusement that was very prevalent here in the Rains', when 'a sub of something less than 300 Rs a month would frequently lose in that period a little more or less than his pay at an anna ($\frac{1}{16}$ of a Rupee) to fish.'[75]

Out in the *mofussil* officers and civilians alike were also able to hunt. The image of the Briton out with his gun counteracted that of the fop who could not pull his own boots on and off. William Tayler's sketch of *The young civilian's toilet* compensates for the present indolence of its subject by showing a racket, saddle, boots and a gun case, littering the room, all of which, plus the dog by the side of his chair, 'shew that our hero is a sportsman'[76] (see plate 2). Hunting on a grander scale allowed the nabob to take on the mantle of royalty. Company officials saw an invitation to accompany an Indian prince on a hunt as an opportunity to demonstrate the equal standing of the British and the Indian nobility. Sport could be used to further legitimize the political position of the British as rulers in India as, by hunting dangerous animals like the tiger, they were able to cast themselves as the protectors of the Indian peasant. Blood sports counteracted the image of effeminacy and promoted the young officer's position as a ruler, but this was undermined by the association of sporting parties with a level of heavy drinking 'to be severely depreciated'. Apart from the risk of ill-health, over-consumption of alcohol was said to lower the British in the eyes of the Hindus, among whom 'drunkenness is in general very much detested'.[77]

The addictive pleasures of alcohol, which it should be noted were not confined to sportsmen,[78] were complemented by those of tobacco. During the eighteenth century the British in India learnt how to smoke the hookah. The habit eventually became so essential to the Anglo-Indian identity that hookah-smoking was one of the first techniques which the 'griffin' (newcomer) was required to master in order to become fully integrated into Anglo-Indian society.[79] Even women were known to enjoy a whiff, although some were irritated by the bubbling, the smell and the ungentlemanly habit of smoking before the ladies. Thomas Williamson complained that 'many gentlemen...give themselves up, almost wholly, to the enjoyment of smoking. Some begin before they have half breakfasted; whiffing away, with little intermission, till they retire to rest: I know not of any custom which becomes so habitual!'[80] Charles D'Oyly can be seen 'whiffing away' at his hookah while he watches opium being weighed in his sketch of himself (see plate 3). Here he cuts the figure of a stereotypical nabob in his coloured coat and white trousers, with a hookah and *chattah* behind his chair. The hookah provided opportunities to enhance one's status with silver attachments, expensive tobacco and a special servant employed solely to service the machine. The medical view of tobacco as a stimulant inadvisable

Plate 3 Charles D'Oyly, a typical nabob with his coloured coat and white trousers, and the hookah and *chattah* behind his chair. 'Sir Charles D'Oyly seated at a table smoking a hookah, his clerks seated nearby, watching opium being weighed.'

in large quantities in a climate where an anti-inflammatory regimen was advocated meant that it was condemned as a low habit. George Spilsbury added hookah-smoking to the list of dissipations which men resorted to in order to pass the time, and recommended reading and drawing as more suitable occupations.[81] Disapproval was strengthened by the association of the hookah with other disreputable practices. Thomas Williamson knew of 'one or two gentlemen' who indulged in the 'folly' of incorporating opium into the tobacco of the hookah, which he assured his readers was 'attended with the utmost degradation'.[82] The smoker was also at the mercy of his servant, and Fanny Parks knew of *abdars* who had administered thorn-apple in the hookah, an overdose of which resulted in delirium.[83] The use of intoxicating drugs was not viewed in the early nineteenth century with the same disapprobation as it was by the end of the century; for example James Mackintosh, Recorder of Bombay (1804–11), is known to have frequently taken laudanum for reasons of pleasure rather than health. But smoking rather than eating opium was regarded as a peculiarly oriental habit, and this added to the disreputable image of the hookah as a luxurious means of stimulation which assimilated India into the persona of the nabob.[84]

In addition to gambling, drinking and smoking, the heat in India was said to stimulate the sexual drive, leading young men into the dangerous area of sexual temptation. Lord Wellesley warned his wife that 'this climate excites one sexually most terribly', and threatened her with adultery when she stubbornly refused to join him in India.[85] The scandal of the court case arising from Francis Grand's allegation that Phillip Francis had been discovered sneaking out of his beautiful French wife's bedroom by means of a ladder at the window seemed to confirm the laxity of Anglo-Indian sexual morals.[86] Each Presidency had its share of taverns where low life and prostitution might be sampled. Thomas Williamson warned 'nothing can be more dangerous than this irregular indulgence; it never failing, first to drain the purse, and, in a few days, or weeks, the constitution also.'[87] An associated Indian form of entertainment which the Anglo-Indians took to with enthusiasm was the *nautch*. Rather than dance themselves, the Indians preferred to watch specially trained dancing girls who were often also courtesans. William Huggins mentions *babus* (Bengali gentlemen) whom Europeans visited, in order to 'indulge with dancing girls, music, and perfumes'.[88] While George Hadley reported 'When a gentleman gives an entertainment, he often gives a dance (nautch) performed by dancing girls.... The entertainer generally compliments his guests with the liberty of chusing their partners for the night.'[89] As it was popularly believed that sexual excess could lead to 'lassitude, weakness, numbness, a feeble gait, ... [and] effeminacy', all of which the climate alone did much to induce, India offered many different ways by which the European might reduce himself to a state of physical and moral corruption.[90]

On a more respectable level *nautches* provided a meeting point for Indians and Europeans. In the Presidency towns wealthy Indian figures who wished to entertain the British socially would invite them to a *nautch* or the celebrations of a religious festival.[91] But it was in their role as Residents, representing the Governor-General at the Indian courts away from the Presidency towns and the cantonments, that the British mixed most with Indians and learned to appreciate Indian forms of entertainment. Johann Zoffany's painting of *Colonel Mordaunt's Cock Match* (1786) shows British residents of Lucknow mixing sociably with the Indians at Asaf-ud-Daulah's court. Some men at the Indian courts used their comparative isolation from British society to adopt a semi-Indian mode of life. A painting, probably of David Ochterlony, Resident at Delhi (1803–6 and 1818–22), depicts him enjoying a *nautch* seated on the floor in Oriental fashion, in native dress, his hookah close by.[92] William Fraser, Assistant to the Resident at Delhi (1806–11), wore the 'dress of the country – a pair of loose drawers and a sort of morning gown cut in the native fashion called the ungurea', ate vegetarian food in the style of Medwin's nabob, wore long native-style moustaches and appears to have kept an Indian mistress at a village not far from Delhi.[93] A number of men acting as Residents married or lived with high-born Indian women and had their relationships celebrated in paintings of themselves with their Indian wives and children.[94] By integrating the Englishman into the extended family of his wife these relationships created a bond between British and Indian society. However, James Kirkpatrick's relationship with Governor-General Wellesley became severely strained as a result of his alleged seduction of the granddaughter of a respectable member of Indian society at Hyderabad. The resulting struggle between Kirpatrick and Khair un Nissa's family was seen to lower the British in Indian eyes. Kirkpatrick eventually married Khair un Nissa and they had two children.[95]

The British Residents at Indian courts, living in comparative isolation from the rest of the Anglo-Indian community, demonstrated the greatest openness towards Indian society and its customs, but nearly all Company officials assimilated India into their bodily practices to some extent. Whether it was in their use of servants to aid them in washing and dressing, their love of *shampooing* or the hookah, their association with a native woman, the abundance of food with which they loaded their tables, or even in their almost brahminical temperance, one way or another India was integral to the bodily practices of every Anglo-Indian. In the colonial context, where the British found themselves in a position of power with regard to an alien people, this appeared to be an appropriate adjustment to circumstances. By allowing India to infiltrate the norms which governed his relationship with his body every Briton in India engaged in a process which made India his own country. The indianization of the Englishman also created an affinity between himself and his subjects. However only certain Indian bodily practices were assimilated, limiting and controlling the process of exchange between the two cultures. For example a mongrel tongue developed among old hands, who interlarded their sentences with Hindi words, but Anglo-Indians tended to learn Indian languages only as languages of command, leaving a large part of one of the central elements of Indian culture untouched.[96] India was allowed to shape the body of the Anglo-Indian but only as long as it did not overwhelm it or make it unrecognizable as an essentially British body. In the same way that Thomas de Quincey could describe his ingestion of opium as a form of inoculation against the terrifying spectre of the Orient, the integration of the Orient into the persona of the nabob could be seen as a protective mechanism.[97] It was integral to the process of making India a British possession but it was controlled so that India was not allowed to encroach too far on the Britishness of its rulers.

A similar process can be observed in Europe where the Orient, interpreted as an exotic and exciting world, was incorporated into the culture as a fashion commodity. After Napoleon's Egyptian campaigns in 1798, crocodile bonnets were all the rage in Paris and London, and a fashion for turbans also developed.[98] Nigel Leask argues that this assimilation of the Orient was a way of neutralizing fears which the encounter with a strange, and therefore potentially threatening, world aroused.[99] The jumble of oriental features incorporated into fashionable life formed a heraldry of the Orient which symbolized and celebrated its conquest by the West. Indeed, the orientalist project to recover an ancient and glorious Indian past which would be reinstated in India through British rule defiantly equated the subjugation of the colonies with 'the imperial triumphs of the classical world'.[100] The adoption of Oriental habits by the Anglo-Indian could therefore be interpreted as a glorification of British achievements in India.

The level of assimilation which was permissible, and even regarded as necessary within the Indian context, aroused anxieties. Assimilation of the Orient might slip into infatuation; a dose of the exotic might become an infection rather than an inoculation. The trial of Warren Hastings did much to stain the East India Company with a reputation for corruption, and the baseness of the Indian body politic was perceived to have filtered down to the level of the bodies of the individual officials. During Hastings' trial Edmund Burke drew on the stock of images used to defame the Mughals to discredit British rule in India, conjuring up an image of the nabob as an Eastern despot, inextricably linked in the European mind with femininity, corruption, cruelty and decadence.[101] Medical environmentalism reinforced the idea of an indianized European body as diseased. The nabob as a hybrid of East and West was primarily the product of cultural miscegenation, but, according to the environmental doctrine, the adaptation of the European constitution to the Indian climate could be interpreted as a process of degeneration into a state of physical miscegenation. The hybridity of the nabob aroused fears that a racially impure and socially inferior creole community would develop in India as it had done in South America. A print of the returned nabob, Paul Benfield, entitled *Count Rupee in Hyde Park* (see plate 4) depicts him as so tainted by his contact with India that his skin has turned brown, while his venality explains his 'title'.

Plate 4 The Company servant has been so corrupted by India that his face has turned brown. 'Count Rupee in Hyde Park.'

Unsurprisingly, the nabob who returned to his native country and who aspired to membership of the British ruling class by building a large country house and seeking a seat in parliament, was met with hostility. As late as the 1820s the Company civilian was portrayed as a miniature Indian tyrant. William Huggins wrote of civilians:

> From a long residence in India, they are deeply imbued with its manners, and acquire something like the pride of nabobs, in their notions of self-importance. Accustomed to a luxurious style of living, which equals that of noblemen in England; to authority over a numerous population; to flattery and submission from underlings, they often acquire a despotic habit of thinking and acting, totally inconsistent with genuine freedom.[102]

Regarded as arrogant parvenus whose fortunes represented ill-gotten gains, upper-class British society deeply resented the intrusion of these upstarts into its domain. A threat to the established social order, they were accused of introducing oriental corruption into British political and economic life.[103] In Samuel Foote's play *The Nabob*, Sir Matthew Mite, the nabob of the title, attempts to outwit an old landed family with the force of his wealth. Sir John Oldham, having borrowed money from Sir Matthew, is entirely at his mercy, and Sir Matthew threatens to mortgage Sir John's estate and marry his eldest daughter. The Oldhams are rescued by Sir John's brother, Thomas, a merchant who Lady Oldham had always looked down upon for being associated with trade.[104] In the end honest British wealth wins out over that of the corrupt colonial. Just as oriental goods were seen to usurp British goods and to introduce an immoral love of luxury into British society, returned Company officials were seen as the agents of excess and ignominy.[105] The play even shows Sir Matthew considering the logistics of setting up a seraglio in London, although he is warned that in a free country the ladies might object to being confined to the house.[106]

His intimate identification with the Orient left the nabob out of place in his native country. The bodily norms of the British in India were seen to re-construct their bodies to such an extent that ordinary civilians worried about the reactions of their families on their return. Frederick Shore wrote in a letter to his sister:

> I do not wish to give way to these Indian customs, which are in fact nothing but the customs of laziness, and it is by giving way to these sort of bad habits in this country, that people find themselves uncomfortable when they get back to England, but I keep up as much as possible all English customs, so that when I come to see you all again I hope you will find me just as much of an Englishman, as I was before I left it.[107]

Although it was no longer possible to make vast fortunes, Indian officials could live well above the social rank which they held in Britain and enjoy comforts and luxuries which would have been unavailable to them there. But in addition to the terrifying prospect of contracting a tropical disease and the risk of premature death, they had to pay the price of bodily corruption and disapprobation within the metropolitan country for the privilege of becoming a nabob.

The limits of indianization

Women were also perceived as being corrupted by India. Their rosy complexions faded and turned sallow, an outward manifestation of the inner deterioration of their constitutions. Like the men they were regarded as parvenus, lower-class women in search of husbands who would afford them a better life than they could ever have aspired to in Britain. The reputation of Anglo-Indian women was helped little by books such as Henry Frederick Thompson's *Intrigues of a Nabob*, which revealed that the woman who passed herself off as his wife in Calcutta society was in fact his mistress and had been a prostitute before accompanying him to India.[108] Mrs Fenton, travelling in India in the 1820s, regarded these upstart women with scorn and remarked with disdain of a woman who claimed that she could not put on her stocking without the assistance of her ayah that she 'seldom had any to wear before she came to India'.[109] Nevertheless, women made up such a small proportion of the British population in India that a clearly defined image of a female counterpart to the nabob never really emerged. Marian Hastings came closest to what might be termed a 'nabobess'. Having amassed a substantial private fortune in India, she acquired a reputation for a vulgar love of money and display. With her splendid clothing and jewellery, on which she spent vast amounts, and her auburn hair unpowdered and loose down to her shoulders, she made a very good nabobess.[110]

The lack of a rounded image of a nabobess makes a pamphlet bringing together a series of letters on the subject of European women's dress, first published in a Calcutta newspaper under the pseudonym B. C., of particular interest. It represents a rare attempt to integrate European women into the process by which the European body was transformed within India. The author of this unusual pamphlet, entitled *The Ladies' Monitor* and published in 1809, was Charles Stuart, an eccentric officer in the Company's Bengal army, who became known as 'Hindoo Stuart' due to his sympathy for and interest in Hinduism.[111] In *The Ladies' Monitor* his main argument is that European ladies should 'throw away their whalebone and their iron, and adopt the *Indian corset*' and the *peishwaz* or Indian robe.[112] In attempting to integrate women into the process of indianization, Stuart thought through the implications of orientalism for the European body to their logical end, but at the same time he revealed the limits of orientalism as a discourse which justified the adoption of Indian manners. He argued that Indian women in their flowing robes reminiscent of those worn in Greece and Rome recalled the classical virtues of grace and harmony. The image of the graceful Indian girl was used as a metaphor for the India of the distant past. By adopting Indian clothing British women would, like the nabob himself, reinvigorate British culture by reintroducing to Britain the charm of the classical past while at the same time celebrating the conquest of the Orient. The adoption of the neo-classical style of dress by the fashionable French women of the Directory period was also invoked to reinforce the argument.[113] White muslin dresses worn with scanty flesh-coloured underwear symbolized the revival of ancient Greek republicanism in modern France.

> Here lighted lustres reflect their splendour on beauties dressed *à la Cléopatre, à la Diane, à la Psyché*;...I know not whether the first of these dancers have any great affection for the republican forms of the Grecian governments, but they have modelled the form of their dress after that of Aspasia; bare arms, naked breasts, feet shod with sandals, hair turned in tresses around their heads by modish hairdressers, who study the antique busts....The shift has long since been banished, as it seemed only to spoil the contours of nature; and besides, it was an inconvenient part of dress...The flesh-coloured knit-work silk stays, which stuck close to the body did not leave the beholder to divine, but perceive, every secret charm. This is what was called being dressed à la sauvage, and the women dressed in this manner during a rigorous winter, in spite of frost and snow.[114]

This defiantly revealing style of dress, a reaction to the puritanism of Jacobinism, was interpreted in Britain as confirmation of the want of propriety in post-revolutionary French society. Stuart used the interplay of differences between the Europeans themselves to complicate the juxtaposition of Britain and the Orient, by playfully using India as a vehicle for the covert introduction of republican bodily ideals into Britain.[115]

Just as the French Thermidorians sought to 'bring nature into the public realm',[116] *The Ladies' Monitor* allied Nature with classicism in the crusade against the stiffness and fussiness of British women's dress. The long, nipped in waists and corsetry of female fashion in Britain was not only restrictive and inelegant, it suggested artifice by the way it disguised the natural female form and moulded it into a fashionable shape. Stuart declared that the purpose of dress was rather to exhibit 'the human frame, as nearly as possible, in the perfection of Nature'.[117] In the same way that European deists used their admiration for what they saw as the rationalism of Asian belief in order to criticize religious orthodoxy at home, Stuart used the simplicity and naturalism of Indian attire in order to attack the artful nature of British fashionable society.[118] He attributed the beauty and proportion of Indian women's forms to the fact that they allowed nature to take its course, only aiding it by frequent ablutions and constant exposure to the air. They never compressed their bodies with unnatural ligatures.[119] Thus, by rationally following the dictates of nature, Indian women's dress celebrated the work of God by exhibiting 'those charms that the bounty of heaven hath so liberally bestowed' upon them.[120]

Stuart's crusade to free the female body of its creaking stays and to clothe it in a flowing robe so that its full grace and beauty might be appreciated as nature had intended was part of an attack on the superficiality and dishonesty of fashionable society and an attempt to subversively introduce republican bodily ideals into Britain. On the other hand, his focus on the female body as the symbol of fashionable artifice was not entirely innocent. It allowed strong sexual undercurrents to run throughout the text. Stuart's frequent disquisitions on Hindu beauty demonstrate his appreciation of the charms of Indian women, and he clearly hoped to transform the British female into an equally desirable sexual object: 'the Hindoo female, modest as the rosebud, blushing at the approach of the amorous sunbeams of the morn, bathes completely dressed . . . and necessarily rises with wet drapery from the stream. Had I despotic power, our fair ones should soon follow the example; being fully persuaded it would eminently contribute to keep the bridal torch for ever in a blaze.'[121] Here the cracks in his argument begin to show. In the Romantic literature of the West, India was used as a space where the imagination might run riot, where the respectable reader might succumb to the attraction of voluptuous, soporific pleasures without challenging the social mores which simultaneously condemned such licentiousness.[122] Following this convention, Stuart used the Orient as a space where he could play out his fantasies. He pictured himself as the despotic oriental ruler with women freely at his disposal. The point of essential difference is that rather than confining himself to fantasies of Indian women, by arguing for the indianization of the European female he was able to transpose his fantasy onto British women.

It is here that Stuart's argument becomes untenable. The dangers inherent in the indianization of the male European body were counterbalanced by the opportunity this provided for self-aggrandizement as well as a symbolic glorification of Britain's cultural heritage and overseas achievements. But for a woman, such an effective indianization of the physique as Stuart envisaged would leave her unprotected by the European rules governing sexual relations which served to preserve a woman's honour. Even Stuart was prepared to acknowledge that white skin revealed by Indian attire might prove so inflammatory that decorum could break down:

> We must not . . . overcharge the scale: – the blooming fruit, so tempting to the eye, viewed through the medium of a Brahmin robe, would make the heart run riot with desire, – 'and in sweet madness, rob it of itself,' till, all surcharged, the overflowing sense of exquisite delight, might,

hapless, urge our youth to force those, yet too feeble, barriers wisely erected by a sense of public decency, to guard the fair 'from the rash hand of bold incontinence'.[123]

A British woman in Indian dress laid herself open to the same sexual gaze which European men cast on Indian women. A nabobess therefore faced the risk of degenerating to the level of the Indian mistress. Thomas Williamson confirmed that when women tried the experiment of 'adopting the entire costume of the natives; a circumstance which, however gratifying it may have been to themselves, [it] by no means raised them in the estimation of those whom they imitated; while, at the same time, it gave birth to opinions, and occasionally to *experiments*, by no means favourable to their reputation.'[124] Although a minority of British women may have experimented with the adoption of full Indian dress, there were good reasons why this did not become common practice.

Even at the masquerade, one arena where it was permissible for respectable men and women to don outlandish and outrageous costumes, the restrictions which prevented women from following Stuart's advice also applied. Men often wore authentic oriental costumes which they brought back from their travels as souvenirs. At a masquerade given for the King of Denmark in 1768 'the Duke of Northumberland appeared in a Persian habit with a turban richly ornamented with diamonds.... An East India Director was dressed in the real habit of a Chinese Mandarin.'[125] Similarly, Captain John Foote celebrated his Indian connection by having himself painted in an Indian *jama*, shawl and sash which he brought back to Britain with him.[126] Women, in contrast, were only able to incorporate the Orient into their personas in a more limited and restrained way by adapting oriental costumes to the styles fashionable in Europe. At the masquerade for the King of Denmark, Mrs Monckton cast herself as an Indian sultana not by wearing authentic Indian dress but by wearing 'a robe of cloth of gold and a rich veil.... embroidered with precious stones, [with]...a magnificent cluster of diamonds on her head'.[127] More popular were the baggy trousers worn under a smock or gown of the Turkish costume, and dresses made of embroidered Indian muslin, or gauze, in a cross-over style with a sash, often complemented by a jewelled headdress or turban, which were accepted as respectable imitations of Indian dress. It was this style which Anglo-Indian women often wore in portraits celebrating their connection with the East.[128]

Resistance to Stuart's call for the adoption of the loose flowing robes of the Indians was firm, despite the fact that similar calls were made by Company surgeons. British doctors at the turn of the century also disapproved of tight-fitting, stiff, unventilated clothing, and they can be found making appeals to classicism similar to those made by Stuart. Hugh Downman's didactic poem on *Infancy or the Management of Children* held up the dress of the ancient Greeks as an ideal to which contemporary dress should aspire.[129] The new medical understanding of the skin as a permeable membrane which needed to be kept clean and supple so that it would remain pervious to the air, led Company surgeons to view the flowing robes of India as compatible with a suitable regimen for tropical climates. If we return to James Johnson, we find him adamantly recommending native vestments and bemoaning the fact that few Europeans actually adopt them.

> The necessity which tyrant custom – perhaps policy, has imposed on us, of continuing to appear in European dress – particularly in *uniform*, on almost all public occasions, and in all formal parties, under a burning sky, is not one of the least miseries of a tropical life! It is true, that this ceremony is often waved, in the more social circles that gather round the supper-table, where the light cool, and elegant vesture of the East, supersedes the cumbrous garb of northern climates. It is certainly laughable, or rather pitiable enough, to behold, for some after each fresh importation from Europe, a number of *griffinish* sticklers for decorum, whom no persuasions can induce to cast their *exuviae*, even in the most affable company, pinioned, as it were, in their stiff habiliments.[130]

Where once 'Gentlemen studied *Ease* instead of *Fashion*; [and]... even the Hon. Members of the Council met in Banyan shirts, Long Drawers... and Conjee... caps', by the first two decades of the nineteenth century only a few old hands still wore the loose drawers and baggy chemise of the Indians during the day, and most men wore them only in the privacy of the bedroom or when relaxing on the verandah in the morning.[131] By the 1810s the days when men like William Fraser, comfortable in his Indian garb and eccentric moustaches, were a normal part of Anglo-India were on the wane. Williamson claimed that 'the same kind of ridicule attaches equally to gentlemen, who at times allow their whiskers to grow, and who wear turbans, &c., in imitation of the Mussulmans of distinction', as it did to women in Indian dress.[132] At the turn of the century the greatest concession most Anglo-Indians were willing to make to the climate and medical opinion was the adaptation of their European dress. The broadcloth and woollens of formal wear were cast off in favour of white linen jackets, waistcoats and trousers even on semi-formal occasions: 'In many instances, these evening visits are paid in a very airy manner: coats being often dispensed with; the gentlemen wearing only an upper and an under waistcoat, both of white linen, and the former having sleeves. Such would appear an extraordinary freedom, were it not established by custom.'[133]

Women tended to wear very loose clothing in private and would even (as would have been much to the *Ladies' Monitor*'s satisfaction) abandon the corset and other superfluous and heavy underwear. In public they were willing to integrate India into their dress in the form of cool Indian muslin. This fabric worked in gold and silver was very popular between 1790 and 1810 as it fitted in well with the glittery Regency taste. Indian beetle-wing embroidery was also regarded as a beautiful curiosity, while cashmere shawls were very desirable and expensive both in Britain and in India.[134] Clearly, British women were more susceptible to Indian cloth and styles as fashion commodities than as a means of preserving health. This was the level at which the conquest of India could be celebrated. The adoption of Indian-style clothing for medical purposes would have suggested a deeper level of Indian integration into British bodily practices. Men could still adopt outlandish modes of behaviour and undergo a high level of indianization without entirely discrediting themselves but orientalism generated a smaller range of behavioural codes for women, who were never able to assimilate India into their persons to the same extent. Although Fanny Parks's interest in India extended to more than the use of Indian materials in dressmaking, leading her to travel up and down India 'in search of the picturesque', the assimilation of India into her own person was necessarily confined to an enthusiasm for tasting Indian dishes, learning how to play the sitar and the adoption of Turkish dress.[135] In fiction a lady was able to fall in love with a brahmin and 'convert' to Hinduism, but only as long as this was presented as a drawing-room flirtation.[136] It was not simply the question of propriety which checked women's behaviour. Women's position in British society as the repositories of morality meant that within India they acted as the ultimate symbols of western refinement and high culture or as the primary indicators of the civilized state of the West.[137] This would no longer be effective if they were indianized. Women's role within the creation of a British self-identity placed greater restrictions on them and stunted the development of the nabobess.

The limits placed on the transformation of women into nabobesses would seem to affirm Percival Spear's contention that what the British 'borrowed from India were the excrescences of Indian customs and not their essence'.[138] Indeed there were clear limits to

British openness to Indian influence. The British were most willing to take from India those practices which harmonized with their idea of themselves as Indian rulers or which accorded with the medical discourse of temperance. Thus, it might be argued that only those practices for which the levels of tolerance required were already present among Anglo-Indians were incorporated into the culture. This qualifies the main thrust of the argument, that the bodies of the early nineteenth-century British in India were remarkably open to Indian influence. Although the nabob was seen to carry the seeds of degeneration in his person, the British were anxious that India should not be allowed to entirely subvert their Britishness. The fact that in certain spheres the British were indianized can even be said to have heightened the Britishness of the body in those circumstances where India was excluded from Anglo-Indian practice; when, for example, the officer was on parade in his British uniform. Despite Indian mistresses and friendly social intercourse with local magnates, the British were careful to preserve a barrier between themselves and the Indian population. While the retinue of servants constructed the nabob's body as a politically hybrid entity, legitimizing the Company official's ruling status by Indian as well as British means, the bevy of peons, stick bearers and umbrella carriers also formed a protective wall around the body of the nabob when he ventured out into public. The reliance on *munshis* (secretaries) as intermediaries between themselves and other Indians ensured that the British only came into contact with certain more desirable sections of the Indian population. A brusque manner, which Bishop Heber was told contrasted with the 'more conciliating and popular manners' of the French, made 'the English wherever they go, a caste by themselves'.[139]

It could therefore be argued that indianization was an easily shed expediency and that the integration of India into the British body appears to have involved no psychological adjustment. But this seems too hasty a dismissal of the impact which colonialism had on the colonizer. It is a conclusion born out of the difficulty of separating out the extent to which India simply fitted in with European orientalist and medical opinion and the extent to which it actually influenced the formation of ideas. The examination of Anglo-Indian bathing and cleanliness practices which follows allows an exploration of how far the British adoption of Indian practices was simply expedient imitation, and how far it was the result of the significant and lasting impact which India had on the British who lived there.[140]

The depth of indianization

Bathing was initially taken up by the British in India for medical purposes. Company surgeons enthusiastically integrated bathing into the battery of treatments with which they attempted to stem the tide of tropical disease. At Madras in 1806 it was agreed that due to the 'great utility of Baths in many disorders of this Climate' they should be installed in all European Hospitals in the Madras Presidency.[141] In 1808 a shower bath was in use at the Lunatic Hospital at Fort St George, and the Surgeon of the European General Hospital reported on the usefulness of a Captain Jekyll's vapour bath in 1832.[142] The surgeons may have been adopting a practice which they had observed in use among Indian doctors, although there was also a revival of interest in warm medicated baths in Britain at the turn of the century. In fact an Indian, Sake Dene Mahomed of Patna, was an influential promoter of the vapour bath in Britain. He was known for having introduced the technique of *shampooing* to Britain, first in Basil Cochrane's baths in London and then at his own establishment in Brighton, where he moved in 1814. Balneology (the medical science of bathing) provided an alternative to conventional medicine's use of harsh remedies. Mahomed asserted that the *shampooing* technique could cure languid circulation and inactive animal functions, all without the need for internal remedies and even in those cases where medicine failed.[143] Warm baths were therefore seen as a curative measure.

The preventative measure of cold baths was of even more interest to surgeons in India. James Johnson recommended cold baths as a prophylactic means of strengthening the constitution's resistance to the effects of a tropical climate.

> Now, there is nothing that steels the human frame, with more certainty, against the effects of [atmospherical vicissitudes], than the cold bath. ... By keeping the skin clean, cool, and soft, it moderates excessive, and supports a natural and equable cuticular discharge; and from the '*cutaneo-hepatic* sympathy,' so often noticed, the functions of the liver partake of this salutary equilibrium – a circumstance hitherto overlooked. The use of the *cold bath*, then should be regularly and daily persevered in, from the moment we enter the tropics.[144]

The medical focus on the cold bath in the tropics was connected to the belief that the body was governed by 'consent of the parts', which meant that 'when *one* [part of the body] is affected by particular impressions, the *other* sympathises, as it were, and takes on a kind of analogous action'.[145] The great heat of the Indian climate caused excessive perspiration leading, it was thought, to the over-stimulation and loosening of the skin. Johnson concluded that the internal organs, acting in sympathy with the skin, were in turn over-stimulated as a result of profuse perspiration. He identified a particularly strong affinity between the skin and the liver (the '*cutaneo-hepatic* sympathy') which meant that immoderate perspiration led to the over-production of bile, which was damaging to the equilibrium of the stomach. Eventually, the prolonged excitement of the organs led to their relaxation, the consequence of which was the torpor which marked out those who had long been resident in the tropics and which made them vulnerable to congestive diseases, especially biliousness. It was therefore imperative that perspiration should be regulated by regular cold baths and moderate consumption of water. Alcoholic beverages were condemned as stimulants which aggravated thirst, leading in turn to over-perspiration.[146] For the same reason Johnson outlawed the use of linen in tropical climates, claiming that it absorbed perspiration far too quickly, stimulating rather than moderating the flow. He noted that the British could learn much from the habits of the Indians, pointing to the fact that in India the efficacy of the cold bath as a preservative of health was widely recognized, the whole population benefiting greatly from their daily bathe. William Tennant, too, remarked with admiration that among the Indians 'Almost every individual bathes once or twice a day, and in a warm climate this must not only brace the limbs, but preserve health by promoting cleanliness.'[147]

Cold baths had long been recognized in Britain as a means of hardening the body and toughening its fibres. Bathing was a practice with which the British were familiar and the Anglo-Indians were therefore willing to integrate cold baths into their daily routine, especially as the heat of the Indian climate made bathing in cold water a pleasure. In his humorous account of life in India, Captain Bellew mentioned that during the hot weather a change of clothes two or three times a day was commonplace and that this would be accompanied by a dousing on the lawn from the '*bhistee's mussack*'.[148] Medical notions of the relaxing effect of the heat and the strengthening effect of cold filtered through into lay thinking about the body. Having quoted Johnson on the efficacy of cold baths, Colesworthy Grant asserted that 'in India, as it should be elsewhere, it is the custom for every person to bathe very frequently, if not every morning *throughout the year*, a practice which many systematic old residents would not neglect for the "sea's worth".'[149] In contrast, in

Britain, although bath tubs were available, a daily splash of water on the face and hands would have been regarded as quite sufficient even among the middle classes. It was only the most genteel, or the most fastidious dandy, such as 'Beau' Brummel, who felt the need to frequently wash and scrub their entire body.[150] Writing in 1801, a doctor commented that 'most men resident in London and many ladies though accustomed to wash their hands and faces daily, neglect washing their bodies from year to year.'[151] Indeed, Richard Reece remarked in his *Medical Companion* that '[in a temperate climate] the propriety of washing the whole surface of the body oftener than once a week, either with warm or cold water, is much to be questioned.'[152]

The chill of the climate was one reason why the British in the metropole bathed far less frequently than their compatriots in India. In addition, cleanliness at the turn of the century was generally associated with clean linen rather than a spotless skin. Bathing, even in India, was regarded as a prophylactic against disease or as a means of relieving the heat, not as a means to cleanliness as an end in itself. But as the practice became commonplace among the British in India they added bathrooms to their bungalows, well equipped with bath tubs, washstands, *chilumchees* (basins), soap and commodes. Bathing gradually became an integral part of the process of changing one's linen and came to be equated with cleanliness.[153] It can therefore be argued that the Anglo-Indians were one of the first sections of British society to define cleanliness as being thoroughly washed and scrubbed. Bathrooms were attached to every bungalow by the 1830s while in Britain, although a washstand might occupy a corner of a middle-class bedroom, it was not until the late nineteenth century that bathrooms became a normal part of the middle-class home.[154]

The Anglo-Indians also followed the example of their Indian subjects where hair was concerned. In Britain combing and powdering was preferred to washing the hair, which was regarded with anxiety and thought to induce head- and toothache.[155] Charles Stuart pointed out 'In all hot countries, where daily bathing is so eminently conducive to health and cleanliness, it will readily be conceived, that the use of hair-powder must be very inconvenient.'[156] This, combined with the fondness which Williamson said that rats and cockroaches had for eating the 'powder and pomatum at the back of [the] head', was certainly good reason to give up powdering in favour of washing the hair.[157] Fanny Parks asserted that hair-washing was a constantly repeated activity in India, and in an appendix to her book included a recipe for 'shampoo', indicating that she thought this something unusual in Britain, where soap was used if and when the hair was washed.[158] The recipe is a mixture of *basun* (a type of pulse), egg yolks and the juice of limes, and very similar to that given by Colesworthy Grant, who described this means of cleaning the hair as a virtue the British had learnt from the Indians, who regarded the head as the symbolic seat of bodily powers. He added that hair-washing was 'an operation to which I suspect more importance is not attached in any part of the world, than in this country'.[159] That the word shampoo is derived from the Hindi *chãmpõ*, meaning 'to massage', suggests that one of the means by which washing the hair with materials other than soap was introduced into Britain was by way of returned colonials from India.[160] It took several more years before shampoo appeared as a commercial product, but by the 1920s *The Englishman* was carrying advertisements which invited ladies to save their hair by massaging their scalps with 'Plomer's Jaborandi Hair Wash' and to make their hair 'soft and lustrous' with concentrated 'Egg Julep'. Both of these advertisements hint at the origins of their product with the use of eggs in one preparation and the association of the action of massage with shampoo in the other.[161]

The compatibility of Indian cleansing practices with British ideas facilitated their integration into the regimen by which Europeans sought to preserve their health in a tropical climate. The heat and the discomfort of perspiration also increased the likelihood that ordinary Anglo-Indians would heed the advice of their doctors. A further impetus to the adoption of washing practices by the British in India was the challenge of brahminical ideas of purity. In his *Description of the Character, Manners and Customs of the People of India* the Abbé Dubois noted that 'the Brahmans have nothing so much at heart as Cleanliness; as it is this quality...that gives them in a great measure the superiority which they assert over the other tribes.'[162] Already at a disadvantage in that the Hindus regarded them as ritually impure in body, and anxiously seeking to establish political bodily legitimacy, early British residents in India could hardly assert personal cleanliness as a signifier of British superiority. As early as 1775 Peter Crosthwaite, a sailor on an East Indiaman, asserted that the spread of cleanliness among Anglo-Indians could only be advantageous on a personal, social and imperial level: 'such a high esteem have the natives of Asia for it, that they count it very unnatural not to wash; and the Europeans a dirty people, because they do not wash; and by what I have learned from that good natured people, the Europeans would be held in much better esteem by them, were they to practice the salutary custom.'[163] This was almost certainly an important motivating factor which facilitated the rapid spread of washing habits among the British in India. The image of the civilian at his *toilette*, bathed and dressed by his servants – already a display of wealth, status and power – took on additional significance as a means of making a claim to bodily purity. In this way personal cleanliness was incorporated into the strategy of rule, as well as survival, in an Indian idiom.

The integration of Indian cleansing practices into Anglo-Indian life can be seen as expedient, adopted merely in order to ensure survival and to reinforce their status as a ruling group in Indian eyes, but the Anglo-Indians did more than absorb the outward features of Indian practice. Anglo-Indians took to cleanliness with great enthusiasm, and reserved special servants and rooms for the rituals of bathing. Increasing elaboration of cleansing practices indicates that the threshold of acceptable standards of personal hygiene gradually rose, revealing a psychological adjustment which redefined what the Anglo-Indians regarded as clean. Once they had been some time in India the British no longer perceived their bodies to be clean if they applied only those practices which were used at home. Much later in the century Reginald Maxwell described this process to his mother, explaining how he and his wife had integrated an Indian technique into their bodily routine: 'Lyle and I hate having baths in the English fashion now: we have for years followed the Indian practice of not getting bodily into the bath but sitting outside it, so that the water we apply to ourselves is always clean!'[164] Here the body can be seen as an active principle in a process of historical change. The bodily experience of being clean in a new way generated a new norm of cleanliness which ensured that the practices of bathing and washing the hair became integral to the Anglo-Indian definition of personal cleanliness. Thus the influence exerted by India was far from superficial as, by these means, Indian norms were absorbed into Anglo-Indian life.

The standards of cleanliness which the British learnt in India not only became a part of the Anglo-Indian self-identity but also played a role in introducing the pleasures of personal cleanliness to the middle class in the metropole. Retired Anglo-Indians brought these practices back to Britain, and ex-Company surgeons recommended higher standards of cleanliness in their popular medical advice books, which were addressed to a British as well as a colonial audience. What was an incipient trend towards higher standards of personal cleanliness among the British middle class was almost certainly strengthened by the influence of Anglo-India on the metropolitan country, where, if the research on Germany can be taken as a guide, cleanliness played an integral part in the development of the bourgeoisie.[165] Other apparently superficial developments such as the adoption of pyjamas also played an important part in re-shaping the British body. Pyjamas complemented the dressing gown, which was a Turkish import, as was the smoking cap. The donning of these items of apparel signified a period of time for a particular bodily activity. The gentleman in his smoking cap signalled that he wished to be left in peace to enjoy his cigar or pipe. The dressing gown and pyjamas signified not only sleep but also an informal period of relaxation, which was particularly apt due to their association with the luxuriant indolent East. Wearing pyjamas and a dressing gown permitted a specific form of deportment unavailable to the fully-dressed individual. Thus, norms of deportment as well as cleanliness, originally developed in the Indian context, spread to Britain where they helped to mark out the emerging private sphere, taking on new meaning within the British social fabric. In this way the colony was interwoven into the corporeal life of the metropolitan country.

A range of possible codes of behaviour which were often remarkably open to Indian influence were generated by the discussion of rule and survival in an Indian idiom. In their search for models of behaviour appropriate to the rulers of India the British drew upon the customs of the European aristocracy as well as those of indigenous elites. The figure of the nabob which emerged was a hybrid construct, integrating East and West into his person.[166] As the British constructed an idea of India in dialogue with their subjects, they attempted to mould themselves accordingly. Thus, a process was set in motion which redefined the body of the Briton and which might be described as a process of transculturation whereby the meeting of two cultures creates a new cultural phenomenon.[167] The nabob was a carnivalesque figure who blurred the boundaries between the political, symbolic and personal areas of life by surrounding himself with splendour and magnificence in all these spheres. Even the everyday acts of washing and dressing were transmuted into the symbolic means by which to claim bodily purity, which in turn was part of the political strategy of rule in an Indian idiom. The nabob disrupted British notions of the social hierarchy by aspiring to wealth and luxury, and the repertoire of possible practices available to the British in India, ranging from extreme asceticism to the heights of indulgence, involved in some cases a startling level of indianization which disrupted metropolitan ideas of virtue and propriety. The ambiguous figure of the nabob was therefore viewed with a mixture of affection and disapproval. As the nineteenth century progressed the latter response began to dominate, arresting the process of transculturation. The next chapter explores the nabob's decline and the rise of the anglicized British official.

2

The Anglicization of the Body

During the first half of the nineteenth century the British in India developed from a disparate group of merchant administrators into an established and closely interconnected community. The introduction of steamers on the Ganges in the 1830s improved the links between the different British settlements within India, while communications with Britain were improved as the overland route to India through Egypt reduced the journey from between five and eight months to thirty-five or forty days.[1] Greater interaction between the colony and the metropolitan country was thus facilitated and as the nineteenth century progressed British influence on the Anglo-Indian community increased on all levels – political, social and cultural. Political debates within Britain converged with debates within the government of India to provide new solutions to the question of how to rule India. A political shift towards utilitarianism was complemented by shifts in medical thinking which, with the arrival in India of the new, middle-class code of morals and manners, converged upon and transformed the body of the nabob. The open body of the nabob was made obsolete as the boundaries delineating how far India and Indians might encroach upon the British body were defined. A process of anglicization gradually sloughed off the Orient and constructed an altogether more British Anglo-Indian persona, more appropriate to the new ruling style. The standardized manners of the new morality narrowed the range of behaviour open to the Anglo-Indian. One of the costs of this process was the deterioration of relations with the Indians. This process can be seen as a colonial reflection of what might be termed the rise of Victorianism in Britain, but the anglicized body of the Briton in India was more than a mirror image of the middle-class body in the metropole. The closed bounded body which emerged was a distinctively Anglo-Indian version of the Victorian body.

Rule in a British idiom

As the nineteenth century progressed the wish to restore India to its golden age by reviving the classical values of the ancient period was eclipsed by a more aggressive belief in the benefits of contemporary British civilization. The rise of middle-class liberalism in Britain brought evangelicalism, free trade and utilitarianism to the forefront of the political agenda, none of which demonstrated the respect for Indian culture and institutions which had guided orientalism. Rather, the representatives of these groups, their scope of action limited within Britain, looked to India as a space where their ideologies might be implemented and tested. The evangelicals sought to reform Indian society through education, which by subtly undermining the attachment of Indians to their own culture and inculcating in them a western viewpoint would eventually bring them to the spiritual redemption of Christianity, freeing them from their bonds of super-stition.[2] James Mill, utilitarianism's most influential proponent, identified the despotic oriental form of government as the root of Indian degradation and therefore saw reform of the law and the administration – particularly land revenue – and the introduction of an accountable and efficient centralized government as the means of reforming Indian society. These arguments instigated a reinterpret-ation of morally responsible British rule as a mission to bring India into the modern age.[3] William Bentinck, whose governor-generalship (1828–35) has been hailed as an age of reform, expressed this new attitude of assimilation and anglicization: 'The introduction of European school-masters or teachers of all the improvements in agriculture, in moral management, in manufactures, in the use of machinery, is one of the greatest benefits that can be conferred upon this country. In all these arts, India has made no improvement; she is as she was ages ago.'[4] More prosaically, the advocators of free trade identified a westernized India as a profitable new market for British goods.

By the 1820s these utilitarian and evangelical attitudes to British rule in India had infiltrated all levels of the Company administration. New staff at Haileybury enthusiastically preached the precepts of utilitarianism to future civilians who went on to fill positions of power and influence in the Indian government.[5] Under Bentinck, the foundations for education in the medium of the English language were laid, reform of the judicial system was set in motion, and measures against what were seen as some of the more disturbing Indian practices such as *thuggee*, infanticide, human sacrifice and *suttee*, were put into place. However, as C. A. Bayly has pointed out, although these were important developments which heralded a new, reformist, anglicizing approach to British government in India, to label Bentinck's period of government as an age of reform would be to exaggerate the impact which these changes had on Indian society.[6] The ramifications of anglicization were in fact far more wide-reaching for the British themselves.

If the body is understood as sustaining a particular view of society by virtue of the fact that it embodies certain values and ideas, then it is clear that the body of the nabob was no longer appropriate in the context of evangelical and utilitarian ideologies which cast Anglo-Indian officials as carriers of western civilization to India. The reconception of good government as the neutral administration of law by honest and upright officials undermined the earlier policy of gathering in the threads of traditional political legitimacy.[7] The British were increasingly reluctant to acknowledge that they derived their political legitimacy from the Mughal emperor and were far less interested in Indian interpretations of the appropriate expression of power. This was reflected in the declining power of the old Muslim court servants, the diplomatists and *munshis* whom the British had been reliant upon in the early days of British rule.[8] A new model of the civilian as a patriarchal guardian of the Indian population developed. British political authority was now said to be derived – ignoring both British economic and military power – from the inherent superiority of the British. Thomas Postans argued in 1842 that 'We govern millions in India by means of a high moral estimation formed of us as a nation by the natives of the country.'[9] According to Henry Spry 'the influence of moral integrity on the part of one European' was sufficient to subdue the 'native mind' so that it was possible for 'a single European officer, at a station sixty-four miles apart from any of his countrymen' to maintain law and order.[10] If the British held India by the force of their moral integrity, the logic of this argument was that every British official must be seen to embody British superiority. Great stress was therefore placed on the preservation of British manners and customs among civilians. John Malcolm admonished in his *Instructions Regarding Intercourse between European Officials and Natives* 'We should always preserve the European; for to adopt their [Indian] manners is a departure from the very principle on which every impression of our superiority that rests upon good foundation is grounded.'[11] As the discourse of orientalism crumbled away so too did the hybrid figure of the nabob for whom it had provided ideological support. The reforming anglicist view of British political legitimacy remodelled the image of the appropriate ruling figure. The indianized body of the nabob was discredited in favour of that of the *burra sahib*, who was characterized by the British qualities of energy, probity and manliness.[12] Although the *burra sahib* was seen as an embodiment of Britishness, he was a distinctively Anglo-Indian figure, formulated as he was as an instrument of authority within a specifically Anglo-Indian ruling strategy.

The new political climate affected the extent to which the British were willing to immerse themselves in Indian political culture, particularly at the courts. The new breed of Resident's reluctance to participate in a process of indianization is demonstrated by the decline in the ornamentation of titles. James Achilles Kirkpatrick, Resident at Hyderabad from 1798 to 1805, was happy to be addressed as 'Magnificence in War, Beloved Son' but Charles Metcalfe, Resident from 1820 to 1825, preferred the more utilitarian 'Regulator of the State'.[13] Residents now took pride in the Britishness of their bodies, clothed in plain black frock coats which contrasted with the sartorial flamboyance of the nabob as well as 'the pretentious glitter of the oriental monarchs they controlled'.[14] The ideal of a more efficient as well as a more upright and honest form of government resulted in a clash between 'the stricter justice and morality in a new generation, with older standards of conduct'.[15] In 1823 Sir Edward West, the King's Judge at Bombay (1823–8), dismissed William Erskine, Clerk of the Court for Small Causes, from his post for allowing his Indian clerk to extort fees for subpoenas which were never issued. Bombay society felt he had been treated unjustly as it was considered commonplace to allow a clerk to manage such affairs even though it provided ample opportunity for corruption.[16] West's ideas about justice were offended by the Indian system in the same way that Charles Trevelyan's moral code and ideas about good government were offended by Sir Edward Colebrooke's methods when he arrived in Delhi as First Assistant to the Resident in 1827. Colebrooke got things done the Indian way by associating with influential members of the Indian community and covertly accepting presents and other financial favours from them. He was exposed by Trevelyan and dismissed from his post.[17] This new atmosphere which styled Indians as untrustworthy, unprincipled and politically corrupt, and those civilians who associated with them as stained by corruption, made the new civilians shy of cultivating Indian friendships. The growing separation of British officials and

Indians was furthered by Bentinck's continued destruction of the old indianized system of government. In 1833 measures were taken to protect British officers' reputations at the courts by ordering that visits made to 'Natives of Rank' should only take place with the permission of the Resident or Political Agent. This was to prevent any suspicion of intrigue tainting the name of an official as Indians were said to be wont to interpret unofficial visits as a sign of special favour. For the same reason British officials were no longer allowed to sell property to natives.[18]

In 1837 Henry Spry remarked 'Free entré of a native house can seldom be granted to any save a medical man, since partly in consequence of the official stiffness of an English functionary, and partly from the desire to preclude a possibility of incurring a taint of suspicion, Anglo-Indians usually avoid that free and confidential intercourse with rich or influential natives which might lead to an intimacy.'[19] Commercial collaboration and intermarriage in the early days of British rule had fostered close relations between the British and the Indians but a dominantly European executive had less to gain from friendly inter-racial intercourse while the new emphasis on probity eroded the conditions under which cordial inter-racial relations could exist. The younger men still mixed on the sports-field but a social environment within which real friendships between British and Indians might develop was rapidly eroding. The theorization of moral and racial contempt for Indian society by the utilitarian and evangelical analyses of Indian society such as James Mill's presentation of India as an uncivilized, degenerate society in his *History of British India* made matters worse by encouraging a tendency towards the denigration of all things Indian.[20] R. N. Cust's response to a *nautch* in 1843 is indicative of the shift in attitude: 'Returned exceedingly disgusted – without any beauty or elegance the motion of the dancers was so exceedingly disgusting . . . that the baboos sit night after night reflects no credit upon their sense and shows how utterly destitute they are of any usual or proper ideals and feelings . . . *but* the sensual.'[21] The atmosphere of mutual enjoyment which had once been present at the *nautch* or the cockfight was lost as British interest in Indian forms of socializing waned. This repugnance for Indian entertainments reflected a moral shift in the metropole, where the evangelical movement campaigned against dissolute sports such as cockfighting.[22] On the other hand the notion of probity and how this should be presented – in clothing and racial distance – constructed a peculiarly Anglo-Indian notion of the presentation of Britishness, which was formulated in reaction to the perception of native customs and ruling methods.

British refusal to adapt to Indian ways meant that friendly social intercourse was hindered as the complex web of practices which surrounded and defined the Hindu body came into conflict with the social proximity which for the British defined friendship. The British reluctance to accommodate to Indian manners and customs coincided with an increase in the hold of brahminical ideas about ritual distinction over respectable sectors of the Indian community. Besides regarding the consumption of beef with disgust Hindus only ate food prepared by, and in the company of, members of their own caste. This meant that the sharing of food around a table, which for the British was one of the acts which cemented friendship, was impossible with respectable members of Hindu society. Muslims, who in the eighteenth century had been content to dine with Europeans despite their repugnance for European consumption of pork and alcohol, were also undergoing a revival of purity and began to avoid eating with non-Muslims.[23] The taboos surrounding food consumption thus prevented an Indian from dining at the house of an Anglo-Indian. Anglo-Indians were sometimes invited to dine with an Indian gentleman but the host would simply sit with his guests while they ate, or he might withdraw and leave his guests to eat alone. Often a visit, as George Latham, an engineer with the Madras railway company discovered, consisted of nothing more than a little polite talk after which the visitor was given a jasmine garland, betel nut and sprinkled with *laudal*.[24] Another disturbing aspect of these encounters for the British was their all-male character. The seclusion of women among both Muslims and high-caste Hindus meant that the women of the family never joined these dinner parties, and it could even be considered bad taste to ask after an Indian gentleman's family. The bodily taboos of the Indians on the one hand and the British expectations of bodily proximity on the other created a formidable barrier to meaningful social interaction between the two.

Caste restrictions meant that the British held the Indians responsible for the increasing gulf between the two races. Many were offended that in the eyes of the Hindus they were outcasts with the power to pollute. William Huggins was indignant that 'if we enter his [a Hindu's] house he will break all his cooking vessels, or if we touch his body, he will wash himself afterwards.'[25] Some members of the ruling race found it galling that a religion which they regarded as nothing but degraded superstition, and a social system which they saw as the degenerate product of years of Mughal oppression, defined them as impure and thus inferior. Even Frederick Shore, who was extremely critical of British attitudes towards India and its people, was of the opinion that a great step in the civilizing process would have been gained if Indians could be persuaded to dine with Europeans and thus to adopt their table manners.[26] It was indicative of the shift in political perspective that the Indians were now expected to accommodate to the manners and customs brought to their country by the British. The decline in British respect for Indian customs created conditions in which tensions between the rulers and their subjects were potentially more volatile. British contempt for Indian ideas of purity and pollution created an atmosphere of distrust which made the rumours which circulated before the outbreak of the Mutiny in 1857 all the more powerful. Apart from the question of the source of the grease for the new Enfield rifle's cartridges, it was rumoured that the British were insidiously undermining the purity of the Indian population in other ways, by, for example, polluting flour with bone-dust.[27]

It is clear from complaints from Indians and advice issued to both civilians and military officers on how to behave on such occasions that official meetings became a flashpoint where the deterioration of inter-racial relations became apparent. Military and political officers would have continued to come into close contact with Indians but for the majority of civilians, especially in the Presidency towns, Indian life would have been remote. Their contact with respectable members of Indian society – the wealthy merchants, local chiefs or rajas and the large landholders – was reduced to acknowledging them at the theatre or at a meeting of one of the scientific societies and the reception of Indian visitors as part of the British official's duties.[28] It was during such meetings that the contemptuous bodily demeanour of the British soured Indo-British relations. Respectable Indian gentlemen attempting to obtain an interview with a British official were frequently put at the mercy of their inferiors within society by virtue of the fact that Indian clerks determined who might be permitted one. These employees had no scruples about exploiting the power of their position, which allowed corruption to infiltrate the administration of British rule. Indian gentlemen would often be kept standing for an unreasonable length of time while waiting for an interview, and once they reached the presence of the British official, they were likely to be confronted by an Englishman with barely a sufficient grasp of the language to converse politely who might well, unintentionally or otherwise, address his respectable visitor in the familiar rather than in the polite form. The inability to converse politely was also a growing problem in the army. Sita Ram complained bitterly of the declining language skills of British army officers: 'the only language they learn is that of the lower orders, which they pick up from the servants, and which is unsuitable to be used in polite conversation.'[29] Worse still was 'the haughty superciliousness, arrogance, and even insolence of behaviour, which the generality of the English think it necessary to adopt towards the natives, by way of keeping up their own dignity'.[30] Many Anglo-Indians felt that British moral integrity was most effectively demonstrated by an arrogant manner. It was Richard Burton's firm conviction that it was 'The tight pantaloons,... the authoritative voice, the procurante manner, and the broken Hindostani' which impressed the Indian.[31]

Those who relied on such a manner to demonstrate British superiority matched this with the firm belief that the bodily demeanour of the Indian should demonstrate his inferiority. The Indian body was thus transformed into a battleground, with chairs and shoes as the weapons. A calculated insult was the failure to offer a chair to an Indian gentleman waiting to visit a British official. In the colonial context the chair was invested with emotional value. Henderson characterized the chair as 'the visible sign of our civilization... as much an outward symbol of our proud distinction from among the enslaved millions of the East, as is the black beaver adornment of the head of our countrymen, or the carefully preserved shape and fashion of our habiliments'.[32] The Indian posture of repose, reclining on cushions, sitting or squatting on the floor, as well as the habit of sitting cross-legged on a chair was regarded as a signifier of the Indians' barbaric state.[33] Therefore the British were reluctant to grant an Indian the right to sit in a chair as this could be read as an acknowledgement that he was in fact civilized enough to possess western manners.[34] For the same reasons many Anglo-Indians were reluctant to accept that Indians who adopted the attire of the British, and in particular British boots or shoes, should be granted the right to keep them on in the presence of a British official. In 1867 the Calcutta High Court were recorded as being 'of [the] opinion that it would be objectionable in obscure and outlying places where the Presiding Officer, judging by popular feeling, would naturally regard it as an indignity if a Native were seen standing upon any carpeted portion of the Court-house with shoes of any description on his feet'.[35] This was despite the fact that the government at Calcutta had adopted a more conciliatory approach, passing a resolution, extended to the whole of Bengal in 1854, which allowed natives the privilege of appearing before government officials on semi-official and official occasions in European boots and shoes. Granting Indians European marks of civility was resisted as it was felt that this conceded to Indians a level of equality with the British which was undesirable. Within Anglo-India a specifically colonial notion of respectful bodily demeanour developed which rested on the notion that British rule was founded upon keeping Indians in their place by imposing supposedly Indian bodily customs upon them.

The strutting manner of the schoolboy as an expression of British superiority was compatible with the new political tone as a particular means of demonstrating Britishness. However, an alternative school of thought identified such intolerance and rudeness as an obstacle to the new British policy of reform. This hoped to anglicize India by fostering a collaborative Indian elite who, through their identification with British culture, would acknowledge the British as the rightful rulers of India. A westernized Indian elite could only be drawn into the mechanisms of British rule if a conciliatory manner was adopted. John Malcolm was a representative of this point of view. In 1821, while acting as agent to the Governor-General in charge of political relations in Central India, he wrote *Instructions Regarding Intercourse between European Officials and Natives* for the guidance of his officers. These repeatedly emphasized the need for courteousness in British dealings with Indians, and came to be regarded as a model guide to conduct for the British official. They were reproduced by John Borthwick Gilchrist in his re-edition of Thomas Williamson's *East India Vade-Mecum* and in John Briggs's *Letters Addressed to a Young Person in India; calculated to afford instruction for his conduct in general, and more especially in his intercourse with the natives.*[36] Briggs, a Lieutenant-Colonel in the Indian army, and other army officers – notably Thomas Postans and Henry Kerr who respectively published *Hints to Cadets* and *A Few Words of Advice to Cadets* – reiterated Malcolm's position.[37] The civilian, Frederick Shore, argued for the adoption of Malcolm's conciliatory approach among members of the civil service in his comprehensive criticism of British rule in India entitled *Notes on Indian Affairs.*

Malcolm's *Instructions* urged officials to ensure that all classes of natives should have 'easy access to personal communication with their European superior'.[38] They were instructed not to keep native officers waiting and, if the occasion were to arise, they were to furnish the officer with a chair.[39] Shore suggested that a chair could be provided for Indian landowners and respectable merchants, a bench for farmers or shopkeepers and a *setringee* (low bench) or carpet for the inferior classes. In this way the civilian would retain his dignity by treating higher-class Indians with respect and others with kindness. Such civilities were written into the 'standing orders' for officers. Both the cadet and the writer were exhorted to learn Hindustani properly. It was not considered sufficient to be able to issue commands or instruct servants. They should be fluent in the language, able to speak it in the manner of the Indian elites with a full command of the proper terms of respect. An ability to make polite conversation would win over the respectable Indian, the sepoy and the lower orders, who would all regard such a grasp of the language as a mark of distinction.[40] Disgusted by 'many a young prig, fresh from the Writers' Buildings, who actually conceived that every native he passed ought to make *him* a salutation', Shore modelled his ideal civil servant on the picture of the responsible country squire.[41] Indeed, he strengthened the conciliatory argument by drawing a comparison between the Anglo-Indians and the British aristocracy. Oblivious to the need to conciliate the lower orders of society the latter had continued to 'lead a luxurious indolent life, associating solely with each other... knowing as little of the people whose support is necessary to preserve their own estates or honours from the clutches of the radical, as they do of the Kalmucs or Hindoos', with the consequent erosion of their authority in the shape of the Reform Act of 1832 which was seen by contemporaries to increase the power of the lower orders.[42] Shore cautioned that without making a concerted effort to understand and gain the support of Indians the British in India might face a similar threat to their authority. The failure of many British officials to follow the advice of Malcolm and Shore certainly contributed to the development of the atmosphere of distrust and antipathy which created the conditions that made the Mutiny of 1857 possible.

The changed political atmosphere brought about a marked change in the person of the Anglo-Indian official. The figure of the nabob was replaced by a *burra sahib* who was expected to be thoroughly British. Among the conciliatory camp, fair-minded honesty and justice combined with a tolerant approach to Indian culture was advocated as the source of British moral authority. At the same time, an emphasis on probity and a determination that the Indians, as part of a process of anglicization, should meet the British on their own social terms, distanced the British from the Indians. An opposing group continued to believe that their credibility as a ruling elite rested on the public enactment of arrogant authority, to be met by deference on the part of their Indian subjects. The resulting battle over the bodily gestures of the Indians reduced the meetings between British and Indians to a formulaic pattern which lessened the risk of a challenge to British authority. Ultimately, however, this more aggressive attitude resulted in a level of tension between the British and the Indian population which was potentially explosive.

The ban on the East

> The nabob of books and tradition is a personage no longer to be found
> among us.... If you go to the house of an Indian gentleman now, he
> does not say 'Bring more curricles,' like the famous Nabob of Stanstead
> Park. He goes to Leadenhall Street in an omnibus, and walks back from
> the City for exercise.... They do not wear nankeen jackets in summer.
> Their livers are not out of order any more; and as for hookahs, I dare
> swear there are not two kept alight within the bills of mortality; and
> that retired Indians would as soon think of smoking them, as their
> wives would of burning themselves on their husbands' bodies at the
> cemetery, Kensal Green, near to the Tyburnian quarter of the city which
> the Indian world at present inhabits.[43]

If the nabob was an increasingly rare figure in Thackeray's London
of the 1830s and 1840s, he was also an endangered figure within
India. The new ideology of rule, which recast the Anglo-Indian as a
representative of British culture, was accompanied by a rejection of
those habits which had incorporated East and West into his persona.
This process was in part the colonial expression of the changing
moral climate in Britain. The improvement in communications
between Britain and India, combined with the arrival of fresh recruits
imbued with utilitarian and evangelical attitudes, facilitated the
transference to the colony of the complex set of social codes which
now governed middle-class society in the metropole. Among the most
visible indications of this were the changes which occurred in colonial clothing styles.

By the 1830s the days were gone when India could act as a space,
like the masquerade, where it was possible to don outlandish costume, try on new personas and revel in the inversion of the social
order. It would no longer have been considered appropriate to attend
a ball and supper to celebrate the king's birthday dressed as William
Hickey was in the 1770s in 'a coat of pea-green, lined with white silk
and richly ornamented with a spangled and foiled lace, waistcoat and
breeches decorated in like manner, being also of white silk'.[44] The
flamboyantly attired nabob had disappeared from view. The respectable Anglo-Indian now wore the black broadcloth of the middle
classes in the metropole to dinner parties, to balls, while going for
the evening drive, or at church – in fact, on nearly all semi-formal
and formal occasions. *The Calcutta Review* remarked in 1844:

> One would imagine that there had recently been a very extraordinary
> atmospherical revolution; for within the last five or six years, we have

noticed a progressive tendency towards heavy vestments, especially in crowded assemblies, at large dinner parties, and on all other occasions where the heat is more than usually intense.... Formerly, white jackets were frequently – white trowsers universally – worn at dinner-parties, in the hot weather.... In the hottest weather now, the fashion is to appear at *burra-khana* dressed in broad cloth from head to foot.[45]

Second-Lieutenant Arthur Moffat Lang complained in 1854 that in Calcutta 'One must always be *en grande tenue*, always when out with a great black hat on, always with a dark coat and so on'.[46] The discomfort this occasioned was reduced at small dinner parties by tolerant hosts who would suggest that their guests, politely arriving in dark jackets, should change into the more comfortable white ones they would have brought along with them. This custom does not appear to have died out until the 1860s when Sidney Blanchard commented with some regret that 'now everybody dresses for dinner as they do in Europe.'[47]

The adoption of the black suit in India mirrored the shift in the metropole from the colourful and varied eighteenth-century code of clothing towards black broadcloth. By 1810 black had become the accepted colour of men's evening dress among the best circles in Britain; the black costume of the dandy as well as the sombre colour of riding wear among the gentry had made the colour fashionable. For businessmen and professionals the black frock coat asserted their right to be considered gentlemen. These tendencies converged until the black suit became all encompassing in men's formal and informal dress, even among the aristocracy.[48] Black was interpreted by contemporaries as a representation of the decency, self-respect, importance and power of the rising middle-classes, and the arrival of such values in India was symbolized by Lord William Bentinck, the Governor-General, himself.

> Lord W. Bentinck, on the throne of the Great Mogul, thinks and acts like a Pennsylvanian Quaker. You may easily imagine that there are people who talk loudly of the dissolution of the empire and the world's end, when they behold the temporary ruler of Asia riding on horseback, plainly dressed, and without escort, or on his way into the country with his umbrella under his arm.[49]

Bentinck's more sober style of government meant that much of the oriental grandeur which had surrounded the nabob was stripped away. By 1844 John Kaye commented 'the race of *chobdars* are extinct – we never see a silver-stick now.'[50] Peons, who also acted as messengers, were the only servants retained as functionaries 'of consequence'.[51] The palanquin, once an important status symbol which obviated the nabob's need to walk even a few yards, was abandoned as a means of transport within the precincts of the town in favour of the English carriage.[52] The reduction in ceremony was complemented by the civilian's black suit, topped off by a black top hat.[53] Among the British, civil servants became known as 'black-coats'[54] and black acquired additional resonance in India not only as the colour of sobriety, decency and uprightness as it was in Britain but as a symbol of the civilian's commitment to utilitarian principles of good government and his political legitimacy as a neutral administrator of the law.

As Anglo-Indian men's dress became increasingly formal and standardized, anxiety about women's dress and behaviour in the tropical climate of India increased. The discomfort caused by layers of constricting underclothing in the intense heat and humidity meant that many women abandoned most of the underwear which they would have worn in Britain. Fanny Wells left off her drawers and wore only one petticoat and a muslin dress during the day, and often left it as late as nine o'clock before she got dressed as she preferred to 'ward off the evil moment of putting on my clothes as long as possible'.[55] In her handbook of advice Emma Roberts roundly condemned this sort of behaviour: 'the indulgence of the indolence which the oppressive nature of the climate is so apt to produce, is but too frequently attended by an unwillingness to give up the comfort of a loose and careless attire for the restraints of the toilet.'[56] A loose and careless toilet carried a suggestion of loose and careless morals.[57] The Anglo-Indian practice of taking a siesta after lunch compounded this impression.[58] Against the background of the evangelical moral imperative to always occupy one's time usefully and a code of conduct which prioritized self-improvement, politeness and correctness, Anglo-Indian women's behaviour was thoroughly reprehensible, especially as such useless indolence was associated with Eurasians, who were said to 'sit in a listless state of ennui during the interval that elapses between the morning and the evening drives, or, what is worse, slumber on the hall sofas'.[59] It was also reminiscent of the behaviour of Indian women in the *zenana*, where 'life . . . passes without any employment bearing the stamp of industry; they will sit for hours in circles wiling away the time in silly obscene conversation, to which none but an experienced Christian female can safely hazard exposure.'[60] Carelessness with regard to retaining and constraining the body therefore carried additional echoes of racial degeneration. The heightened value of women in the colonial context as repositories of the values of western civilization meant that their behaviour was carefully monitored. Advice books urged women to keep up their accomplishments and to spend their time engaged in elegant cultural pursuits, and by the middle of the century the middle-class behavioural code can be seen to have gradually taken effect in Anglo-India.[61] Augusta Becher commented that the laxity of loose clothing and siestas were fast going out of vogue.[62]

The adoption of the middle-class social code within the colony was facilitated not only by increased communication with Britain but also by changes in the structure of Anglo-Indian society itself which meant that the British community in India were particularly receptive to the socially exclusive code developing in the metropole. In *The Civilizing Process* Norbert Elias links the monopolization of power by developing nation states and the consequent complexity of the relatedness, and intertwining, of the effects of individual acts, to changes in the personality structure of individuals. Elias argues that the more complex a society becomes and the less social control is imposed by external powers, the more the individual has to exercise self-restraint.[63] Throughout the period 1800–1857 the British were gradually consolidating their power in India, while at the same time the size of the British community was growing. In 1800 the number of covenanted civil servants in the three Presidencies was 681. By 1835 it had risen to 869.[64] In 1837, 6,000 officers of the Company's and the Queen's regiments were stationed in India along with 37,000 British soldiers.[65] Their numbers were complemented by the non-commissioned Europeans working in the districts as indigo planters, missionaries and artists. In four districts within the Bengal presidency alone, fifty-five such non-commissioned Europeans are listed for 1830.[66] Women formed only a small proportion of the entire community, but their numbers were also gradually rising from the 250 European women which Thomas Williamson estimated were to be found in Bengal in 1810.[67] Increasing regulation of the Anglo-Indian body can be seen as a response to this consolidation of British society in India. The potentially oppressive social code operating in the metropole as a guide to one's own behaviour and how to judge that of others acted in the colony as a means of social differentiation which separated out the growing community into discrete groups. Within the official community civil servants were at pains to distinguish themselves from the military and this was facilitated by their black suits, which contrasted with the red coats of the military, drawing attention to the separation of powers within the British government of India into a civil government and a subordinate military establishment. W. D. Arnold remarked with pride that a 'black-coated civilian' among a crowd of red-coated officers looked 'quiet and gentlemanly' in contrast.[68] On the other hand the official community as a whole distanced themselves from the growing unofficial community of planters and businessmen, who in turn used the adoption of a rigid social code of manners and behaviour to distance themselves from the growing medley of disreputable and poor Europeans and Eurasians.

The pressure towards self-restraint and social differentiation intensified the social gaze on the body as greater attention was paid to self-discipline in clothing, posture, table manners, and personal neatness and cleanliness as signifiers of gentility. This gaze though was now firmly fixed on the outer body as a signifier of gentility rather than on the body's internal equilibrium, indicating a shift in the way in which the body was perceived as a category of discourse. Criticism of Anglo-Indian society shifted in the same direction, away from the dangers of inward bodily degeneration consequent upon indianization, towards the outward signs of social degeneration. In the 1844 edition of his handbook on India J. H. Stocqueler pronounced that 'residents in India necessarily degenerate, in an intellectual sense, and also in what are regarded as good manners and social habits in England...they are at last not only backward, but bigoted.'[69] One indication that this change was a response to larger social processes is the comparable shift in focus towards codes of conduct or civility in Indian society in the same period. The decline of the British nabob was paralleled by that of the old Indian nawabs. The policy of anglicization and assimilation replaced them with a growing western-educated elite with an interest not only in European learning but also in European customs. In conjunction with this, the ranking and grading of Indian society, stimulated by (among other things) the British administration of brahminical law, fostered an increasing interest in ritual purity and practices of differentiation among Indians.[70]

According to Norbert Elias, a by-product of increasing self-restraint and refinement is the construction of an 'affective wall' distancing the body from the bodies of others as well as from itself.[71] In the same vein, Terry Castle argues that the disappearance of the carnivalesque was hastened by the Romantic spirit, which concentrated on the individual: 'The scene of transformation moves inward, in both a literal and a figurative sense and transgression is figured in more psychological ways.'[72] Similarly, the bourgeois retreat into the black suit has been interpreted as a retreat into the body. The black suit erected an affective boundary around the body, closing it off from bodily contact with others, sealing it away from contact with the surrounding environment in a way which eighteenth-century

clothing styles had not.[73] The disappearance of the flamboyantly
attired nabob indicates a similar withdrawal among Anglo-Indians.
The black suit, however, was an extremely impractical form of attire
in the tropics. Frederick Shore commented with exasperation that the
adoption of the black broadcloth suit 'affords an additional proof of
an opinion I have seen great reason to entertain: viz. that the English
are nationally the most bigoted and illiberal people I have ever seen
or heard of.... I think the climate of India is quite debilitating
enough without our giving it adventitious aid by wearing a dress
unsuited to it; and I act on that principle.'[74] What Shore chose to
ignore was that the suit gained additional symbolic significance in the
colonies by the fact that it made no concessions to context. Any
modification of the suit which would have adapted it to the Indian
climate would have stripped it of its social and political significance
as a symbol of its wearer's British nationality. Enveloped in Britishness, the Anglo-Indian body in a black suit may have been thoroughly uncomfortable, but it was also thoroughly anglicized. In
India the suit performed an additional distancing function, not only
signifying a retreat into the body but also into Britishness to the
exclusion of the Orient.

As successive boundaries were drawn around the Anglo-Indian
body, limiting and defining more clearly its relationship with the
Indian environment, it gradually became more insular and less open
to Indian influence. The adoption of the metropolitan code of appropriate middle-class dress by the British in India did more than mirror
changes in British society – it incorporated them into the complex
process of sloughing off all taint of indianization. This can be seen
most explicitly in Anglo-Indian women's dress. While the fashionable
world of London continued to integrate the Orient into women's
clothing, women closer to the source of such finery rejected it altogether. By the 1820s and 1830s even the use of the once popular gold
and silver fabrics was outlawed among Anglo-Indian women, who
wished 'to avoid the appellation of *nautch* girls' and to disassociate
themselves from lower-class Eurasian women who were notorious
for their gaudy clothes.[75] Mrs Fenton was frustrated by the fact that
it was 'the extremity of bad taste to appear in anything of Indian
manufacture... when I wanted to purchase one of those fine-
wrought Dacca muslins I was assured I must not be seen in it as
none but half-castes *ever* wore them. These dresses sell in London as
high as £7 or £10.'[76] Instead, Anglo-Indian women went to great
lengths to import their clothing from Britain. The papers were full of
advertisements for the latest in home fashions: a Mrs Carberry
assured her customers in a newspaper advertisement that 'the above

goods left Europe at the end of November and are the freshest in the market.'[77] During the cold weather a thoroughly anglicized 'Home' look of dresses made of thicker materials and worn with shawls was the height of Anglo-Indian fashion.

Despite the dominance of standardized black dress, the anglicization of the British body in India was not a uniform process. The ornamental Orient was not entirely drowned in a sea of black. The officer's uniform remained an area where colourful sartorial display continued to be acceptable, and in the 1820s the Orient resurfaced in the uniforms of British officers in the irregular cavalry corps. Inspired by the flowing robes of their *sowars* (cavalry) and the example of Skinner's Horse, whose officers wore yellow coats reminiscent of those worn by the Rajput warriors of old, irregular cavalries abandoned their old uniforms in favour of the *alkaluk* (a long coat with an embroidered bib) and the *poshteen* (a skin coat worn over the *alkaluk*). Underneath they wore pyjamas and cummerbunds, and for headwear they sported decorative turbans. This Indian uniform, which contrasted with the stiffer more compact British uniforms of their fellow officers, gave irregular cavalry officers a romantic dashing air, associated with the bravado of the frontier regions.[78]

Indian forms of clothing never entirely disappeared from the Anglo-Indian sartorial repertoire. Pyjamas were worn to sleep in, and in the cool of the morning men might lounge on the verandah in a picturesque manner reminiscent of the nabob, in pyjamas and sleeping jacket, drinking their tea.[79] The standardization of manners in Anglo-Indian society meant that aberrations from the norm were pushed into the background areas and activities of life. Exotic clothing and the lax posture which accompanied it marked out a backstage area where the individual could take respite from the formality of public codes of behaviour. A distinctively colonial hierarchy of possible forms of clothing and the deportment which accompanied them developed. This placed Indian costume at the bottom and British forms of dress at the summit. Somewhere in between lay the white tropical suit of shirt, waistcoat, jacket and trousers, all made of white linen. British in terms of the items which made up the suit but colonial in its colour and cut, the white tropical suit was to develop in the late nineteenth century into a distinctive signifier of the sahib. Thus, while the process of anglicization re-fashioned the Anglo-Indian body into a British body, it also retained distinctively colonial characteristics.

The same process of hierarchization which placed India and its practices at the bottom can be seen at work in the sphere of Anglo-

Indian dietary habits. The change in direction which took place in the discussion of food is particularly revealing of the way in which the nature of the body as a category of discourse altered during the first half of the nineteenth century. In the days of the nabob, even outside the medical discourse, the culinary discussion focused on how best to preserve the body in a state of equilibrium with its environment, as was illustrated by David MacFarlan's exchange with his brother over the benefits of a vegetarian diet. Gradually, although the medical concern with temperance did not abate, the discussion shifted away from matters of health and the inner state of the body to those of etiquette and outward signifiers of gentility. Against a pattern of changing dietary habits in the metropolitan society, Anglo-Indian eating habits began to stand out as not only different but also inferior. The Anglo-Indian table was characterized as lavish but lacking in civility.

> There is always a mixture of meanness and magnificence in everything Asiatic; the splendid appointments of silver and china, which deck the board, have not their proper accompaniment of rich damask, but appear upon common cotton cloths...All the glasses are supplied with silver covers to keep out the flies: but the glasses themselves are not changed when the cloth is removed. It will easily be perceived that there is an air of barbaric grandeur about these feasts, which reminds a stranger of the descriptions he has read of the old baronial style of living.[80]

Gluttony and love of feasting were both associated with the urban *nouveau riche* in Britain.[81] Like the metropolitan social upstart, his inability to display a grasp of the etiquette which now regulated food consumption in polite British society marked the Anglo-Indian as a parvenu. Charles Day's handbook on etiquette warned 'Nothing indicates a well-bred man more than a proper mode of eating his dinner. A man may pass muster by *dressing well*, and may sustain himself tolerably in conversation; but if he be not perfectly...au fait *dinner* will betray him.'[82] J. H. Stocqueler viewed the backwardness of Indian dinners, which he dismissed as 'far behind the home *cuisine* in every material respect', as just one more symptom of the parochialism of Anglo-Indian society.[83] But many refinements had found their way to the Anglo-Indian dinner table from metropolitan polite society by the end of the 1830s.

In Britain between 1815 and 1850 breakfast had become a light meal, eaten early. Lunch was now a cooked meal followed by afternoon tea; and dinner, where the most significant changes of all took place, was eaten much later and was significantly influenced by

French practice.[84] Dinner was now divided into a number of courses and more attention was paid to the appearance of the food, which was presented dressed or in the form of 'made' dishes, rather than as plain joints of meat. Large joints of plain meat now tended to be regarded as distasteful, and they were relegated to a side-table for carving.[85] Eaten from good china with silver cutlery, each course was accompanied by different wines drunk from the best glassware, and the tablecloth, of good quality stuff, was removed, along with the first set of glasses, before the dessert was served.[86] George Johnson, who visited India between 1838 and 1840, found that Anglo-Indian dinners had undergone a similar reform: 'French cookery is generally patronized, and the beef and mutton oppressions of ten years since are exploded. . . . Dinners in India now resemble those of the best regulated establishments of England.'[87] Even Stocqueler felt able to omit his depreciation of Anglo-Indian table etiquette from the 1854 edition of his handbook.

The presentation of the food and the order in which it was served was complemented by the attention paid to the tableware. A print of 1863 (see plate 5) shows Mr and Mrs Gladstone Lingham enjoying a civilized breakfast with their friends, the table spread with good tableware and decorated with flowers, just as it would have been in the best homes in Britain. From their earliest days in India the British

Plate 5   The black-coated civilian at breakfast, using British crockery and cooled by a punkah. 'Mr and Mrs Gladstone Lingham at breakfast with their friends Colonel Austin Thompson and Captain Bailey.'

had brought their crockery and cutlery with them, finding what they required unavailable in India, or of inferior quality, but as the century progressed the insistence that such goods should come from Britain rather than India or anywhere else in the East was less a matter of practicality than ideology. Frederick Shore remarked on this development with some disdain.

> Innumerable articles of daily use are procured at a high price from England...which might be produced equally good [sic] in India, at much less expense. Indeed the whole of the eastern world seems sometimes to be placed under the ban. Some years ago, hardly any one in Calcutta would place upon his dinner table any but the plainest white English crockery ware. Even English china was objected to for fear it might be mistaken for real China, and not perceived to be of English manufacture.[88]

The tableware on Mr and Mrs Gladstone Lingham's breakfast table was almost certainly brought from Britain, where Josiah Wedgwood remarked that he received orders for his chinaware from Anglo-Indians who held it 'in much higher estimation than the finest Porcellain' even though Chinese porcelain could be bought cheaply in India.[89] Here, the same trend which encouraged ladies to abandon Indian muslin was at work. The rejection of things of Eastern manufacture was part of the process of throwing off the taint of indianization which had characterized the habits of the nabob.

This ban on the East was also applied to the food eaten off the English crockery. The improvement, from the late eighteenth century onwards, in techniques for preserving food, combined with the economic pressure to sell British goods in India, led to the importation of large quantities of European foodstuffs (see plate 6).[90] Thus, the conditions for the development of a preference for European foodstuffs were created. Imported foods were accorded pride of place on the table: 'The delicacies of an entertainment consist of hermetically-sealed salmon, red-herrings, cheese, smoked sprats, raspberry jam, and dried fruits; these articles coming from Europe, and being sometimes very difficult to procure in a fresh and palmy state, are prized accordingly.'[91] Transporting the goods added hugely to their cost and in the *mofussil* tinned goods were sold for immense prices. Emma Roberts noted that 'a jar of preserves that sold in London for 4 shillings could fetch as much as 24 and was seldom sold up-country for less than 16 shillings.'[92] Indian merchants responded to the demand for British food by setting up shops dealing in imported goods. Market gardens sprung up on the outskirts of large European

TULLOH AND CO.'S ADVTS.

SOFT FLANNEL.—Messrs TULLOH and Co. have for sale at their New Rooms, a few pieces of Rogers' improved 4-4 and 8-4 Patent Flannel, which is decidedly preferable to every other species of Flannel, for its peculiar softness and not shrinking in washing; it likewise affords warmth and comfort to the tenderest habits when other Flannel are found unpleasant. For Waistcoats and under garments it is particularly recommended.

FASHIONABLE QUILTINGS, for Gentlemen's Waistcoats.—Messrs. TULLOH and Co. have just received for sale on Commission, a case of beautiful London Printed Quiltings, for Gentlemen's Warm Weather Waistcoats, of a variety of new and pretty patterns. Also a few pieces of Plain, Coloured and Figured Valencia, for Dress and Waistcoats.

FRESH FRENCH and SPANISH WINES, imported within the last few days.—Messrs. TULLOH and Co. have much pleasure in announcing to the Public, that they have received an extensive Investment of the undermentioned WINES and LIQUORS, the qualities of which Messrs. TULLOH and Co. can with the utmost confidence recommend as the freshest for sale in Town. The Investment comprises Sparkling White Champaigne, in quarts and pints, warranted the growth of Ai Vintage 1827, without exception the finest Wine for sale in Town.

First Growth Clarets, confidently recommended.

Chateau Latour, vintage 1825, possessing a remarkably rich flavour, with a fine full body, and well calculated for sending into the Mofussil.

Chateau Margaux, vintage 1825, in quarts and pints, a very superior Wine.

St. Julien Medoc, a fine flavoured Wine.

White Wines, for the hot weather, the qualities of which will be found very superior, Haut Pregnac, Haut Sauterne, White Hermitage, Burgundy Chambertin, Dessert and other Wines, Albaflor, Revesaltes, Calcavella, Cotie Rotie, genuine Maraschino de Zara, Delicious Liqueurs, of different sorts. In addition to the above, Messrs. TULLOH and Co. have received a batch of remarkably fine London-bottled Pale Sherry and Port Wine, from William Harper, London, Old Cogniac Brandy and Genuine Hollands.

OLD MADEIRA, SERCIAL, and MALMSEY, in whole and half pipes, for sale at Messrs. TULLOH and Co.'s Godowns. These Wines are of the best quality, and strongly recommended.

SUPERIOR PALE SHERRY, in butts, hogsheads, and quarter casks, for sale at Messrs. TULLOH and Co.'s Godowns. Price per butt 500 to 700 Rs.

CORDIAL WHITE AND CHAMPAIGNE BRANDY.—Messrs. TULLOH and Co. have received a small quantity of singularly fine Old White and Champaigne French Brandy, which they recommend as some of the best imported for many years.

SPARKLING WHITE CHAMPAIGNE, warranted the growth of Ai and vintage 1825.—Messrs TULLOH and Co. have for sale a small batch of White Sparkling Champaigne, which they have no hesitation in declaring to be the freshest and finest Wine for sale in Town.

FRENCH and ENGLISH BRANDY, of the most unexceptionable quality, for sale at the Godowns of TULLOH and Co. Tank-Square.

JAMAICA RUM and HOLLANDS.—Messrs. TULLOH and Co. have for sale some particularly fine old Jamaica Rum and pure Hollands, which they warrant to be of the finest quality.

HAMS and CHEESES.—Berkeley, double Glo'ster, Chedder and Pine; and Plump Yorkshire Hams, ex. *Hindostan*, for Sale at TULLOH and Co.'s Godowns.

EUROPE-MADE BUGGY [illegible] LOH and Co. have for sale at their Commission Rooms, a few sets of well finished brass mounted Buggy Harness. Also, a few sets of Driving Reins. Prices moderate.

SHEPPARD AND CO.'S ADVTS.

AMERICAN OX-TONGUES, even *superior* to the English, may be had for *Cash*, at No. 57, Old Fort Street, at Sa. Rs. 24 per dozen. 24th March, 1834.

LONDON BOTTLED SHERRY.—A few six dozen cases of *Mackenzie's* London bottled Pale Sherry, *a dry and very superior Wine*, just imported on the *Hindostan*, may be had on application to Geo. Sheppard and Co.

57, Old Fort Street, March 4, 1834.

MESSRS. SHEPPARD and Co. have for Sale at their Godowns, No. 57, Old Fort Street, Pine, Warwickshire and Berkley Cheeses, at one Rupee per pound, pure Olive Oil in quarts, Salad Oil in pints, Mustard, Vinegar, Sauces, Pickles, *Sardines*, *Whole Anchovies*, Capers, Olives, Red Herrings, hermetically sealed Oysters and Salmon, Hyson Green Tea, in whole chests and 10 catty boxes, Picked Mocha Coffee in frazils, Bloom Raisins, *Genoa* Pipe and French Macaroni, Vermicelli, Fruit for Tarts, Hoffmann's Cherry Brandy, *fine little* PLUMP YORKSHIRE HAMS, and supplies generally.

1st March, 1834.

Plate 6 Flannel, wines and a wide variety of hermetically sealed foods were imported from Britain to satisfy the Anglo-Indian desire for British food. Advertisements from *The Englishman*.

stations and in the hill stations to supply the towns with 'British' cabbages, cauliflowers, peas, runner beans, spinach, lettuces, artichokes, celery and beetroot. On the foothills of the Himalayas apples and pears were cultivated.[93]

The Anglo-Indian demand for European foodstuffs reveals the body as an active agent of change. The Anglo-Indian response to the flavours of food which devalued, for example, the flavours of Indian vegetables (the glutinousness of okra) and valued those of European vegetables (the crispness of cabbage), was less to do with biology than a mindset encoded in the body.[94] The tastes expressed by the Anglo-Indian body were the expression of a mental map of flavours which placed European imports at the pinnacle of a hierarchy of foodstuffs. The body as the site where food preferences were encoded actively shaped the culinary discussion and the economy of food production and importation. Even Indian food culture was affected as Indians gradually incorporated a taste for European vegetables into their bodily map of acceptable flavours. Cabbage, peas, beans, potatoes and a whole host of vegetables introduced to India by either the British or the Portuguese were integrated into, and remain essential ingredients in, Indian cuisine.

Food preferences were not simply a matter of flavour but also of discernment. Food was a means of claiming membership of polite society. In India British food gave a meal extra symbolic resonance.[95] The fact that heavy hot dinners were unappealing in the Indian climate and that the methods of preserving food often meant that the taste was impaired merely served to underline the determination of the exile to preserve the proprieties of British society within an alien land. The food practices which developed between 1830 and 1850 constructed an Anglo-Indian body more in harmony with the new ideology of rule which cast the British as carriers of western civilization to India. Here, as with clothing, the Anglo-Indians took what in Britain were seen as defining aspects of the middle class and gave them wider resonance as signifiers of British nationality in the colony.

It was not of course possible for the British to entirely abandon Indian food. British vegetables could only be grown during the cold season. During the hot weather, and in the more isolated areas, the British relied on Indian vegetables or expensive tins, and subsisted mainly on the Indian staples: mutton, fowl, and eggs, occasionally varied by much-relished game. Even in the 1920s in the hot season potatoes, pumpkin, papayas and bananas were the only available vegetables and fruit in isolated areas.[96] The continued incorporation of Indian foodstuffs into the Anglo-Indian diet, as well as a continuing preference for abundance, ensured that the British body in India remained distinctively Anglo-Indian. This was not only a matter of necessity but also of choice. The Anglo-Indians made certain Indian dishes their own. Kedgeree, a combination of fish, eggs and rice, which was an adaptation of the dish of the Indian poor known as *khichri* made of rice, dhal and spices, was indispensable at breakfast. It also made its way to Britain in the eighteenth century where, ironically considering its origins, it was integrated into the breakfasts of the aristocracy. Curry and rice was another staple of the Anglo-Indian diet, eaten for breakfast, lunch and dinner. Exactly what was meant by 'curry' is difficult to determine, but the term probably covered a variety of dishes with a spicy sauce adapted from Indian cookery to suit the tastes of the British.[97] Anglo-Indian eating habits were never simply a pale reflection of the eating patterns of British middle-class society. They retained a distinctive, partially indianized character of their own.

Despite the fact that remnants of Indian influence survived the process of anglicization, the ban on the East extended into all areas of life where the integration of India had once made the nabob's body distinctive. One of the practices most symbolic of bodily indianization was smoking the hookah. Within the context of the shifting political climate, the hookah was no longer considered an appropriate accoutrement for the British official in India. This status symbol was now considered too opulent for the more sober *burra sahib*. By the 1820s the hookah was decidedly unfashionable and by the 1830s some members of society appear to have made it clear that the hookah was unwelcome at their dinner tables by printing 'No hookahs' on their invitations.[98] Although there were some smokers, especially in Calcutta, who clung to their hookahs well into the 1840s, by then this had almost entirely been replaced by the cheroot. Once looked down upon as somewhat vulgar, smoked only by 'the lowest classes of Europeans, as also of the natives', the cheroot was now favoured as a more independent way of inhaling tobacco.[99] Necessitating neither a special servant nor fancy paraphernalia, it was less associated with a process of indianization.[100] In addition it involved solely the inhalation of tobacco, while the hookah was associated with stronger stimulants and other indianizing practices: 'Now [the 1860s], the scent of a hookah in a house is considered almost disreputable – more especially as it gives rise to surmises that it is not the only manner in which the master of the house accommodates himself to native habits.'[101] The disappearance of the hookah, identified with an indianized lifestyle of *nautches*, Indian attire, an Indian concubine, and possibly even the use of narcotics, was essential to the process of anglicization.

The demise of the hookah was accompanied by the disappearance of those customs which were associated with it, including the common practice of keeping an Indian mistress. In 1844 *The Calcutta Review* asserted that a comparison of recent handbooks with that of Thomas Williamson's *The East India Vade-Mecum* (1810) demonstrated the improvement in Anglo-Indian social morality. Beginning with the work of Williamson, the reviewer wrote:

> There is evidently no consciousness, in the mind of the writer, that his work, almost from first to last, is characterised by a looseness of morality, destined in a few years to be regarded almost with loathing. Let the reader, anxious to estimate rightly the moral improvement of the English in India, within the last five and thirty years, compare this *Vade Mecum* of 1810, with the Handbooks, recently published, of Mr. Parbury and Mr. Stocqueler.[102]

Indeed, Williamson, writing at the beginning of the century, was completely at ease in his discussion of the native mistress. He described the advantages of the system, which avoided the expense of a European wife and children while it also compensated for the lack of European women in India. He discussed the cost of the practice, the 'infatuation' of many men with their mistresses, and the problem of the duplicity of Indian women as well as the possibility of polygamy.

> The mention of plurality, may possibly startle many of my readers, especially those of the fair sex; but such is common among natives of opulence, and is not unprecedented among Europeans. I have known various instances of two ladies being conjointly domesticated; and one, of an elderly military character, who solaced himself with no less than SIXTEEN, of all sorts and sizes![103]

Williamson was firm on the pre-eminent charms of European women and on the point that marriage to a native woman was inappropriate, although he reiterated that concubines should not be confused with prostitutes. Convinced that the system was the one best suited to the circumstances, he argued 'that matrimony is not so practicable in India as in Europe; and that, . . . it is impossible for the generality of European inhabitants to act in exact conformity with those excellent doctrines, which teach us to avoid "fornication, and all other deadly sins".'[104] Aware of the scandalous nature of some of his comments (his style occasionally slips into bawdiness), he covered his frank references to sexuality with none of the layers of disapproval and propriety which later veiled the discussion of such matters. In contrast, an open discussion of the advantages of keeping a concubine would look entirely out of place in Stocqueler's *The Handbook of India* (1844). His only mention of the system was in a footnote on the origin of the Eurasian community: 'We should here explain that by the "original source" is meant the illicit connections between Europeans and native females, a sort of connection that is happily falling into desuetude.'[105] In the 1854 edition of Stocqueler's handbook no mention was made of these illicit connections, an indication that by mid-century civilians would not have considered keeping an Indian mistress, even covertly.[106]

The natural companion of the nabob, the native mistress no longer suited the needs of the new type of civilian for a number of reasons. Firstly, an Indian companion created an intimate bond with the Indian people. Marriage to high-born Indian women had brought the British into friendly contact with their wives' Indian families. On another level, Richard Burton said of the mistress that she taught her companion not only Hindi but also the 'syntaxes of native life'.[107] A mistress also necessitated that the official should live at least to some extent in the Indian style because most of these women would have lived in purdah. Her presence therefore undermined the new definition of the Anglo-Indian official's body as untainted by Oriental contact. A second problem was that it was possible to equate the position of the Indian mistress with that of a slave as their families were normally paid a dowry.[108] Against the background of the evangelical campaign against slavery in Britain and the Anglo-Indians' own efforts to abolish the practice among Indians, the keeping of an Indian mistress put the humanitarianism of the Anglo-Indian official in question. Many of the British protested, as did General Claude Martin in his will, that 'they were not as we term slaves tho' paid a consideration for, but the sum I paid was a present to the relations that I might have a right on her.'[109] Nevertheless a native mistress who had apparently been bought from her family was something of an embarrassment.

Thirdly, the rejection of the Indian mistress is often attributed to the growing numbers of respectable European women coming to India. They are usually held responsible for deteriorating relations between the British and the Indians.[110] Their availability as marriage partners meant that British men found it more difficult to justify turning to the indigenous population for companionship. Nevertheless, European women remained few and far between. The dearth of women combined with the fact that civilians and officers could rarely afford to marry until late in life must have left many men single, and presumably celibate, over a long period of the time they spent in

India. Native mistresses would have conveniently alleviated the frustrations of this situation, and yet by mid-century, as the morals and manners current in Britain spread to the colony, they were viewed with great disfavour. The moral misgivings which such liaisons had always provoked, even in the special context of India, were now made manifest. The growth in numbers of European women played an important part in this process because women were appointed the guardians of morality.[111] Further moral pressure was exerted by the educated Indian elite who, once they had become conversant with western culture and values, became increasingly critical of Anglo-Indian morality in the press. The momentum for a tightening up of moral standards was therefore also generated within the colony itself in response to the threat of criticism from respectable Indian circles.

Moral judgements were given greater power by the question of 'moral restraint', which Malthus's theory of population growth put on the agenda in Britain. It was argued that populations could be limited if men were to abstain from sexual intercourse until they were in a position to marry and support their offspring. Out of this discussion emerged a conceptualization of the human libido as transformable: 'the idea came to be in the air that sex-drives would be moderate in the properly circumstanced individual (hard-working, mentally active, envisaging or enjoying a comfortable domesticity), and would become more temperate in society over time.'[112] The notion was introduced into the morality of the period that the substance of the body was actually physically altered by social circumstances; a moral body could be moulded by conduct which conformed to the moral code. The Anglo-Indian man living with an Indian mistress in the over-stimulating heat of the Indian climate could hardly be described as living in proper circumstances, and his consequent moral degeneration was inextricably linked to the spectre of physical decline as well as uncontrollable population growth.

Finally, probably the most important factor which led to the demise of the Indian mistress was the enduring link between the British and the Indian population created by the offspring of such unions. Higher officials tended to send their Eurasian children home to Britain.[113] Neil Edmonstone, who went out to India as a civil servant in 1783, had four children with a native mistress. They were sent to Scotland to be cared for by the sister of a fellow officer in the East India Company's army. Edmonstone saw to it that the two boys were educated and placed in a career (John in the army and Frederick in a manufacturer's business in Glasgow) and like many such children they would have been integrated into the lower levels of British society. Nevertheless, a patriarchal concern that Indian families should not undermine the British family unit meant that any children from a legitimate British marriage remained the heirs to their father's estate. When Edmonstone married twenty years later the existence of his Indian sons was never known to any of his subsequent children, who inherited his estate.[114]   Separate trust funds often solved the problem of Indian children while ensuring a racially pure line of inheritance. This should not be taken as evidence of an uncaring attitude towards their Indian families on the part of these men. Francis Fowke, who died without European connections by marriage, divided his estate between his sister and his 'natural son' while he also made provision for his mistress, named as 'the mother of my son, William'.[115] William Holland became so attached to his mistress that despite his sense 'of the impropriety of it yet I have many times determined to grant a request she has often made to me which is to go home with me and the children as their Ayah.'[116] The majority of such children were kept in India, however, where as Mrs Sherwood noted, the sons were usually 'accounted unpresentable'. They were found employment, as clerks for the Company or on indigo plantations, or more commonly in the army.[117] The daughters, who presented no threat to the British family line, were regarded as presentable and were married off, generally to members of the Company's military establishment. The children of ordinary soldiers were placed in orphanages where they were trained for menial jobs or married off to soldiers who attended regular match-making dances at the orphanages.[118] This meant that in the late eighteenth and early nineteenth century Eurasians were well integrated into Anglo-Indian society, especially military circles.

As the century progressed, resentment of this incursion of Eurasians into respectable society grew in force. Their inclusion implied a tacit acceptance of the practice of keeping an Indian mistress, which offended the increasingly sensitive moral code. As early as 1813, George Spilsbury noted that polite society was beginning to reject them.

> I heard the other day that Lady London had refused to invite half casts to her house. This seems to have caused a great sensation as I suppose a third of the people in this country are either married to this race or have children grown up by Hindostanee women. Should the example be set below of not receiving them no doubt it will be followed. The two refused at least left out in a general invitation are two ladies that have hitherto moved in the highest rank. It has caused a great sensation in the army.[119]

The exclusion of Eurasians progressed patchily, often according to the reputation of individuals. In the early years of the century moral disdain was as much an expression of class as racial prejudice: Eurasians were usually illegitimate, their mothers of low breeding. As the century progressed, scientific ideas of race intensified the fear of degeneration by the mixing of racial blood. Racism became increasingly overt as the British consolidated their rule and thus felt a greater need to assert both their Britishness and their superiority. Growing racial awareness transformed moral disdain into a desire for bodily distance which made moral boundaries manifest. By mid-century Eurasians had virtually disappeared from official Anglo-Indian circles. The disappearance of the native mistress and the exclusion of the Eurasian formed further vectors of a protective racial barrier which was developing around the British body in India, ensuring the separation of the colonizing society from that which it had colonized. It was this racial element which sharpened the British moral code in the colonial context. Although young men's entertainments in the metropole were supposedly less rakish by the 1840s, the prostitute and the mistress remained commonplace.[120]

If the middle-class code was effective in India in the sphere of sexual morality, it also appeared to be taking hold in other areas of Anglo-Indian life. In 1830 Fanny Parks noted that 'Methodism is gaining ground very fast in Cawnpore; young ladies sometimes profess to believe it highly incorrect to go to balls, plays, races, or to any party where it is possible there may be a quadrille. A number of the officers also profess these opinions and set themselves up as New Lights.'[121] But most evangelicals who came out to India with the same intention as W. D. Arnold's fictional hero, Edward Oakfield, to join in the 'grand work' of civilizing India by 'bringing religion into daily life' were deeply disappointed to discover that it was Anglo-Indian society itself which was in need of civilizing.[122] Arnold's novel presents Anglo-India, and especially the military, as morally and socially degenerate.[123] Oakfield vigorously resists the ungodly influences of his new life. Meanwhile his pitifully gentle and effeminate friend Vernon expires in a pathos-soaked deathbed scene. Arnold used Vernon's death to demonstrate that within a colonial society a stronger, more active religious spirit was required than the clerical attitude of Christian humility, no matter how virtuous. Indeed, it was when evangelicals in India and Britain united in an aggressive campaign that they had most success in influencing Anglo-Indian affairs. Evangelicals were concerned that the East India Company acted as a patron of Indian religions. Officials attended Hindu and Muslim religious festivals as part of their duties, the Company protected temples and mosques, and collected the pilgrim tax which not only financed the upkeep of Hindu shrines but also made a profit which went into government coffers.[124]   Under pressure from evangelical campaigning British attendance of Indian religious ceremonies declined. British dissociation from Indian religion was nevertheless slow and patchy. Although a despatch of 1833 ordered the abolition of the pilgrim tax, it was largely ignored.[125]

When it came to the observance of their own religion, Frederick Shore observed that Anglo-Indians tended to divide into two camps, 'the religiously inclined [who] are generally enthusiasts beyond all bounds of reason' and 'the greater number who are apparently without any care at all on the subject'.[126]   Many bemoaned the lack of churches and the neglected state of cemeteries in India, but this was more because religious ritual was accorded importance as an enactment of the basis of British superiority.[127]   The church service was also an important site for the delineation of the social divisions in Anglo-Indian society with the officials occupying the first rank of pews and the unofficial community, ordinary soldiers, Eurasians and poor whites relegated to the pews behind in descending order of their place in the hierarchy. Despite this rather lax religious climate, a further comparison of Williamson and Stocqueler's handbooks would seem to suggest that Anglo-India was no longer viewed as a place of vicious temptations for the young writer or cadet. In 1844 Stocqueler wrote soothingly:

> The important question of general morals...may justly be decided in favour of an Indian residence over a London one.... In our Oriental cities there are none of those lures and haunts which prove so attractive and fatal to the young Londoner. His Indian contemporary almost *must* spend his evenings in a decorous manner, for not only would he soon become marked if he frequented such scenes of debauchery as there are...but there is not that field for 'lark' which tempts the London ...youths.[128]

Even Williamson commented that most men were in bed by midnight, except those that played cards. Williamson did give a detailed description of the taverns of Calcutta, however, as places which can ruin a man's reputation while Stocqueler gave taverns only a cursory mention. Williamson described the 'sottishness' caused by drinking brandy and water in such a climate and the 'odium' which attached itself to all those who indulge while Stocqueler dismissed heavy drinking as a thing of the past.[129]   The comparison of the two handbooks indicates that by the 1840s vice within the Anglo-Indian community was perceived to have declined. Other evidence would suggest that such confident assumptions were misplaced. George Johnson detailed the ruinous activities of writers: 'Horses, gambling, champagne tiffins, dinners and suppers, the billiard-room, the fives-court, nautches, "Hindoostanee nights", &c. &c.'. He added a tantalizing footnote in explanation of 'Hindoostanee nights': 'The initiated will know what I mean... but the obscenity of their orgies forbid my being more particular.'[130] The tenor of these dissipations did, however, alter, reflecting a shift towards anglicized rather than oriental debauchery. The place of the *nautch* was taken by the officer's mess, the use of opium and other narcotics declined, arrack (an Indian spirit), brandy and punch were replaced by imported French wines. Sita Ram was of the opinion that this shift, which he identified as one of the causes of the Mutiny, was due to the increasing influence of religion among army officers. He complained that while in the old days 'the Sahibs often used to give *nautches* for the regiment... Nowadays they seldom attend *nautches* because their Padre sahibs have told them it is wrong.' [131] It seems more likely that the increasing distance between officers and their men within the Indian army was the product of the wider process of anglicization than a growing sense of religious fervour but, whatever the cause, the outcome was an ever-widening gulf between the British and Indians.

The body was at the centre of the process which transformed the nabob into the *burra sahib*. It reinforced the social trends operating in Anglo-India by generating practices which harmonized with the dominant ideologies of the period, demarcating the official's body as a British body in an Indian setting.[132] The body of the nabob was envisaged as an open body, in flux with its environment. The practices which surrounded it allowed adjustment to the circumstances of life in India. As the century progressed the body was reconceptualized as a category of discourse. Increasingly it was envisaged as an entity in itself, sealed off from the environment. The process of sealing off the body promoted the bodily distance of the British from the Indian community, forming a racial boundary around the body of the official which reinforced the process of anglicization. The rejection of the nabob was accompanied by increasing pressure towards social conformity. Norms which were perceived to demonstrate greater physical control replaced the fluid moral and behavioural codes of the eighteenth century. Britishness was defined within India by the markedly rigid, less flexible set of bodily norms which now governed Anglo-Indian behaviour. In this way the colonial environment transformed the codes of middle-class respectability and virtue into signifiers of British nationality. However, Britishness took on a distinctive character of its own within Anglo-India. The Anglo-Indian bodily map of tastes, desires and deportment – a preference for British vegetables combined with a continued love of curry; the restraining black broadcloth suit alternating with the tropical white suit; the cheroot; British wives tempered with 'Hindoostanee nights' – constructed a distinctively Anglo-Indian body, clearly distinguishable from the Victorian body in the metropole.

Survival in a British idiom

The process of anglicization received additional impetus from changes in the medical discourse. During the early years of the nineteenth century the indianizing regimen recommended by Anglo-Indian surgeons was the product of a belief that the European could adapt to the tropical climate. One of the earliest writers on tropical disease, James Lind, asserted that 'by length of time, the constitution of Europeans becomes seasoned to the East and West Indian climates.'[133] By the 1820s and 1830s, Company surgeons were a great deal less optimistic about the ability of the British to survive for any length of time in the tropics. The dominant environmentalist influence in Anglo-Indian medicine, which linked disease to topography, meant that the early nineteenth century saw a great deal of activity on the part of Anglo-Indian surgeons conducting medico-topographical surveys, detailing climatic, geological, botanical and urban conditions, in different areas of India. The aim was to identify those areas most suitable as British stations, the most important criterion being the similarity of their climate to temperate climatic conditions.[134] The general conclusion was that for the European the Indian landscape was pathogenic. India was defined as a dangerous and exotic environment, inhospitable to the European, who shrivelled in the heat in the same way that a tropical plant withered when transported to a cold climate. The Anglo-Indian was portrayed as an exotic within the exotic space of India. This was confirmed by Arthur Thomson's analysis of mortality rates in an article for the *Madras Quarterly Medical Review* of 1840 which suggested that the longer the length of residence the higher the death rate of Europeans.[135] Rather than adapting and becoming more resistant to the threats of the tropical climate over time, the British constitution appeared to weaken progressively.

The Portuguese were considered living proof that prolonged residence in a climate inimical to the European constitution led inexorably to deterioration: 'Who, without being told, could suppose that the wretched creatures we see creeping about Calcutta were Portuguese derived from athletic forefathers?'[136] The pale and sickly hue of British children born and raised in India suggested that British colonists would eventually find themselves as physically and mentally enfeebled as the Portuguese.[137] The indianized nabob also acted as a warning: often his indianization was described as so complete that return to Britain would endanger his health.[138] It was thought impossible for the European to survive in India unaltered in substance, or in racial terms, for a people to remain 'fertile and healthy from one generation to the next in an alien climate'.[139] Company surgeons concluded that it was absolutely necessary that all children should be sent back to Europe, preferably by the age of seven, to be raised in their native environment; that British rule in India was dependent on a constant regenerative flow of newcomers to India, and that eventual return to Britain for all Anglo-Indians was desirable.

Meanwhile those Europeans entrusted with the maintenance of British interests in India now sought some means of ensuring their survival during their sojourn which did not involve altering their bodily substance. Rather than seeking to adapt the European body to Indian conditions and learning from the example of the Indians, as early Company surgeons had advocated, Anglo-Indian medical men now set about opposing the effect of the climate and maintaining the colonist's temperate constitution unaltered despite the change of climate. In other words, the medical effort shifted towards opposing any indianization of the European body and maintaining as much of its British essence as was possible in the hostile conditions of India. This attitude was reinforced by the racial explanations for differences between the British and the Indians which began to overlie climatic ones. Differences between Indians and Europeans were increasingly attributed to their possession of fundamentally different physiologies rather than to the impact of different climates on physiologies which were essentially the same. Although the Indian body appeared to be more resistant to certain tropical ailments, it was thought to sink much faster than the average European body once it was attacked by disease. The inability of the Indian to withstand the vigorous European remedies of bleeding, mustard blisters and mercury was interpreted as a sign of intrinsic weakness. Indian remedies were therefore said to be more suitable for the Indian body, while the robust European required more aggressive interventionist treatments. The utilitarian critique of Indian society which encouraged the Company surgeon to view the Indian body as weak, the Indian climate as poisonous and Indian medical practice as nothing but despicable quackery also reinforced the argument that it was less the climate than Indian cultural norms which fostered disease.[140]

The positive impression of high standards of personal cleanliness among Indians was countered by impressions of the filthiness of Indian towns: 'in the hot season, an intolerable effluvia is constantly exhaling from numerous pieces of stagnant water and the filth, which is indiscriminately thrown into the streets, and there left to rot and bake: the whole producing a rare compound of villanous smells which can only be perfectly appreciated by those who have perambulated an oriental town or city.'[141] Any number of tropical diseases, especially ague, were attributed to the inhalation of miasma – air poisoned by the emanations given off by putrefying vegetable and animal matter, or dense rank vegetation and stagnant water. Thus the poor state of Indian health could be attributed to the filthiness of their surroundings. If health was a matter of cultural habits and personal responsibility, the Europeans were cheered by the prospect that the adoption of certain precautions would enable them to survive, European physiologies intact, despite the harshness of the climate. Confidence in British superiority reassured them that they would be able to adapt to climatic circumstances, not through acclimatization and its necessary concomitant, degeneration, but by erecting protective barriers around themselves.

The influence of the medical discussion on the preservation of the European body can be seen in the layout of Anglo-Indian urban and domestic space. Financial limitations and the fear of arousing opposition from the Indian population meant that rather than intervening to clean up Indian towns the British adopted the solution of separating native and European living quarters. European cantonments and civil stations were built at a distance, and upwind, from what was termed the 'black town', which Europeans avoided entering.[142] In this way medicine played an essential role in the process of anglicization in that medical precautions erected boundaries around the Anglo-Indian body, separating it further from India. Filthy Indian towns were not the only source of noxious emanations. Damp areas of dense vegetation were supposed to be particularly productive of miasma, especially at certain times of the year when heat was most likely to combine with exhalations from the vegetation. This was said to make miasma particularly fatal. The poisonous haze was believed to be denser than ordinary air and therefore more concentrated close to the ground and in gullies and valleys, where it might become trapped. The British therefore tried to avoid building close to such terrain or to jungly patches of ground, marshes and swamps.

Within the stations trees, mango groves and bamboos were discouraged as prejudicial to health, particularly during the rainy season, as they engendered a stagnant atmosphere by obstructing ventilation, besides harbouring filth and insects.[143] In order to facilitate the free circulation of air the houses were well-spaced and laid out along wide streets (see plate 7) which were watered in order to lay the dust. In fact, Anglo-Indian urban space was structured in opposition to the perception of Indian urban space. The wide avenues of the British stations were juxtaposed to the narrow streets of Indian towns; regularity of form contrasted with an unplanned irregularity of layout, and cleanliness opposed filth.[144] In her novel, *Life in India*, Mrs Monckland described the ideal station:

> Barrackpore, though a large station, presents an air of quiet and retirement like a country village; which joined to its military neatness and propriety, make it one of the sweetest places in India. The bungalows in four lines stand each separated from the others, every one surrounded by its corn-garden, flower-garden, and neat trimmed hedge; while the whole cantonment is at right angles intersected by well kept roads, smooth as bowling greens.[145]

Plate 7 In the Anglo-Indian station wide well-watered roads separated the bungalows, and the English-style church was reminiscent of home. 'Our station.'

The contrast of the neat clean British station with the Indian town was interpreted as a sign of British superiority. Constructed around concerns for health which were distinctively Anglo-Indian, the station nevertheless recalled the English country village. Anglo-Indian urban space gave visual expression to the need to protect the British body in India while simultaneously providing it with a British setting.[146]

Domestic space was arranged with the same concern to avoid miasma. Thick vegetation in the compound was discouraged, while elevation above the level of the heavy miasmic air was a crucial principle behind the plan of nineteenth-century Anglo-Indian dwellings. In early houses the living rooms were situated on the first floor, well above the level of miasma, and the ground floor consisted of storerooms. Later on when bungalows became common these were raised on a platform above ground level. Ventilation throughout the entire bungalow was assisted by its open-plan layout with each room interconnected by a series of doorways where curtains replaced doors. Miasma was thought to be more of a risk to the body at dawn and dusk, therefore Anglo-Indian sleeping arrangements were adapted to these dangers.[147] Allan Newton Scott's photograph of a man in his bed admirably illustrates the Anglo-Indian arrangement of the bedroom (see plate 8). The bed is raised high off the floor, above the level where dense miasma might unconsciously be inhaled. This contrasted with the Indian manner of sleeping on mattresses on the floor. It stands in the middle of the room, which is open to the garden so that the sleeper might benefit from a free circulation of air. The mosquito curtain is draped above him. Mosquito nets were thought to block the passage of miasma, which was a fortuitous idea as they would have erected a barrier not only against an illusory putrid atmosphere but also against the real carrier of malaria – mosquitoes.[148]

The protective structure of Anglo-Indian urban and domestic space demonstrated British ingenuity in the construction of effective barriers against the threat of the tropical environment. David Arnold argues that their ability to change their surroundings to suit their needs gave the Anglo-Indians greater confidence.[149] Paradoxically, the need to structure their world around the threat of India also demonstrated just how vulnerable the British were outside their own environment. Their vulnerability was highlighted by their need to create a familiar world around themselves evocative of the metropolitan country. This was a need most successfully fulfilled by the hill stations. During the 1820s and 1830s the East India Company began to explore the foothills of the Himalayas as well as the southern

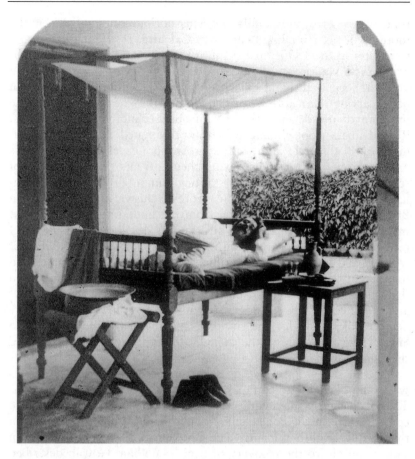

Plate 8 Protected from miasma by the high bed and the mosquito net. 'Rest, warrior, rest.'

mountain ranges in search of possible sites for sanatoria for troops. Detailed reports by medical men on the meteorological conditions in the hills confirmed their suitability for convalescents. J. O. Walter, the surgeon in charge of the convalescent station in the Mahabaleshwar Hills asserted that 'by assisting and regulating the remedial efforts of the constitution, under the tonic and salutary influence of a cooler atmosphere, we may...hope to succeed in many instances, in permanently reestablishing the equilibrium of the circulation, and the healthy action of the whole system, where long continued derangement of function has not already induced organic disease.' He appended case histories of his patients to his report which confirmed that men sent to the hills generally improved in health and robustness.[150] By 1830 Simla and Mussoorie were established in the foothills of the Himalayas; closer to Calcutta, Darjeeling grew up a little later in the 1850s; in the south Ootacamund and Mahabaleshwar served Madras and Bombay.

It was suggested that if hill stations were a solution to the problem of preserving the health of British troops, they might also solve the problem of the degeneration of European children in the tropics. Reared in the cool climate which approximated the temperate climate of Britain, children would grow up just as robust but less distant from, and expensive to, their parents.[151] A number of schools were set up in the hill stations, but Anglo-Indians still preferred to send their children to more exclusive establishments in Britain where absolute isolation from the undesirable influences of India was ensured.[152] Instead, hill stations developed into places of retreat from the heat, and from India itself. During the hot weather women, and those children who had not yet been sent home, retired for the entire period to the cool safety of the hills. The men joined them during their leave to snatch some relief. By the 1850s district and provincial administrations were moving their headquarters to the nearest hill station for the summer, and the government moved to Simla. After the Mutiny the desire for escape from India increased their popularity further.

The hill stations were seen as havens of Britishness. The houses were built like country cottages and given suitably countrified names. The gardens were filled with European flowers and vegetables which could survive in the cooler climate, and here the British engaged in thoroughly English pursuits. The Britishness of the hills was even seen as an aid to the recovery of health. William Gowan described the delights of the hill station: 'the temperature is such that Europeans may be out of doors all day with comfort and advantage – partaking of occupations and diversions the same as at home, and delighting in the association excited by scenery and climate ... resembling so exactly those which distinguish and exalt in his mind his distant and Dear Native Land.'[153] Despite the fact that with increasing numbers diseases quickly found their way to the hills,[154] and the British towns were rapidly complemented by rather squalid Indian counterparts, the hill stations, founded entirely for British purposes, became one of the most powerful symbols of the separation of the British from the Indians and one of the most significant indicators of the Britishness of Anglo-Indians: a concrete sign of the British inability to acclimatize.

Apart from advising separation from the Indian population and the creation of a protective environment for the European body, medical men continued to recommend a regimen adapted to the tropical climate. On the whole this differed little from the regimen prescribed by James Johnson in the early years of the century except that the tendency to hold up Indian habits and customs as examples to the British declined. Temperance in all things continued to be the keynote of medical advice. Bathing remained an important aspect of daily routine and, following developments in Britain, this was advocated in conjunction with daily exercise, which was said to not only help prevent and cure indigestion but also to stimulate the healthy action of the skin while maintaining muscular and moral fibre by disciplining the body. One area where the regimen did develop further was in the sphere of clothing as a protection against the vicissitudes of the climate. The cold was now identified as the other half of the climatic configuration which made the European body so peculiarly at risk in the tropical climate.

> Let every man, residing in a tropical climate, beware, above all things, of the *cold*.... The heat is an evil to be mitigated, chiefly on account of the danger to be apprehended from the cold. The relaxation, consequent upon the increased temperature, renders the frame so peculiarly susceptible to the impression of cold, that the utmost care should be taken to escape the influence of these distressing atmospherical vicissitudes. There are few of the ordinary diseases in India, which may not in the majority of cases be traced to the action of cold on the surface of the body, relaxed by the antecedent heat.[155]

As a defence against the shock of the cold on a relaxed body doctors and handbooks recommended flannel underwear: 'Whatever may be said upon the subject of wearing flannel in India, I am quite certain that no one thing is more essential to health in warm climates than the continual use of flannel.'[156] Flannel, considered to be a better absorber of perspiration than cotton or linen, allowed sweat to evaporate gradually, ensuring that the body cooled down slowly and providing it with an extra protective layer. Tulloh and Co. advertised soft flannels, which they particularly recommended for underwear, in *The Englishman* (see plate 6). Flannel underwear would have been unbearable during the hot weather, but it was particularly then that it was recommended as this was the period when the body was believed to be most susceptible to the cold. Elisabeth Bruce recorded in her diary that in Simla as the weather got hotter 'Her E[xcellency] spoke seriously to Dr F. about wearing winter clothes in such circumstances. He answered, "No underclothing was to be changed."'[157] In particular flannel was used to protect the stomach, which was identified by the theory of cutaeo-hepatic sympathy as the area of the body most vulnerable to the dangers of rapid cooling. Drawing on Indian customs, Johnson had pointed to the cummerbund as a practical means of protecting the stomach, and a flannel cummerbund or waist-belt which covered the entire abdomen had been developed. The flannel belt was universally recommended as an excellent means of warding off bowel complaints, especially cholera, which many Company surgeons associated with the evaporation of perspiration from an over-heated stomach. For this reason it became known as the 'cholera belt' and was used in both Britain and France during cholera epidemics, while 'Instructions to Army Medical officers for their guidance on the appearance of spasmodic cholera' advised that each soldier should be issued with two cholera belts.[158] Even once the cholera bacillus had been identified and the etiology of the disease was understood, the cholera belt remained a standard item of Anglo-Indian clothing, worn well into the twentieth century at night-time if not during the day.[159] When her family was packing to leave for India in 1913 Lady Chapman remembered 'a pile of these, knitted in wool and worn next to the skin round one's middle. They warded off chills which could be fatal if one became over-heated and was then exposed to a draught resting under a punkah for example during the mid-day heat.'[160] Even though the cholera belt developed out of a piece of Indian apparel it accentuated the Britishness of the Anglo-Indian body, acting as it did as a constant reminder that the British in India inhabited an alien and threatening environment.

Apart from temperature changes, the sun itself was identified as the other great threat to the European in India. The weak points of the body with regard to the sun were identified as the head and the spine. This latter part of the anatomy was provided with extra protection by a strange contraption known as a spine pad which was 'about seven inches long and three wide from the collar of the coat to about the lower angle of the back-bone...constructed of cork shavings, a material which while acting as a non-conductor of heat, is light, and sufficiently soft not to occasion inconvenience even if laid upon.'[161] The spine pad was worn by sportsmen in particular, who spent a lot of time in the sun when out hunting. Initially the British protected their heads from the sun with the Indian *chattah* and ordinary hats. James Johnson suggested following the Indian example and exchanging hats for turbans but most soldiers probably wore forage caps or 'havelocks' covered in white cloth with a piece of cotton attached to the back in the manner of the Indian *pugri* to protect the back of the neck from the sun. By the 1850s a specialized hat made out of a wicker frame, covered in quilted cotton cloth with a *pugri* at the back had developed.[162] The sola topi probably developed out of this form of headwear. The frame of the topi was fashioned out of the pith of the sola plant, which, according to Fanny Parks, meant that it was 'very light and [provided] an excellent defence from the sun'. Fanny Parks went on to describe how 'At Meerut they cover them with the skin of the pelican, with all its feathers on, which renders it impervious to sun or rain; and the feathers sticking out beyond the rim of the hat give a demented air to the wearer.'[163] She made this comment on the sola topi in 1833, but it is unclear when the first topi was worn by a European and how widespread they were before the 1850s. A complaint in an 1836 edition of *The Meerut Universal Magazine* that 'ten years have passed away since I saw a hat', there being 'an insuperable objection to...the covering for the head worn in this country...bearing the honourable title of HATS!', suggests that topis were already widely worn by the 1830s.[164]

The Mutiny gave the development of the topi a further boost. In response to the rebellion of the Bengal army the British substantially increased the number of British troops in India and stationed them in the plains rather than the hills so that their presence would be felt by the Indian population. It was clear from the sickness and mortality rates among troops that better means of protecting them from the climate needed to be found. Julius Jeffreys, in his book on the pre-servation of the British army in India, written in response to the problems highlighted by the Mutiny, went so far as to suggest that having observed with satisfaction the 'sickliness of Europeans in India' the Indians had felt bold enough to challenge British rule and had deliberately planned to rebel in the hottest season.[165] Jeffreys came up with a series of plans for providing troops with better protection against the climate, including a bizarre sun-screen tunic and a topi of great sophistication and complexity, both of which would have been absurdly impractical.[166] The topi did however become standard wear for all British soldiers, and all other Anglo-Indians dutifully wore their topi from sun-up to sun-down, or, during the cold weather, the soft felt terai hat, in combination with a *pugri*.[167] In 1912 Clarmont Skrine described his headwear for his mother: 'I have got two topees, one khaki one in Bombay and one white one here.' The white one was a full dress topi 'with a puggaree and every European without exception wears one as best both here and at Bombay and I believe all over India. No question of their being "only worn by globe-trotters" or anything of that sort.' The khaki one 'everyone wears for everyday use and for shikar [sport].

They are exceedingly uncomfortable head gear topees, and we all hate them: directly the sun goes down we appear in Homburgs, straw hats and caps. Bowlers [are] not worn at all.'[168] So ubiquitous was the topi that it appears in almost every photograph of the Anglo-Indian. In plate 11 Reginald Maxwell has removed his for the photo-graph and holds it on his lap. It became so powerful a symbol of Britishness that Eurasians took to wearing topis in order to assert their racial affinity to the British, and Gandhi was criticized for wearing one when recruiting for the British war effort in 1917.[169]

Goggles were an additional protection against the sun as it was thought that 'sunstroke [might]...be communicated to the brain through the eye.'[170] In the 1890s Elisabeth Bruce records a Captain Ponsonby wearing a 'white veil tied in a large knot behind, and green spectacles',[171] but goggles were never as popular as flannel under-wear, cholera belts, spine-pads and the sola topi. This array of protective paraphernalia lived on well after medical advances brought their efficacy into question. This may in part be due to the anachronistic nature of Anglo-Indian medicine between 1858 and 1914. The longevity of medical advice books meant that the medical advice which reached the ordinary Anglo-Indian family was increas-ingly outdated. James Johnson's *The Influence of Tropical Climates, More Especially the Climate of India, on European Constitutions*, first published in 1813 and revised by James Martin in 1856, was still available in 1861. H. H. Goodeve's *Hints for the General Manage-ment of Children in India*, first published in 1844, went through countless editions and several editors and was still available in the version issued by C. R. M. Green and V. B. Green-Armytage in 1913.[172] The failure of Anglo-Indian medical texts to keep up with medical advances was compounded by the fact that an older gener-ation of doctors continued to dominate the Indian Medical Service into the latter half of the nineteenth century. This was a result of the system of promotion on the basis of seniority which, despite the high death rate among Indian surgeons, meant that young men with new ideas took a very long time to climb the Anglo-Indian medical hierarchy.[173] Out-moded concepts of the body and the texts which expounded them were thus given a longer life than they deserved. More importantly, the British clung to their protective clothing as it gave them a sense of security. Dane Kennedy, writing on colon-ial Africa, suggests that it allayed those climatic fears which reflected the socio-psychological dislocation which the European felt in the tropics.[174] A further compelling reason for the longevity of flannel underwear, cholera belts, spine pads and sola topis was that they gradually became essential elements of the uniform of the sahib. This was especially true of the sola topi, the ultimate signifier of Anglo-Indian group membership and the authority and prestige which went with it. The other forms of protection began to drop out of use in the inter-war period but the Anglo-Indians did not relinquish the topi until the 1940s.

The variety of measures which the Anglo-Indians took to protect themselves within the hostile environment of India served to underline their incongruous position in India. The earlier conception of the British body in India as an open entity in dialogue with its surroundings was substituted by the idea of the body as a closed entity bounded off from its environment. The medical discussion abandoned hopes of acclimatization by means of the assimilation of India and turned towards the preservation of an intact British body. Medicine now highlighted the vulnerability of the European and in doing so constructed the Anglo-Indian's body as an occidental body which was perceived to be highly sensitive to a non-temperate climate and in need of a host of protective mechanisms. This creation of a vulnerable occidental Anglo-Indian by the medical men allowed them to preserve their authority as a profession while ensuring that they remained indispensable to the project of empire building.

The paraphernalia of medical protection marked out the Anglo-Indian body as idiosyncratic within the tropical setting. The increasing numbers of women and children in India in need of special care probably added to this image of the weakness of the European. The precautions which the British adopted thus compounded the effects of the process of anglicization by virtue of the fact that they underlined the status of the Anglo-Indians as exiles and thereby their Britishness. British vulnerability was thus transformed into a strength as it symbolized British superiority as well as otherness.

The medical occidentalization of the body coincided with those political and social developments that encouraged a shift in the cultural norms which created an anglicized Anglo-Indian body.[175] The image of the Anglo-Indian of the 1830s and 1840s, dressed from head to foot in a broadcloth suit, possibly concealing flannel underwear, with a sola topi adorning his brow, eating foodstuffs imported from Britain at his table in a cottage-like bungalow in the hills, contrasts markedly with that of the nabob, reclining on cushions to watch a *nautch*, enjoying his hookah and the company of his Indian mistress. This contrast demonstrates the extent to which the shift in the political, social, moral and medical discourse stimulated a radical change in the construction of the Anglo-Indian body. The rejection of things Indian, the adoption of signifiers of Britishness and the medical occidentalization of the Anglo-Indian body, combined to draw in the boundaries which marked the extent of Indian influence on the Anglo-Indian and, as a result, a web of Britishness was woven around the body. A process of the separation of ruler from ruled, of different social groups within the Anglo-Indian community from each other, and of the self from the body, was set in motion. These tendencies coincided with a political policy of anglicization and assimilation which placed less emphasis on creating traditional lines of political legitimacy. British rule was now justified by its role in bringing the benefits of western civilization to India. Britishness was therefore seen as an essential quality of the Anglo-Indian ruler. Thus, the anglicized official body harmonized with the shift in the discourse towards rule in a British idiom.

3

The Limits of Anglicization

There were limits to the process of anglicization just as there were limits to the process of indianization. Although the middle-class code of respectability and virtue was translated in India into a code of behaviour which signified Britishness and superiority, anglicization was neither a uniform nor an uncontested process. The Anglo-Indian body was not passively moulded by a monolithic discourse. British moral and behavioural codes were reformulated as they were trans-ferred into Anglo-Indian life, creating a distinctively Anglo-Indian body. The process of anglicization may have removed the figure of the nabob from the Indian scene, but the spread of respectability from Britain was not all-encompassing. In certain spheres of life the British in India remained remarkably open to their surroundings. This chapter explores the limits and inconsistencies of anglicization in the spheres of Anglo-Indian childcare practices, domestic space and relationships with Indian servants. These were all areas of life where the British neglected to draw the boundaries closer to the body or to clearly demarcate where India ended and Britain began.

The 'baba logue'

In many ways Anglo-Indian children, the *baba logue* as they were referred to by their servants, retained that openness to India which had characterized the nabob, and which was gradually lost by adults during the first half of the nineteenth century. As with the decline of the masquerade, which saw costume parties relegated to the sphere of children's entertainment, the openness of the nabob was relegated to the sphere of childhood.[1] Late eighteenth-century portraits of

children frequently show them in Indian-style dress. In John Zoffany's portrait of *The Impey Family Listening to Strolling Musicians*
(*c.*1783–4) the parents are depicted in European dress and it is the
children in their Indian-style dress, especially Impey's daughter in the
attitude of a *nautch* girl, who make the Indian connection apparent.[2] Contemporaries described Anglo-Indian children's clothes,
even outside portraiture, as an adaptation of Indian styles. They
took the form of 'a single garment, a frock body without sleeves
attached to a pair of trousers, with a rather short, full skirt gathered
into the body with the trousers, so as to form one whole'.[3] Not
dissimilar to the muslin frock and long drawers which children
customarily wore until the age of five or six in Britain, this costume
was admirably suited to the climate.[4] By mid-century a touch of
Britishness was added by the topi, which every child wore from
sun-up to sun-down (see plate 9).

The openness of Anglo-Indian children's bodies to India is made
apparent by the intimacy which existed between Anglo-Indian children and their Indian servants. The child's first servant was generally
an Indian wet-nurse, the *dhaye*. In the absence of safe substitutes for
breast milk and in a climate where fatigue and anxiety affected many
European women's ability to breast-feed, the majority of British

Plate 9   Anglo-Indian childhood was marked by pony rides and sola topis.
'The young Churchill Arthur Luck in the 1860s.'

babies born in India were suckled by a *dhaye*. For many women this was the only means of ensuring that their child was properly nourished in the first few months of its life. Although Mary Ann MacFarlan managed to nurse her first child, with the birth of her second child she suffered from jaundice, felt 'quite worn out' and was forced to employ a *dhaye*.[5] Even when the mother was able to produce milk and wished to feed her child herself, many argued that the quality of a European mother's milk was inferior to that of a sturdy Indian woman who was constitutionally fitted to withstand the climate.[6] Wet-nursing had gradually been going out of fashion from the middle of the eighteenth century in Britain, but in the special circumstances of the colonial environment it was considered essential for the delicate European child well into the nineteenth century.[7]

The employment of a wet-nurse presented mothers in India with a set of problems similar to those which they would have faced in Britain.[8] The dependence of the child on its nurse meant that women of an inferior social status gained a position of power within the household. The wet-nurse in both countries could demand high wages and perquisites such as clean clothes, plenty of nourishing food and numerous little presents.[9] In Britain this dependency disrupted class relations but in India, at a time when racial barriers between the British and the Indian population were hardening, it undermined the ongoing process of racial segregation. It placed European women in the uncomfortable position of having to endure the bad temper not only of an inferior servant but also of a member of the subject race. On discharging her *dhaye* Mary Thornhill 'never was so thankful to be rid of a nuisance – her temper and falsehood are something terrible to contemplate.'[10] One of the most powerful reasons for creating distance between themselves and the Indian population was the Anglo-Indian fear of disease, and yet the *dhaye* threatened to bring the diseases of India into the household both on her person and through her habits. The British therefore made every effort to regulate the *dhaye*, whose body was subjected to extremely close scrutiny before she was allowed into contact with the child. As in Britain, medical handbooks carefully described how to inspect her for signs of illness and listed desirable bodily qualities. On entering the household the woman was bathed and given a new set of clothing, and employers were warned to supervise her weekly bath in order to ensure her personal cleanliness. *Dhayes* were frequently banned from all contact with their own families until the task of suckling the child was over in order to reduce the risk of illness to the child.[11] Employers also sought to monitor the quality of the *dhaye*'s milk by ensuring that she only ate food provided by themselves. The

Stewarts, living in Cawnpore in the 1860s, rejected a woman despite the fact that she was healthy as she 'positively refused to eat out of any plates but those of her caste and not even to have her dinner cooked in our kitchen. This was too much and she was today changed for another.'[12] It was feared that unless properly monitored the *dhaye* would indulge in spicy foods which would upset the baby's stomach. The other great fear was that the laziness of the *dhaye* would result in the child being doped with opium in order to keep it quiet. This was not a problem confined to India; wet-nurses and nannies employed the same methods in Britain.[13] Large doses of opium could have tragic results. 'One night a witch of a Dhye gave [George Spilsbury's godchild] such a dose of Opium that it was with the greatest [illegible] I could recover him. From ten to midnight I had great doubts if I should bring him thro'.'[14] Parents worried about older children as well. Fanny Wells was concerned about putting her son's bed in another room because 'he is so troublesome that I am afraid . . . lest his bearer should give him opium, as no native will bear getting up [at] night.'[15]

If the quality of the food the *dhaye* ate was thought to affect her milk, more disturbing was the belief that the moral characteristics and the temperament of the nurse could be transferred to the child through this medium. In Britain this meant that great stress was placed on finding a wet-nurse with a good moral character, but in India, where the majority of the population were viewed as morally degenerate, this was more difficult to achieve. In the early part of the nineteenth century John Gilchrist tells us that *dhayes* were 'commonly Moosulman women of better, though decayed families', but by the latter part this was no longer the case and *dhayes* were 'obtained generally from among the poorest classes of natives'.[16] At a time when it was thought that prolonged exposure to the Indian climate could bring about a process of indianization, the belief that breast milk had the power to convey the characteristics of the Indian nurse to the child must have aroused great anxiety. This was compounded by the revulsion some European women felt for Indian women. Edith Lytton was upset by the need to hand her son, born in 1876, over to a 'horrid dirty woman' and believed that the dullness of the *dhaye*'s personality was transferred to the child, who was said to have livened up a great deal once he was weaned.[17] Indeed, there were those who refused to expose their children to such intimate contact with the natives. Alfred Lyall wrote to his sister on the birth of his son, 'Cora is looking wonderfully well, though the duty of nursing rather pulls her down, but we are determined to eschew black foster mothers, and our triumph over other households who maintain negresses is great and deserved.'[18] The possibility that suckling at the breast of an Indian woman might bring about a form of miscegenation was rarely articulated however. Need, as well as the principle of the European woman's delicacy in the tropical climate and the belief in the child's need for an Indian form of sustenance, helped the British to overcome their qualms about using a *dhaye*. That they were prepared to relax the increasingly secure racial barriers they were constructing in order to employ Indian wet-nurses, demonstrates that these barriers were to some extent flexible and could be adapted to the requirements of the British community.[19]

Once the services of the *dhaye* could be dispensed with, children were handed over to an ayah or into the care of a bearer. A review of *The Child's Wreath of Hymns and Songs* in *The Calcutta Review* of 1844 deplored this system of childcare.

> Setting aside for the present the evils of the climate, there remains the terrible drawback of native servants. . . . a child brought up in this country. . . [presents] a fair prospect of becoming in after-life a lover of eating, and of all other bodily indulgences. . . . Yes, even little girls are entrusted to native *men*! . . . Under any circumstances, can a mother think it favourable to her daughter's delicacy, to be always with a man, to listen to his talk, romp with him, and be in all respects tended by him?[20]

Indian servants in sole charge of Anglo-Indian children were seen to be in a position to initiate them into Indian culture. In particular it was feared that the servants would teach the children 'all the dogmas and obscenity of their religion'.[21] Mrs Sherwood described how she sobbed with fear on seeing her son's forehead daubed with powder, his having attended a *puja* with his ayah and bearer.[22] In one of her salutary tales for children she painted a picture of a child left too much in the company of Indian servants.

> He used to sit in the *verandah* between his *bearer*'s knees, and chew *paun* and eat bazaar sweetmeats. He wore no shoes nor stockings; but was dressed in *pangammahs*, and had silver bangles on his ancles. No one could have told by his behaviour or manner of speaking that he was not a native, but his pretty light hair and blue eyes at once shewed his parentage.[23]

Thomas Williamson warned that without constant watchfulness on the part of the parents, '*ayahs*, will initiate their young charges in many practices, and especially in language, such as must require infinite assiduity to subdue; and, after all, may not be completely suppressed. Besides, they are usually very slovenly and offensive in their persons.'[24] The first language of most Anglo-Indian children was Hindustani and they were 'very seldom taught a word of English until they are five or six years old, and not always at that age'.[25] Colesworthy Grant saw their grasp of Hindustani as an indication that their ideas were as oriental as the language in which they expressed them.[26] Fluency in an Indian language created a strong bond between Anglo-Indian children and the country of their birth.

Despite the anxiety of commentators, many Anglo-Indians remembered their childhood with great affection as an idyllic period of daily pony rides (see plate 9) and adoring servants.[27] For parents, the indulgence which Indian servants showed children made the task of disciplining them a tiresome one. Fanny Wells had great difficulty with her son because she could not teach the servants not to give him everything he cried for.[28] The respect Indian servants showed Anglo-Indian children also did little for their moral character as it tended to foster in them, as it did in John Rivett-Carnac, 'a very great idea of my own importance, so much so that in later life it never crossed my mind that I could be killed or be in any danger from an Indian.'[29] Anglo-Indian children had a reputation for being spoilt and wilful, like Mary Lennox in *The Secret Garden* who 'by the time she was six years old ... was as tyrannical and selfish a little pig as ever lived'. On arriving in Yorkshire Mary behaves very much like a tiny nabob, issuing commands to the servants in a peremptory manner and holding out her hands and feet, waiting for her maid to dress her.[30]

The intimate relationship between Anglo-Indian children and their Indian servants was a substantial area of life where Anglo-Indians failed to erect an effective barrier between themselves and the Indian population. Some efforts were made to anglicize children, especially in the sphere of diet, as food was thought to affect their temperament. Alfred Lyall concluded that 'the hideous temper which possesses the majority of British babies is to be traced to the ill advised diet allowed by mothers.'[31] Great emphasis was therefore placed on a bland and simple diet of broths, bread and milk, rusks, eggs, cutlets, and simple puddings, avoiding hot curries and stimulating foods.[32] Augusta Becher also vetoed the Indian practice of feeding the children seated on the floor.[33] Nevertheless India was integrated into the body of the Anglo-Indian child through the ingestion of the *dhaye*'s milk, the wearing of Indian-style clothing, and his or her intimacy with Indian servants and Indian culture. The special case of children demonstrates that the boundaries which were constructed around the Anglo-Indian body during the first half of the nineteenth century were not consistently drawn. The permeability of children's bodies qualifies the argument that a process of closure was occurring. The relatively relaxed attitude of Anglo-Indian parents towards the integration of India into their children's world can only be explained by the fact that the children were sent home at the age of six or seven. It was not only worries about the children's health but also the need for the inculcation of British culture which provided grounds for their removal to the metropolitan country. The failure to prevent the pollution of their children through intimate contact with Indians reflected the confidence of their parents that the taint of India would be purged from them on arrival in Britain: 'It is our proud boast, that wherever our children are born, we send them home to be educated; we give them the sentiments, and the pride, and the independence of our natural character. Whereas in all the Dutch, French, Portuguese, and other foreign settlements, they keep their children with them, and in two generations they are natives in their minds, if not in colour.'[34]

The bungalow

An examination of Anglo-Indian domestic space, by establishing the thresholds of intimacy within the family and the wider household, suggests that here too openness continued to be a defining factor. The structure of the social space in which the body moves reveals the shared values of a community by uncovering the formalities which govern behaviour. In Anglo-India the segregation of races that structured urban space contrasted with the openness of the bungalow. The anomalies in the structure of Anglo-Indian domestic space are further exposed by a comparison with middle-class domestic space in Britain. The middle-class house in the metropole was generally several storeys high, ascended by means of front and back staircases, with each room separated by landings, hall- and passageways. In contrast, the bungalow, by the 1830s the most common form of Anglo-Indian dwelling, was a single-storey, open-plan structure with most rooms leading out of a central hallway, and with each room separated by a curtain rather than a door. Since the late eighteenth century the structure of the British middle-class house had been characterized by the separation of spheres: work from home, children from parents, men from women, guests from the family and servants from masters and mistresses. Within the home 'It was considered undesirable for children, servants and parents to see, smell or hear each other except at certain recognized times and places.'[35] Far less separation existed within the bungalow. The very different use of space and the more relaxed family relationships this suggests, demonstrates the limits of the transferral of the metropolitan code of respectable behaviour to India.

In Britain children were confined to the nursery and, as they got older, the schoolroom, for most of the day. In India children generally ate and were taken for their evening drive separately, but while they might sleep in a nursery they were not shut up in one throughout the day. Emma Roberts, not apparently a great lover of children, commented sourly:

> It is possible to penetrate into the drawing-room of a mansion in England without being made aware that the house contains a troop of children, who, though not strictly confined to the nursery, seldom quit it except when in their best dresses and best behaviours, and who, when seen in any other part of the house, may be considered in the light of guests. It is otherwise in India. Traces of the *baba logue*, the Hindoostanee designation of a tribe of children, are to be discovered the instant a visitor enters the outer verandah.[36]

The constant attendance of servants meant that not only the children, but also their domestics, had to be endured wandering about the house freely. Even when they were not in sight Emma Roberts considered the noise of the children at play or being entertained by their servant to be a 'concert of the most hideous description'.[37] Fanny Wells, although less embittered than Emma Roberts, found the structure of the bungalow impractical where children were concerned: 'a bungalow is so different from a house, no upper storey, every room with five or six doors in it all of which are open and no possibility of having a minute's quiet, I always am so thankful when both the children are asleep.'[38] The layout of the bungalow meant that children were inevitably more of a presence within the Anglo-Indian domestic space than they were in Britain, while the constant attendance of Indian servants allowed the security provided by spatial barriers to be replaced by people. The entire Anglo-Indian attitude towards children thus exhibited a laxity which would have been unthinkable among the metropolitan middle classes.

In British homes the structure of the house underlined and ensured the division of the genders. The library and smoking room were considered male preserves, while the boudoir, bedroom and drawing-room were feminine spaces. Men and women used separate bathrooms. Bungalows in India were far too open for any effective segregation of the sexes. Social practices such as withdrawing at the end of a meal were observed, but the idea that this should be in order to leave the men to their masculine conversation in peace was more theoretical than practical. Ellen Thornhill wrote:

the houses at home are so different to this you know... our hall, dining-room and drawing-room all lead one out of another. ...The drawing-room is on the left hand side as you come in but you must go slap thro the dining-room and the only partition is a curtain which is very seldom drawn except on dinner party nights when there is [illegible] with a great noise after the ladies leave the table.[39]

Although Mrs Sherwood remarked that curtains in the Anglo-Indian home were 'as strong a barrier as an iron-bound door', in a house where bedrooms might lead off the drawing-room the need for privacy was acknowledged rather than realized.[40]

One explanation for the failure of the bungalow to accommodate the separation of the genders is that when the bungalow evolved there were fewer European women in India. Bungalows were designed for a single male with perhaps a native mistress living in separate quarters. Even once the numbers of European women had increased, Anglo-Indian society still largely consisted of bachelors and young people for whom divisions on the basis of gender were possibly less important. The constant moves which were a normal part of Anglo-Indian life meant that bungalows were standardized and that it would not have been worthwhile to construct differen-tiated bungalows for bachelors and married couples. In addition, bungalows originated as a fixed form of encampment, and even once the British were more established in India civil servants and their wives spent a great deal of time touring the countryside living in tents. The bungalow retained the air of an encampment, especially as camp-furniture was often used to supplement more permanent fix-tures. The need to adapt space to the climate also hampered rigid divisions within the home and encouraged a flexible use of space, with verandahs turned into drawing-, dining- and even bedrooms when the weather was hot. Under these conditions a rigid separation of genders and age groups was impracticable. The pattern of daily life in India may also have allowed time to replace space in the separation of the sexes. When men and women were both in the home they were generally engaged in common pursuits, which did not necessitate separation. The daily routine left very little need for elaborately divided homes except in the case of bathrooms and bed-rooms. In addition, while the separation of spheres may have func-tioned well for the middle classes in Britain, the isolation of many of the British in India may have substantially decreased their desire for segregation within the family. Indeed, Anglo-Indians were said to be more domestic than their compatriots in Britain. Frances Wells wrote to her father 'I fancy married people are much more fond of each other in India than in England, you will laugh at the idea but I really think it is the case, they are thrown so much together and for so many months in the year are so dependent on each other for society.'[41]

Anglo-Indian society was also renowned for its hospitality, and when guests needed a room the bungalow demonstrated its flexibility. Harriet Tytler reminisced 'I have learnt long since that English homes are not built so elastically as our own Indian homes, where we make room somehow or other for any amount of visitors, not only for friends but even for utter strangers.' Especially in the isolated up-country areas a stranger might arrive at a house while his hosts were in bed, or even away, and still expect to be shown to a bedroom by the bearer. 'At breakfast he would appear and introduce himself without much apology...He was welcomed and made at home at once.'[42] This policy of open house contrasted with visiting customs in Britain where visitors were usually formally invited and were expected to observe certain conventions governing the separation of host and guest at appropriate times of the day. Indian hospitality grew out of the fact that British official society in India was so small and homogeneous that Anglo-Indians could afford to open their houses to strangers without running the risk of being embarrassed by social inferiors abusing their kindness. In fact such generous hospitality was essential to the British in India as it helped to cultivate a sense of community.

Climate and practicalities imposed an open-plan on Anglo-Indian domestic space but the structure of the bungalow can also be read as a representation of less formalized familial relationships. Fewer lines of demarcation were drawn around the body within the family. Anglo-Indians were much more open to contact with other family members and more relaxed in their attitude towards guests. The Anglo-Indians were eager to adopt metropolitan codes of conduct when they were applicable to their lives and carried symbolic meaning within the colonial context, as was the case with regard to food and clothing, but conditions in India clearly made the middle-class code of separation less practicable as well as less meaningful. Anglo-Indian society was a predominantly bachelor society, children were permanently separated from their parents from a young age, and companionship between husband and wife was of great importance given the lonely situation of most postings. Given these factors it is unsurprising that the process of anglicization had very little impact on the structure of domestic space and the interaction of those individuals sharing that space. The colonial context therefore placed clear limits on the process of bodily closure which can be observed over the nineteenth century in Britain and in India.

The household servants

In the British middle-class home the most important division within the household was that between servants and the family. Servants stayed out of sight in their part of the house – the basement kitchens and sculleries, and attic bedrooms – unless they were wanted, when the bell system made the practice of calling them unobtrusive and convenient. Servants did not enter rooms which were occupied without having been summoned. They got up early to perform household tasks in rooms in use during the day and cleaned bedrooms once their occupants had left them. Hallways, corridors and back stairs ensured that the servants moving around the house came into as little contact as possible with the family.[43]

In the bungalow, separation was achieved by siting the kitchen and the living quarters of the servants in another part of the compound altogether. In addition, all bathrooms had two doors, one opening into the dressing-room or bedroom and the other into the compound so that the bathroom servants could enter without intruding on the privacy of the bedroom. Many of the servants would only ever have appeared on the verandah to be paid or to receive instructions. That still left a large number of servants whose tasks involved entering the living-rooms: the *khansaman* and the *khidmutgar* who waited at table, the bearer and his assistants who were responsible for the master's clothes, bedmaking, dusting and lighting the lamps, the *ayah* in the capacity of ladies' maid or children's nurse. To her irritation Emma Roberts found that these servants moved about the house much more freely than servants would have done in Britain.

> None of the inferior domestics keep themselves, as in England, in the background . . . all the others, down to the scullions, make their appearance in the state apartments, whenever they deem it expedient to do so; and in Bengal, where the lower orders of palanquin-bearers wear very little clothing, it is not very agreeable to a female stranger to see them walk into drawing-rooms, and employ themselves in dusting books or other occupations of the like nature.[44]

Not only did Indian servants fail to observe the rule of never entering a room when it was occupied unless they had been summoned, but the open-plan nature of the bungalow meant that they necessarily moved from room to room using the same routes as the occupants. Indian servants also had an unnerving tendency to move about the bungalow silently on their unshod feet. Charlotte Canning found this disconcerting: 'I am not sure,' she wrote home, 'that I do not regret creaking footmen. These gliding people come and stand by one, and will wait an hour with their eyes fixed on one...if you do not see them; and one is quite startled to find them patiently waiting when one looks round.'[45] Even when they were not wanted, at least one servant would wait on the verandah ready to be summoned by the shout of '*Qui hy?*'.[46] The verandah was also the workplace of the tailor and the punkah bearers during the hot weather. Day and night a number of servants might be found dozing across doorways or working on the verandah. The night-watchman's or the punkah bearer's snores might even keep one awake at night. No bungalow was ever free of various Indian servants, and their presence was much more intrusive than that of their counterparts in Britain.

The structure of the bungalow and the habits of the Indian servants meant that the bungalow was flawed as a private space. Frederick Shore was astonished to discover that the majority of Anglo-Indians seemed to regard these arrangements with equanimity and made few attempts to improve segregation within the household.

> English readers will scarcely believe, that such a thing as a bell to call the servants scarcely exists in India...while the substitutes for these conveniences are the most vulgar, clumsy, and offensive, which can well be imagined. Conceive an English lady, calling out at the top of her voice, 'Kooye hye' (Who is there?) and receiving no answer, the servants being all asleep; going to the door of the room, and stumbling over a half-dressed, snoring attendant, who is lying outside, (in order that he may be within call) and who, if he keeps awake, is a sort of spy, and by no means an inattentive observer of all that passes in the private apartment of his mistress.[47]

In his own home Shore 'had bells hung in all the rooms of the house, after the English fashion' as his wife didn't like the 'natives lying about the house'.[48] His description of the Indian servant as a spy was not entirely hyperbole. The presence of Indian servants in the bungalow opened up the private sphere of the British in India to the gaze of members of the Indian population. In Britain there was also a danger of the middle-class private sphere being revealed to the servants, and this put pressure on the family to exercise restraint in their presence. However despite concerns about '"domestic promiscuity" [which] expressed itself in warnings against dressing and undressing in front of the servants',[49] the extent to which servants intruded, and thus the power which they had to affect behaviour, was much more regulated. The relaxation of boundaries demarcating family and servants is more surprising in the Indian context, where race complicated the servant–employer relationship. The domestic space of the tiny British elite was laid bare to the view of members of a subjugated race. The failure to regulate contact with Indian servants within the home meant that the behaviour of the British could be monitored by their subjects not only in public but also in private. A sphere which the British claimed to cherish as a closed area of life was laid open to Indian view and judgement. The racial segregation established by the structure of urban space was undermined by the failure to demarcate a strict racial boundary within the household. The openness of the bungalow is even more striking when it is considered that British colonists at the Cape were in the 1830s making concerted efforts to increase privacy within their homes. They were moving away from the open-plan houses of the Dutch towards more English houses with halls, corridors, 'greater specialization in the use of rooms and a greater emphasis on the space around individuals'.[50]

The exposure of the private side of Anglo-Indian life contrasted markedly with the shroud which respectable Indians threw over their homes, and especially over Indian women, who were carefully protected from the sight of other men. No male servant would have been allowed to intrude into the intimate sphere of Indian women as they did in Anglo-Indian homes. In Britain, too, only female servants would have entered a lady's bedroom. Anglo-Indian women, who were initially shocked by the semi-nudity of lower-class Indians, soon grew accustomed to it.

> Nowhere, more than in India, is the truth of the apothegm, 'Habit is second nature,' more fully illustrated; for ladies, who would fly dismayed from a naked footman in England, here with perfect *nonchalance*, allow themselves to be fanned by naked bearers, rowed by naked boatmen,...and do not feel delicacy outraged by finding the sirdar-bearer and his mates in a similar state of nudity, performing all the household work of the bed-chamber.[51]

Emma Roberts wondered 'How such a custom could ever have originated...since every body, in the slightest degree acquainted with the native character, must have known that nothing could be more likely to shock its prejudices than so unnecessary an invasion of female privacy.'[52]

Paradoxically, the British may have allowed the racial boundary around their bodies to be undermined in this way because Anglo-Indian households were structured to some extent by the servants' notions of how things should be done. The employment of large numbers of servants to perform menial tasks underlined the elite status of the British. The organization of the compound translated the idea of the Anglo-Indian official as a patriarch surrounded by dependants into concrete form, with the bungalow at the centre and the living quarters of the servants arranged around it.[53] By creating lines of patronage stretching into the Indian community the servants affirmed British political legitimacy. However, in seeking to establish themselves on Indian terms the British were also obliged to accept Indian notions of how a 'great man's' household should be run. In Indian households there was an extended notion of the family which encompassed the whole household. Indians were therefore less disturbed by the presence of servants.[54] In the *zenana* women would while away hours in the company of their women servants, who then expected to behave in the same way in a British household. Frances Wells found this unbearable and sent her ayahs away

> as soon as I can after breakfast for they do irritate me so I can hardly bear it. Fancy a woman squatting down by baby's side, doing nothing but watching your every movement, and fixing her eyes full on your face, hardly ever even blinking them: it is the custom of ladies to allow this but it almost drives me wild, and I am never happy till I have got rid of these creatures, for whom I entertain the most profound aversion.[55]

When the British resisted Indian notions of how the household should be run they were generally told that it was not the custom. In this way a subtle shift in the balance of power was brought about. Indian servants expected to perform even the most menial tasks such as picking up something that had been dropped, moving a chair or letting the blinds down. This meant that they needed to be in constant attendance, and thus the openness of Anglo-Indian family life was to some extent imposed on the British by their servants, who by restricting the movements of their employers 'assert[ed] the boundaries of their domain'.[56] Servants were also able to turn the colonial power relationship on its head by employing a variety of techniques – failure to hear or understand instructions or to perform them properly, unruly behaviour, or protesting behaviour such as 'snuffling...loudly and offensively' while serving dinner,[57] embarrassing levels of sycophancy, delays in passing on messages or the failure to give vital information – which undermined British authority. The ability of servants to subvert the power relationship of master and servant as well as the level of Indian percolation into the domestic sphere frequently exasperated the Anglo-Indians and created tensions within the home.[58] Such an air of tension is conveyed by Hilda and Jim Bourne's photograph of themselves with some of their household servants. The Bournes, staring in opposite directions rather than at the camera, present an air of isolation despite being encircled by their servants. (see plate 10).

Anglo-Indians developed a number of mechanisms to control the level of tension which the contradictions of the master-servant relationship generated. These were similar to those used by the middle-classes in Britain to defuse the tension caused by the presence of members of the lower classes within the household. De-humanization of the servants was a common technique. Some British households would allot a standard Christian name to a particular domestic position. In India only the bearer and *ayah* were likely to be addressed by their forenames; the rest of the servants were referred to by the name of their position. Anglo-Indians also tended to type-cast servants, ascribing a certain character trait to each position, so that the bearer was normally seen as faithful, the *khansaman* as sly, the cook as a cheat who would try to squeeze as much money as possible out of you through the vehicle of the grocery bill. This allowed them to think of the servant as a presence which indicated the performance of a task. John Kaye remarked 'after a little while, one is wont to get wondrously indifferent to the presence of these black automata, and after a few months one learns to think of them no more than of the chairs and the tables.'[59] The offence caused by the semi-nudity of certain servants was negated by the European

Plate 10 Tension marks the relationship between employers and servants. 'Taken to shew the servants. Arkonam 1904.'

trick of adjusting their perception of brown skin. Bishop Heber remarked that the colour of Indian skin removed 'any sense of indelicacy' which would have been the effect of a similar exposure of white skin.[60] This was because it could be perceived as 'a sort of mahogany coloured covering' which 'has the effect of dress'.[61] In the European mind the brown skin of the Indians acted, like the fur of animals, as a form of clothing. This pattern of thought thoroughly de-humanized the Indian to the extent that even when surrounded by large numbers of Indian domestics many Europeans felt alone.[62]

Language also served as a barrier which shut Indian servants out of the world of the family. Most Anglo-Indians preferred to employ servants who were unable to speak English and took comfort in the idea that nothing of what was said was understood by them. Indian languages in the mouths of Anglo-Indians became a means of reinforcing the colonial situation. The books of set dialogues which were produced as aids to newcomers give an indication of the way in which Anglo-Indians would have addressed their servants. Almost every verb was expressed in the imperative: 'hand me the toothbrush and powder'; 'dress my hair'; 'come take off my boots.'[63] The familiar form of address was usually given even for conversations with higher servants such as the *munshi*, denoting a lack of respect. Communication was thus reduced to the bare bones of a colonial interchange.[64] Even while performing the most intimate tasks, attending to the bodily needs of the Anglo-Indian, the servant was reminded of his inferior status. The simplicity of the language allowed no room for familiarity while it exacted deference.

The books of dialogues give the impression of a formal and controlled interaction between master and servant. Other evidence suggests that the tensions inherent in the relationship frequently got the better of the Anglo-Indian. Frederick Shore asserted that 'the language of Billingsgate is in hourly use towards servants in the situation of butlers, footmen, and even clerks.'[65] In fact, Alfred Lyall found that this was the only way he could capture his servants' attention.

> I am much troubled by the conduct of my menage as the servants mistake my natural politeness, and laziness in noticing faults for imbecility, and hence attempt various illegitimate frauds. Consequently I am forced to simulate a frightful ferocity of manner and language on certain occasions, and having previously looked out some abusive phrases in the dictionary, and cooked up some fierce sentences I fulminate these to my astounded domestics, who assume abject attitudes, which always make me laugh and the scene is spoilt.[66]

Others were less jovial and foul language easily spilled over into brute force. The relationship between many Anglo-Indian masters and Indian servants in the early nineteenth century appears to have been characterized by casual brutality. Even the set dialogues hint at physical violence. In William Carey's *Dialogues* the newcomer is instructed as to how to order one servant to pull another's ears; Gilchrist's dictionary contains a revealing sentence: 'I will not speak to him, as I may get angry and beat him, but give him his wages and dismiss him.'[67] But even this example suggests a level of restraint which evidence from travel literature, letters, and newspaper reports indicates was rare.

The Reverend James Cordiner, who travelled in India between 1798 and 1805, was of the opinion that Indian servants were treated as badly as West Indian slaves.[68] George Spilsbury, a surgeon in the army, writes of servant beating as a commonplace event: 'Chesney is my chum... he licks his servants a great deal... it is remarkable how soon the Europeans get the habit of tyrannizing over the natives if it is not guarded against in the first outset it grows rapidly on you it is a bad practice.'[69] When Edward and Lucretia West went to Bombay they were astonished to find that it was possible to send a native to the Police Magistrate with a note saying 'Please flog the Bearer', and it would be done without any further investigation.[70] The evidence of the newspapers suggests that employers frequently responded to their servants' trivial misdemeanours with violence. Numerous cases were reported in which, although the courts did not condone violence, the payment of a small sum of money was seen as sufficient compensation for an injury.[71] The savage treatment of servants was extended to the lower orders of Indians – the coolies, porters, box-wallahs, *dandies* and *dak* runners – that the British encountered in the public sphere. Mrs Sherwood described her sense of shock on first seeing the treatment meted out to them. 'The gallant captain ...inflamed my zeal... by pushing a native aside with a little cane, using at the same time some word of contempt.'[72] G. O. Trevelyan was surprised to discover that 'whenever the Sahibs saw a dawk [*dak*] runner asleep or loitering, they always got out and beat him with their feet.'[73] To some extent the brutal treatment of servants in India seems to have been a simple transference of metropolitan behavioural norms. Servants in some households in Britain would have been accustomed to being sworn at, and outbreaks of physical violence were not entirely out of the ordinary.[74] In an area of life which leaves such an ambiguous historical record it is difficult to make meaningful comparisons, but violence does seem to have intensified in the colony. The tendency to de-humanize servants combined with racist contempt seems to have legitimized greater levels of brutality in the eyes of a large number of Anglo-Indians. Perhaps influenced by the Indian notion that members of the upper castes have the right to exact labour from the lower castes, as well as their own perception of Indians as so indolent that only physical force could make them work hard, once they had been some time in India the British came to see high levels of violence as appropriate within the Indian context.[75]

The conciliatory policy which some officials in favour of anglicization were trying to promote countered this view of violence. The 1830s and 1840s saw the development of an alternative paternalistic model of the district officer as protector of the simple villager, the head of the household, or the officer of a sepoy regiment, as a father figure. Those who adopted this role tended to think of their servants and sepoys as simple but faithful, and childlike in their dependence. The paternal model of Indo-British relations reduced the tensions created by the colonial situation. Within the household the perception of servants as members of an extended family neutralized the anxieties aroused by the intrusion of servants into the private sphere. This counterbalance to more violent conduct reflected an awareness of a number of factors: the diminution of aristocratic power in Britain; the incursion of polite opinion; increasing surveillance of officials by the government, and also the rising numbers of missionaries in India.[76] Bentinck also set an example by abolishing flogging in the Indian army.[77] Handbooks, such as J. H. Stocqueler's, which were aimed at the Civil Service, reminded readers that, while they would need to treat their servants strictly, they should not strike them.[78] Violence, rather than physically demonstrating the authority of the British in India, was seen as undermining that authority. Although the British took care not to come into direct physical contact with their victims by using their cane, their sword or their booted feet, the intensity of verbal and physical animosity created an intimacy between the Indian and his assailant. Violent behaviour thus threatened the principle of racial separation which was the hallmark of the process of anglicization. Regarded in British and Indian circles as equally degrading for the aggressor as for the victim, violence on the part of representatives of the Company lowered the British both in the eyes of their compatriots and in the eyes of all ranks of Indian society. Lieutenant-Colonel John Briggs deplored the striking of a native who was not in a position to defend himself, or even return the blow, as an unmanly, cowardly act.[79] Frederick Shore asserted that servants preferred to work for those Anglo-Indians who were accomplished in Hindoostanee as this was taken as a sign that they must have 'mixed with the native nobility and gentry; [and] ... consequently observed their habits, among whom beating or abusing servants is looked upon with great disgust.'[80]

Despite the policy of conciliation, the reality of brutal physical violence on the part of the British in India undermined inter-racial relations. Endemic brutality combined with the shift away from Indian methods of rule, the emphasis on probity and keeping one's distance, the lack of sympathy for Indian notions of purity and pollution, the reluctance to participate in Indian leisure activities as a result of the influence of evangelical religion, combined with an arrogant and disrespectful manner towards Indians on official occasions, created an atmosphere of distrust. Under these conditions it was easy for economic hardship to unite with cultural reaction to British rule to create an atmosphere in which an uprising like the Mutiny could occur.[81]

During the Mutiny in 1857 the physical impact of colonialism, which violently imprinted the power of the colonizer on the body of the colonized, was reversed. This was what made it so shocking for the British. As John Kaye expressed it, the 'first bitterness of our degradation [was] – the degradation of fearing those whom we had taught to fear us.'[82] The British felt outraged and insulted by 'what had apparently been done to the bodies of British people'.[83] By visiting the revenge of bodily degradation on the British, the actions of the Indian rebels reversed the colonial order. The sepoy at Segowlie who murdered his commandant and his wife and then donned his 'full-dress uniform (on which were his two medals) and sword' appeared to be consciously turning the pattern of power relations in India on its head.[84] Despite the persistence of revolts and armed rebellions in India throughout the first half of the nineteenth century,[85] the British did not regard the Indians as a threat to their personal safety. Women travelling alone by palanquin across India in the early nineteenth century worried more about the possibility of illness or theft than personal attack.[86] This meant that when the mutineers massacred Anglo-Indian women and children the British were profoundly shocked. In Britain *The Times* used the language of religious sacrilege: 'Having once torn away the veil, [they] rush with voracious relish to the pollution of the sanctuary... to soil the marble surface of the temple with the vilest filth.'[87] The murder, and possibly the rape, of British women, constructed as the repositories of all that was best in western civilization, was interpreted as the ultimate violation of the British nation itself. Despite the fact that enquiry into the question after the event found no evidence of the rape of British women by Indian rebels,[88] so powerful was the image of the violation of white women's bodies as the worst degradation the British could suffer, that it lived a life of its own, particularly within the novels of late nineteenth-century Anglo-India, without need of grounding in fact.[89]

The Mutiny was therefore an immensely traumatic bodily experience for the British in India. Survival reduced many to a semi-Indian state. Mrs Goldeney, who was sheltered by a Rajah, found herself and her three children squatting on the floor gnawing roast goat meat 'in our extraordinary half-English, half-Hindostanee dresses'.[90] Fleeing through the countryside, in hiding or under siege, their clothes reduced to rags, they were exposed to the humiliation of living in overcrowded cramped quarters, plagued by rats, mice, flies, fleas and lice, without servants, obliged to wash and mend their own few clothes, often without soap.[91] L. E. Rees detailed the insanitary conditions in which the British were forced to live at Lucknow: 'The inside annoyances are dreadful. The stench from human ordure, from decaying horses, dogs, and men, assails the olfactory nerves most awfully, and little is done to mend matters.'[92] The food supply was meagre and was generally rice and dhal, the meal of the Indian poor.[93] Malnutrition and disease killed many, especially the children. Although the British tried to keep up the proprieties – at Agra everyone went out for an evening promenade at sunset – the Mutiny reduced the British to a state of bodily exhaustion, humiliation and degradation.

That the actions of a small number of Indians could reduce the British so rapidly to such a state highlighted the vulnerability of the British in India. It might be expected that the British would have responded by drawing in the boundaries around their bodies even further, accelerating the process of anglicization. In particular the Mutiny made apparent the dangers inherent in the openness of Anglo-Indian domestic space to members of a subject race. Servants usually 'so obsequious and cringing in manner' became 'insufferably insolent' as the news of the Mutiny spread, demonstrating that good relations between employers and servants were maintained by structures of power rather than goodwill.[94] Mary Gilliand, who survived the uprising at Sialkot, felt that 'the servants are all quite as pleased to see us English killed as the Rebels are to do it.'[95] After 1857 the principle of urban segregation was implemented more strictly and the popularity of the hill stations as places of escape increased, but this was not matched by a stricter policy of segregation within the home. Rather than sealing off this weak point in the boundary the British had constructed around their bodies the Anglo-Indians turned the openness of the bungalow to their advantage, using it as a site in which to display British prestige. Indeed, the fact that, in the latter half of the nineteenth century, the British went on to develop an ideology of rule which was based on a seemingly unshakable notion of the superiority and inviolability of their bodies, suggests that the place of the Mutiny in the bodily chronology of the British in India is ambiguous.

Thomas Metcalf argues that the Mutiny had a powerful impact.[96] Certainly it greatly influenced British policies of how to govern India, which in their turn played an important part in re-defining the appropriate ruling body for the Anglo-Indian official. But late nineteenth-century changes in Anglo-Indian bodily norms developed gradually out of the changes which had been taking place since the 1820s and 1830s. A sharp break after the Mutiny is difficult to discern. As the next chapters will explore, the Mutiny provided a certain impetus for processes already in motion, but the process which continued to close the British body off from India was strengthened and propelled by considerations other than the fears which were its legacy. Although the hatred and fury whipped up against the rebels strengthened racism, especially towards Muslims, who were seen by many as the instigators of the revolt, racial prejudice was also strengthened by the European discourse of scien-tific racism. And it was new concerns with public sanitation which were largely responsible for the distance between British and Indian settlements. What the Mutiny did confirm for the British was their own racial superiority, and India's need for civilization.[97]

Perhaps the Mutiny's most important legacy on the level of the history of the British body in India was its transformation in the Anglo-Indian imagination into a trope for the worst fate possible. It acted as a mythical warning, fuelled by the creation of 'mutiny sites' such as the well at Cawnpore. A tour of these sites almost took on the character of a pilgrimage.[98] Countless Anglo-Indian novels of the late nineteenth and early twentieth century used the Mutiny to conjure up the fear of the Indian, and also the heroism of the colonial official, whether civilian or military. Whenever the Anglo-Indians felt threatened by mass Indian protest, as they did at intervals throughout the twentieth century, particularly in 1942, their response was to invoke the Mutiny as a justification for the brutality of their response.

PART II

The Sahib, 1858–1939

4

The Sahib as an Instrument of Rule

In 1858, with the abolition of the East India Company, India officially became part of the British Empire. British officials in India now saw themselves as representatives of an imperial power. The shift in power from the Board of Directors to Whitehall quickened the pace of bureaucratization within the Indian administration, while the introduction in 1853 of open competition for entrance into the Indian Civil Service meant that civilians were now selected according to merit rather than social connections, and this gradually brought about a shift in the social background of civil servants. These changes stimulated debate about the representation of British authority. For the first time the body became a distinct category within the official discourse of rule as the government discussed whether the competition-men, recruited by the new system of open examination, were suitable representatives of the imperial power. This, combined with the growing influence of the pseudo-scientific discourse of race and class, resulted in the production of an image of what might be termed a legitimate Anglo-Indian official body, in other words the sahib. The body of the sahib provided the basis for an ideology of rule by prestige which visualized the body as an instrument of British rule. The body of the sahib, as an embodiment of British virtues, was employed in the public sphere in the reformulated ceremonial of the state, which sought to create an illusion of the continuity of British rule. Meanwhile the increasing power of the bureaucracy carried the weight of modernizing India. In these different spheres of rule the body of the sahib divided into a symbolic ceremonial body and an active, self-disciplined bureaucratic body. Even as British authority in India was formalized, groups within India were forming which were to effectively challenge British authority. During the twentieth century the violence of the British response to Indian resistance began to reveal the hollowness of prestige, severely undermining the power of the body as a representation of those British virtues which legitimated their rule.

The competition-wallah and the ideal official body

In 1853 open competition by examination replaced patronage as the means of entry into the Indian Civil Service (ICS) and the Indian Army.[1] As the first waves of competition-wallahs began arriving in India they became the focus of fierce attack.[2] A dispute about their physical fitness for the service raged throughout the nineteenth and twentieth centuries. Competition-men were said to lack the 'fresh and undrained energies' of the old Haileyburians.[3] Civilian and government circles as well as the papers in India and Britain vigorously contested the physical robustness of competition-wallahs. Much of the debate about how India should be ruled and by what sort of men therefore centred around a discussion of the body of the civilian. What emerged was an image of the ideal civilian as a man with a particular physique.

The physique of the competition-wallah was a consistent source of anxiety to the Indian government. Whenever it enquired about the suitability of the men recruited by the new system, general expressions of satisfaction were punctuated by complaints such as that of W. Hudleston of the Madras Presidency, who claimed that competition-men suffered from 'a deficiency generally of elasticity, mental and physical'.[4] In 1882 the Bombay government sent in a list of civil servants who had joined the service since 1862 with comments on their fitness which 'in our opinion ... shews that too many gentlemen have been sent out who were not sufficiently robust to stand the work'. Remarks on individual men characterize them as 'not strong physically', 'physically feeble and unable to stand hard district work', 'weakly: unable to stand the Deccan climate', as well as possessing 'inferior manners and temper'.[5] In addition competition-men were said to be unable to ride, a skill which it was argued was essential to the execution of their duties.[6] In other words competition-wallahs' bodies were perceived to be inadequate.

Criticism of the competition-wallah was usually combined with nostalgia for the old Haileyburians: brawny, if rather wild and dissipated, young men who would not have stood a chance of passing the examination but had 'true English grit in their composition'.[7] Enthusiasm for the Haileyburians was in part a reflection of renewed enthusiasm for Sir John Lawrence's despotic Punjab-style of government which had proved so successful during the Mutiny.[8] While *The Englishman*, in an article on 'Typical civilians', styled the competition-man as a 'myopic secretary' it cast the old Haileyburian as a physically active 'equestrian administrator who hears reports while out shooting, who goes out with the greyhounds to visit a disputed boundary; to whom the whole world is a wide and open cutcherry, in which he rules with whip and spur; a Cromwell in a *solah topee*, or a glorified Squire Western'.[9] The romantic myth of the 'courage and pluck'[10] of the Haileybury civilian revealed a tendency in the civil service to value physical over intellectual power. The novelist R. W. Lodwick suggested that, faced by a similar uprising to the Mutiny, their more intellectual colleagues would be unlikely to show the same mettle.[11] Behind these unflattering physical comparisons lay class prejudices which George Birdwood stated explicitly in a paper read before the East India Association: 'the government of the country has at last been gotten into the hands of men born outside the hitherto governing families of the land, into hands bred for generations to other work than man government.'[12]

In the eyes of many the introduction of open competition, which had aimed to consolidate the hold of the old order of the landed gentry on administrative power, had failed in that it favoured the middle classes looking for new avenues for employment.[13] Over the years success in the competition was achieved by increasing numbers of graduates from Irish and Scottish universities, while the representation of men from Oxbridge fell steadily.[14] The number of men joining the ICS without any university education at all also increased, and even after the age limit for the examination was lowered in 1874, in an attempt to attract the best students from the old public schools, the number of recruits who had attended one of the nine most prestigious public schools fell.[15] Between 1860 and 1874 men from lower social backgrounds were also successful in the competition. Fifty-three of the men who went out to India as civilians in this period were the sons of tradesmen (mostly farmers).[16] Although a large proportion of entrants were still drawn from the middle classes, the ICS was now seen as a possible career by men from a wider range of educated families, reflecting a similar trend in the Home Civil Service.[17] These families tended to prepare their sons for the examination by sending them to crammers. Entrance by examination was therefore seen as a test of a man's ability to cram rather than of his real intellectual ability, and a means by which the 'unkempt genius from the Hebrides' or the 'shop-boy of Ludgate Hill' – men from the periphery and the lower orders – could infiltrate the service.[18] *The*

Times claimed that 'aggravated eccentricity, intolerable manners, unmanliness, and a sort of half and half imbecility, all to be traced to this mad "fad" of cramming, are to be met with everyday now in the ranks of the once proud Indian Civil Service.'[19] The newspapers' attack on cramming was, like the focus on the weedy physique of the competition-wallah, a coded attack on the social class of the new recruits.

In the descriptions of the competition-man as a weakling contemporaries would have recognized a colonial version of the 'gent', the petit-bourgeois parody of the dandy, a familiar figure of fun in *Punch*.[20] The gent embodied metropolitan concerns about the strength of the lower orders in British society, particularly after the apparently rapid pace of democratization following the Second and Third Reform Acts. The new recruit was portrayed as vulgar and ill-mannered as well as weakly, reflecting the same fear of the incursion of the lower orders into colonial society. Where once friction between British and Indians had been attributed to the behaviour of the 'Company's hard bargains', the competition-wallah was now blamed for bringing the name of the ruling elite into disrepute. These careerists, with their lack of manners, their attitude towards India, which they were reputed to regard as an 'infernal hole', towards Indians, who they were said to refer to as 'black fellows' and their intolerance of cultural difference, were identified as the root cause of poor relations between the races.[21] James Cassidy, writing about the problem of British violence towards Indians, argued that it was due in part to the fact that, 'the Indian Civil Service Competitive Examinations...pass into India a constant stream of Englishmen of not the highest social standing in their own country.'[22] This was a problem which was perceived to have spread throughout the empire. A correspondent to *The West African Times* complained in the 1860s that ill-educated and ill-refined gents rather than gentlemen were now arriving in Africa and treating educated African gentlemen with contempt.[23] Those who wished to protect the position of the old order claimed that Indians could recognize a true gentleman and preferred his rule. George Birdwood argued that 'In India efficiency is quite of secondary importance; it, indeed, bores the natives desperately. But a high tone, down to the drummer-boys, is everything, at least to the stability of the British Government in the country.'[24] The implication was that the high tone of the gentleman by birth was something to which no middle- or lower-class competition-man could aspire. Unable to compete with the middle classes in intellectual competition, the old order resorted to claims of birth and bodily inheritance to protect their position.[25]

Following the same pattern of bias which they applied to themselves, the British raised very similar objections to those Indians who entered the Civil Service through open competition. Very few western-educated Indians were able to enter the competition as the examination was held in London, but between 1868 and 1883 twelve Indian candidates passed the examination and by 1909 five per cent of civil servants were Indians.[26] Many of the British viewed competition as a means by which upstart Bengalis were able to use the channel of education to compete with the strong and manly races of India who the British perceived to be its natural rulers. The same codes as were deployed against the competition-wallahs were used to denigrate the successful Indian candidates, who were characterized as weakly, ineffectual and lethargic specimens of an inferior Indian race, drained of energy and masculinity by the steam bath of the Bengal climate and, like the competition-man, exhausted by cramming.[27] Especially during the 1860s and 1870s, the British government made great efforts to ensure recruitment into the covenanted Civil Service of often unsuitable members of the Indian nobility, who were said to be far superior to the educated Bengali in terms of vigour and courage.[28] The reaction to western-educated Indian recruits was an extension of the competition-wallah debate transferred onto the level of the relative status of different racial groups within India.

The centrality of the body to the debate about the competition-men reveals the peculiar position which the British in India occupied at the interface of anthropological and ethnological debates about race and class. The belief that different environmental conditions generated specific forms of habitual behaviour worked in conjunction with the generally received opinion that acquired characteristics were hereditary, leading to the conflation of race, physique and culture in late nineteenth-century racial theory.[29] Late nineteenth-century anthropology conceived of the body as the physical outer map of the moral inner man. It was believed that, along with racial characteristics, cultural and moral characteristics could be read off from the body. The ethnological techniques of phrenology and craniometry, anthropometry and photography, defined and classified racial groups according to measurements of the skull, height, length of arms and legs, and breadth of chest, details of skin, eye and hair colour, as well as their manners and customs.[30] Volumes of photographs of different castes and tribes were published as a means of cataloguing and ordering the different types of mankind. From these photographs of bodies the cultural characteristics of different races were deduced. In all the pictorial studies of the various peoples of India the white European body was an unstated presence. Without it being necessary to depict the European, the various bodies of these others were implicitly held up against it. At the same time, however, this subtly deflected racial theory back onto the Europeans themselves, setting a physical standard to which they felt the need to aspire.

In Britain racial theory deflected back onto the European body more directly. Here the 'sciences' of phrenology, physiognomy and craniometry were employed in the search for the racial origins of the various peoples making up the population of the British Isles.[31] John Beddoe (physician and president of the Anthropological Society 1869–70), and the British Association Anthropometric Committee (1875–83), set about measuring samples of the British population. The results of these investigations were used to explain class differences in racial terms. The Celtic heritage of the working classes was supposedly still discernible in their prognathous skulls, darker complexions and sensuous natures. This equation of class and race, strengthened from the 1870s onwards by eugenics, treated class position as though it were hereditary. This was a notion which was used to define and control deviants such as criminals and lunatics, as well as the working classes in general, in European society.[32] Meanwhile, the upper-middle classes used racial theory to strengthen their social position by claiming a worthy Anglo-Saxon heritage in compensation for their lack of aristocratic lineage. The Anglo-Saxon gentleman was depicted as muscular in build and supremely athletic in habits, as evinced by his horsemanship and capacity in sports and hunting. His physique was perceived as 'an index to [his] character and disposition', which was said to be energetic and daring; decent, considerate and independent; marked by a sense of 'fair-play and justice', while he possessed a strong sense of moral duty and responsibility towards his country.[33] The focus on the Anglo-Saxon heritage intensified in the 1870s, fed by fear, combined with admiration, of the Prussians. Contemporaries well-versed in the racial language of class would immediately have recognized in the descriptions of the robust Haileyburian a representative of this superior Anglo-Saxon stock.[34] In contrast the physical characteristics of the degenerate and inferior petit-bourgeoisie were attributed to the competition-wallah. Within the context of late nineteenth-century racial theory physique was such a potent indicator of social rank and character that attacks made on the physical robustness of competition-men were a natural way of voicing concerns about the social status of new recruits.

While the conflation of race and class created the illusion within Britain that the social order was natural and inevitable, the concept of racial hierarchy fed imperial ideology by describing colonial rule as a natural phenomenon. The idea of the superiority of the British was given greater force now that their supposed attainment of a higher level of civilization, demonstrated most notably by their intellectual and technological triumphs, was seen as the product of their racial predisposition. In contrast, the capacity of certain races to attain civilization was questioned by hardening racial concepts.[35] Craniologist Carl Vogt connected the cultural potential of human races to the differential development of the skull: 'We have already pointed out, that in races capable of civilization, the anterior structures [of the skull] remain open longer... the reverse being the case in races incapable of high culture.'[36] British rule in India could then be legitimized as the guardianship of a people incapable of physical and moral progress rather than simply the paternal supervision of the childlike Indians' progress towards maturity. While the racial gaze fixed the Indians in a position of inferiority it intensified scrutiny of the representatives of British imperialism. A racial justification of British rule in India demanded that the Anglo-Indian official should epitomize the ideal Englishman of Anglo-Saxon heritage. If the representatives of British government failed to confirm the superiority of the British as a race, then imperialism would surely rest on insecure foundations. John Malcolm's plea for the preservation of European manners as a strategy for demonstrating British moral integrity was now extended to the level of the body as a physical manifestation of that integrity.

The focus on the physique was so intense that the body, for the first time, became a distinct category within official discourse. The body of the civil servant was envisaged as an embodied legitimation of the British presence in India. The debate about the competition-wallah thus gave rise to a powerful image of the ideal body of the Anglo-Indian official constructed at the interface of debates about class, character and physiognomy in Britain, as well as about race, virtue and legitimacy in India. The popular literature of Anglo-India reinforced this construction of the ideal civilian in the persona of the sahib. Meadows Taylor's hero in his novel *Seeta* typifies the ideal. Cyril Brandon is 'descended from an ancient family' and possesses the grace of the aristocrat and the irregular but handsome features of the gentry. His broad forehead is indicative of intellect, his strong features signify the qualities of the gentleman, and his rude health and vigour and his love of field sports betray the determination, energy and moral character of his class. He possesses innate governing abilities, speaks the vernacular, studies the manners and customs of the people and 'w[ins] all hearts'.[37] In reality few civilians could hope to actually embody this ideal, but this view of the legitimate

official body became so pervasive that comments on a man's physique became a shorthand in informal debates about character, as in
John Rivett-Carnac's praise of Sir Richard Temple as a man with 'a
splendid constitution' or H. G. Keene's description of a friend as
'muscular as a tiger'.[38]

The intense emphasis on a manly, muscular and physically robust
physique paralleled changes in the conception of masculinity within
Britain. During the last half of the century a shift towards a hard,
tough masculinity was expressed in a growing distrust of effeminacy
and aestheticism, accompanied by an ever more virulent attack on
homosexuality, culminating in the Labouchere Amendment of
1885.[39] The emphasis on a powerful manliness may also have been
in response to the increasing confidence of women in society as
women began to claim an education, new legal rights and the
vote.[40] The Anglo-Indian ideal therefore reflected the ideal of masculinity within the metropole, but the racial element which crept into
almost every aspect of Anglo-Indian self-presentation was more specifically colonial. In the photographs of the British in India, the
European body, captured on paper, supplies the lacuna in the ethno-
graphies. Self-consciously constructed as the sahib, European officials present themselves in their photographs as the physical ideal
against which all other types can be compared (see plate 11).

The manly and athletic body of the ideal sahib was perpetuated
and sustained by sports and hunting, both of which achieved what
might be termed cult status during the latter half of the nineteenth
century. The ideology of athleticism, developed within the public
schools and Oxbridge, saw sports as a means of moulding the perfect
Englishman. Indulging in an evening game of polo, squash, or tennis
before a bath and dinner, the athletic civilian displayed his possession
of an appropriate physique while simultaneously demonstrating his
possession of the essential qualities of the ruling race: the ability to
observe rules, loyalty and comradeship towards his team members,
fair play to the other side – in other words, honesty, uprightness,
courage and endurance.[41]

In the same period the 'entertaining and joyous... business' of
early nineteenth-century hunting was transformed into a highly
defined area of Anglo-Indian life laden with moral overtones.[42] A
collective myth of the hunting experience was fostered by the accu-
mulation of the formulaic recitations to be found in the hunting
literature of memoirs, sporting periodicals and other publications,
which were on the increase in the latter half of the century.[43] All
these accounts were governed by a set of conventions which resulted
in the appearance of a limited set of situations and themes, to the

Plate 11 Reginald Maxwell as the bureaucratic sahib. 'Group. Clerks and peon and police naik. Belgaum. R. M. M. Ass. Collector, Belgaum.'

extent that those condemned to read a number of them can only agree with G. O. Trevelyan that 'People have been so over-done with howdahs, and bottled beer, and hair-triggers, and hair-breadth escapes, and griffins spearing a sow by mistake, that they had rather face a royal Bengal tiger in his native jungle than in the Sporting Magazine.'[44] The close association with noble animals which hunting necessitated cast an aura of nobility over the sportsman. The symbiotic relationship between horse and rider, which made the horse an extension of its rider's body, deflected the glory of the pure blood of the thoroughbred back on to its owner.[45] The importance which the civilian attached to his association with horses, and also dogs, is clearly indicated by the central part which these animals play in the family photograph albums of Anglo-Indians. The hunter's prey – noble beasts like tigers, or aggressive boars – also affirmed his manly qualities. Hunting required skill, courage and patience, and thus it enabled the civilian to demonstrate his possession of some of the essential qualities which made Englishmen racially superior.[46] The Anglo-Indian as hunter frequently appeared in the photograph albums, for example, Major Lumsden proudly lying, gun in hand, before his collection of trophies epitomizes the genre which constructed the bold hunter as the ideal sahib

Plate 12　The sahib as noble and manly hunter. 'Major Lumsden lying in front of animal skins.'

(see plate 12). Strewn throughout bungalows, clubs, and messes, trophies such as the skins behind Major Lumsden were a striking affirmation of the prowess of their owners.

We have already seen that the Bombay government complained that the competition-wallah could not ride (a sure sign of a lowly social background) but worse still, it was also claimed by many that he did not hunt. Indians who joined the service were also said to demonstrate their unsuitability for the job by their lack of interest in field sports.[47] Baden-Powell insisted that the Indian people would be more impressed by a sportsman than 'a stay-at-home "clerk-in-an-office young man"'.[48] *The Calcutta Review*, in an article on the competition system, reminded the reader that shooting 'support[s] our national prestige, and impress[es] on the native mind a belief in our skill, energy and resources, and physical strength'.[49] Essential to this construction of hunting as a display of English qualities was the presentation of Indian forms of hunting as unsportsmanlike. Indian hunting methods such as shooting at animals as they were driven past a platform – placed at the bottom of a hierarchy of hunting techniques ordered according to skill, patience and risk – reinforced the sportsmanship of the painstaking and dangerous stalking of the English huntsman.[50] The cult of hunting coincided with the era of the competition-man, and despite claims to the contrary, new recruits enjoyed the fact that an occupation confined to the very wealthy in Britain could be sampled by the ordinary middle-class man in India where game was plentiful, horses affordable and servants cheap.[51] A defence of a competition civilian in *The Calcutta Review* used the language of hunting to affirm his credentials as a legitimate sahib. His ownership of aristocratic greyhounds is used to confirm his breeding,[52] while a description of his horses implies that their qualities were also shared by their master.

> And now as we draw near to the camp, we mark incidentally the evidences of the manner in which the young Civilian occupies his leisure. Picketed close to the tents stand three knowing looking Arabs, stripped of their clothing to be groomed; the laid-back ears, the uplifted hind-leg as the syces rub them down, the glancing eye, their satin skins, their muscular arms, with curious tracery of veins and ligaments, all speak of spirit, power and endurance.[53]

After the First World War the quality of new recruits to the Indian Civil Service continued to cause the Indian government anxiety. Ironically, the days of nineteenth-century competition were now looked back upon with nostalgia as a time when an intellectual elite was recruited. The focus of concern had shifted from the physical to the intellectual suitability of the new recruits. The best candidates in the civil service examinations now preferred to join the Home or the Colonial services rather than the ICS.[54] In 1934 the Indian government gloomily concluded that those Europeans entering the ICS were of an 'inferior type'.[55] The political situation in India in the twentieth century had done much to undermine the popularity of the ICS in Britain, and the Montagu-Chelmsford Reforms of 1919 resulted in a significant increase in the number of Indians in the service. By 1939, 589 members of the ICS were Indian compared to 599 Europeans.[56] Power-sharing broke down the authority which the British derived from the physical separation of European and Indian. The British civil servant frequently found himself with Indians as colleagues, and even his superiors, a situation which some found galling. Edgar Hyde's wife commented that although her husband's District Commissioner seemed 'very nice' and anglicized, 'Indian DCs are not popular, the white men hate being under them.'[57] By siting the authority of the sahib in the idea that he embodied racial superiority, the competition-wallah debate had transformed the body of the official into one of the essential tools of power. Many, like W. O. Horne, opposed the recruitment of Indians into the ICS with the argument that they lacked the bodily legitimacy from which the British derived their authority: 'A Parsi, or for the matter of that a Panjabi, a Mahratta, a Bengali, or a Rajput is, in a Madras district, just as much a foreigner as is any Englishman, and he does not enjoy the compensating advantage of prestige which is, or was, the latter's heritage.'[58] The admission of large numbers of Indians into the ruling elite eroded the idea that authority was inherent in the British body. Their presence demonstrated that the possession of an Anglo-Saxon body was not necessarily a precondition for effective rule in India. But despite the fact that the sahib's authority was undermined, the British proved incapable of constructing an alternative official body, relevant to the political requirements of the colonial situation in the twentieth century. The ideal of the manly Anglo-Saxon sahib survived until 1947 even though it became increasingly difficult to demonstrate authority by virtue of his physical presence.

Imperial ceremony and the symbolic body

After 1857 a new consciousness among the British, of their position as representatives both of an imperial power and a superior race, resulted in a reworking of the British ruling style. In a manner characteristic of regimes which base their claim to legitimacy on 'inherent superiority', the British relied heavily on 'lavish display, ...regalia, and public acts of deference or tribute by subordinates'.[59] Reviving the flamboyance of the nabob, a theatrical ceremonial style was developed which employed and, at the same time, developed the body of the new ideal sahib. Ceremonial was reworked as a distinct means of expressing political authority. The other, bureaucratic, side of government was separated off into the world of the office and the court. The functional aspects of ceremonial were emptied out to create rituals in which relationships of power and submission were symbolically, rather than manifestly, enacted.

The changes the British made to ceremonial after 1857 are exemplified by the reinvention of the durbar. Throughout the first half of the nineteenth century the British cemented their relationships with other Indian rulers in the Indian idiom of the durbar, a ceremony which enacted a form of mystical bonding, whereby the donor, or protector, incorporated the receiver of the *khelat* into his body. The surgeon Edward Raleigh, who accompanied Lord Amherst on a diplomatic tour through Bengal in 1827–8, described how the Indian visitor would be embraced on entering the durbar tent and conducted to a chair. Plate 13 depicts such a moment – Lord Hardinge can be seen disappearing inside the embrace of the King of Oudh. During the ceremony the Governor-General might inspect the presents arm-in-arm with the visitor. Lord Amherst even went so far as to rise at the same moment at the end of the durbar given for His Highness Mirza Selim and walk to the tent door hand-in-hand with the Indian prince.[60] These acts of physical intimacy denoted respect, acknowledged a certain level of equality, even affection, all of which were integral to the creation of a mystical bond between the two men. Although they did not relish participating in them – Lord Auckland, according to his sister, 'detest[ed] great part of the ceremonies, particularly *embracing* the rajahs!'[61] – their retention of these ceremonies in their original format suggests that the British were willing to acknowledge their mystical importance.[62] The British acceptance of Indian structures of power meant that they were also forced to submit to such indignities as standing in the presence of the Mughal Emperor, from whom, theoretically, they derived their authority.[63]

The removal of the Emperor of Delhi into exile and the proclamation of Queen Victoria as the new monarch of India in 1858 resolved the paradox of the British position as *de facto* rulers deriving their authority from a virtually powerless Indian figurehead. British authority was now firmly centred in the monarch's representative, the Viceroy, and British officials clearly occupied a place in the social hierarchy above the Indian princes. India was re-envisaged as a feudal confederation of disparate states, castes and peoples unified under the British administration with the sovereign at its head.[64] The durbar, reinvented on the national level as the imperial assemblages of 1877, 1903 and 1911, became a place where the Indian princes, redefined as feudal allies, expressed their allegiance to the British. Any suggestion that British officials might be symbolically subordinate to Indian rulers was removed. In the new form of the imperial assemblage the British rid themselves of unwanted physical contact with their subjects, gone was the two-way exchange of gifts, the physical contact of embracing and hand holding. Plate 13, where Lord Hardinge submits to the King of Oudh's embrace, contrasts markedly with plate 14, where Lord Curzon retains his dignity and asserts his authority by maintaining physical distance, occupying a dais up which the Nawab of Bahawalpur has to climb in order to pay his respects by shaking hands. The new format transformed the physical performance of the Indian princes from one which symbolized incorporation, equality and respect, into one of homage, particularly in the case of the 1911 durbar when the Indian

Plate 13 The embrace created a mystical bond between Indian prince and Governor-General. 'Durbar scene showing Wajid Ali Shah (King of Oudh 1847–56) embracing the Governor-General, Lord Hardinge.'

Plate 14 A formal handshake marks the relationship of patron and client. 'Presentation of H. H. The Nawab of Bahawalpur, Delhi Durbar 1903.'

princes actually knelt before the King Emperor in the 'homage tent'.[65] The mysticism surrounding the relationship between the two men was transferred to the person of the Viceroy, and in 1911 of the King Emperor, of whom the Indian princes took *darshan* (a viewing of an august or holy person). The changed use of the body by the two parties exposed the altered relationship, which the protocol of a formalized style reformulated as one of patron and client, removing the personal element which the old-style durbar had favoured.

These changes significantly altered the function of the durbar. It was no longer the site where power relationships between two people were cemented but rather a place where the relationship between abstract entities was symbolically enacted. In the new form of ceremonial, authority was depersonalized, sited in the official role rather than in the person.[66] The British officer was present only as an impersonal representative of the British government, the Indian prince as a loyal subject. Whereas the substance of the body had been integral to earlier ceremonial action, in the new form the *tableaux vivants* created by the actors operated as a blank space on to which could be transposed symbolic meaning. The Anglo-Indian officials were transformed into human icons of dignity, respectability and order. The experience of the body as a cipher was captured by Herbert Maynard in a letter to his mother about the 'Grand Durbar of a Native Prince'.

> As I walked up the steps to the hall of audience between the soldiers who were drawn up on each side, the military band struck up God Save the Queen. I cannot tell you how powerfully I was impressed by the feeling that I was ... the sole representative of such glory and greatness as that of England. My heart quite swelled within me as I thought that such a hymn was actually being played in my honour, and I believe that the novelty of this sensation gave me the dignity in which I might otherwise have been deficient. ... it came like an inspiration.[67]

Entering into a ceremony meant stepping into a set of ready-made actions or, in other words, making a 'ritual commitment' to a set of ceremonial actions demarcated from practical, rational, everyday activities. Here the official's own intentions and thoughts became irrelevant in that they had no impact on the performance of the ritual action.[68] Attention was thus concentrated upon the action itself, resulting in great emphasis being placed on outward appearances and the observance of circumscribed postures and gestures in the ceremonial of the Raj. The British retreated into a reserved distance and wooden posture while they expected the Indian princes to adopt the bodily demeanour of deference. Hence the furore which surrounded the Maharajah of Baroda at the 1911 durbar when he apparently turned his back on the 'Imperial Presence', wore too much jewellery and swung his stick in a jaunty manner.[69] Indeed, the reduction of the officials' bodies to symbols meant that retaining one's dignity and keeping to protocol became all that mattered. Reginald Maxwell was amused when the Prince of Wales, on his visit to India, in 1921–2 upset Anglo-Indian notions of appropriate symbolic behaviour and walked among the crowd at the races, entering the third-class enclosure.

> It rather made me chuckle to see H. E. the Governor, who would never move a step himself without a red carpet and a full programme stating in detail the order of the procession, trotting round behind H. R. H. in the crowd and dust ... I'm sure it did much more good than the official bundobust with everyone at the regulation distance of 15 yards, which I believe annoyed H. R. H. very much.[70]

At the imperial assemblages the play of imperial authority and Indian submission was set against a backdrop of semi-feudal pageantry. At the 1877 assemblage Lord Lytton created a neo-Gothic ambience with the princes presented with coats of arms, the durbar stage peopled by yak-tail whisk bearers in livery and European and Indian troopers, and decorated with banners depicting fleurs-de-lis, the shamrock thistle and for good measure the Indian lotus. Curzon, who wanted more explicitly to recall the Mughals, chose an Indo-Saracenic theme for the decorations in 1903.[71] Taking their lead from the revitalization of the ceremonial surrounding the British monarchy between 1870 and 1914, the viceroys of the period used India as a stage on which the dream of the feudal past could be lived out to the full.[72] Although the British argued that it was their Indian subjects who were particularly susceptible to pomp and display, it would appear that it was more the viceroys themselves who were captivated by the show and splendour.[73] Herbert Maynard, who had grown more cynical by 1903, described the durbar as a mere vehicle for the 'private glorification and advertisement' of Curzon, who he referred to as a 'Petrified Peacock'.[74]

A major obstacle to the full realization of the appropriate level of grandeur was the lack of a dress uniform for civil servants. This became a bone of contention between most viceroys and the administration in London. In India it was argued that the changed status of civilians as representatives of the Queen rather than of the Company should be reflected sartorially. In particular it was argued that civilians should be dressed appropriately when participating in the ritual assertion of British power. Lord Mayo 'was amazed, indeed shocked, at his state entries to observe in his train the large number of Indian civilians...who rode in all sorts of costumes with their trousers "strapless" and well up to their knees'.[75] In the absence of a designated uniform civilians generally wore evening dress, which made them appear very drab beside the European military officers and the gorgeously clothed Indian princes. Lord Lytton complained that the 'inconvenience and embarrassment [of this] were sensibly felt on the occasion of the Assemblage held at Delhi in the year 1877'.[76] Indeed Alice Massy, a spectator at the durbar, felt 'quite sorry' for the civilians, who looked absurd with the swallow tails of their dress coats blowing around in the breeze.[77] Lytton argued that with a civilian uniform 'the ceremonial of the Viceregal Court in India should be placed on a recognized Court footing.'[78] The debate dragged on without resolution throughout the century due to lack of enthusiasm in Whitehall. While civilians in the political service adopted a version of court dress, outside the political service they had to put up with less impressive evening dress, which by the turn of the century was replaced, during the day, by the frock coat and trousers of morning dress.[79]

There was more to these complaints than the fanciful personal whims of individual viceroys or the desire of civilians to look as smart as their military compatriots. During the last half of the nineteenth century public ceremonial 'assumed...a central place in the construction of political authority' in British India.[80] Replicas of the grand imperial assemblages were held simultaneously all over India in 1877, 1903 and 1911.[81] In the localities smaller durbars were held throughout the year to distribute honours to the local Indian notables and to celebrate a variety of events.[82] G. R. Elsmie described the opening of the Indian Exhibition at Lahore in 1864: 'To-morrow is fixed for the grand durbar or levée for the reception of the Native Princes, etc. The Civilians have to appear in evening dress at twelve noon!... On Tuesday H. H. the Lieutenant-Governor gives a grand fête at Shalimár to all residents and visitors. On Wednesday the Exhibition is to be opened with all possible pomp. On Thursday come a grand review and ball.'[83] Just as enormous effort had gone into the creation of the setting for the imperial assemblages, the British in India set about creating appropriate public settings for the ceremonial display of authority. Public gardens provided one venue, railway stations another, themselves a celebration of the introduction of technology to India by the British.[84] In the same way, the clock towers which the British erected in the centre of even the smallest stations celebrated the bringing of order and discipline, through time-keeping, to India. With the completion of geometrically ordered New Delhi in 1931 the British were finally provided with an appropriate setting for the seat of British authority.

By means of the ritual enactment of Indian allegiance in ceremonial the British sought to construct a feudal relationship with the princes as well as leaders of local communities, thereby creating a body of allies within the Indian community. In order to veil the newness of these feudal links, which the now formal Empire relied upon, and to create an illusion of continuity, the new ruling style which the British developed was consciously archaic. The evocation of the ancient institution of the British monarchy gave credibility to performances which sought to forge a powerful sense of historical continuity almost overnight.[85] David Cannadine has pointed out that 'the aim of those who stage-managed [spectacles]...was to create feelings of security, cohesion and identity, in an era of anxiety, uncertainty and social dislocation.'[86] Even at the height of their power the British were not immune from threats to their imperial position posed by rival powers such as Germany and Russia, while the memory of the Mutiny remained vivid. In all likelihood the symbolism and ritual which the British employed had a far greater psychological resonance with the British themselves than with their Indian audience.[87] Ceremonial provided the British with a concrete enactment of their own ideology of rule, making manifest their own understanding of their position in India.[88]   As such, it was probably most effective at persuading the British themselves of their own superiority, power and authority, and of the security of their position within India.

Ritual is often interpreted as disguising the exercise of power. It can be argued that by surrounding the relationship between their Indian allies and themselves with splendid pageantry the British hoped to distract the public gaze from the actual lack of Indian participation in government. Nevertheless, ceremonial was not just an edifice. The bureaucratic workings of the administration were no longer integrated into ceremonial, but it still functioned as a site of political action.[89] For the British, Indian participation signified loyalty as well as the adoption of civic values. For the Indian politicians and notables who participated, ceremonial was an opportunity to create and cement personal bonds and to assert their claim to political leadership of their communities.[90] Indeed, the 'crucial centrality of ritual occasions to the constitution of political authority' was demonstrated by the vigour with which the Gandhians set about

undermining Raj ceremonial after the First World War.[91] Non-cooperators in the municipalities sought to undermine British ceremonies
by boycotting them, thus rendering them ineffective as a means of
incorporating Indians into the power structure. They also organized
counter-demonstrations, weakening the British belief that Raj splendour had a favourable impact on the masses of ordinary Indians. The
Indian reaction to the visit of the Prince of Wales in 1921–2 contrasted markedly with the warm welcome his parents received in
1911. While the newspapers reported the enthusiasm and splendour
with which royalty were welcomed in Bombay on both occasions,
even the most sycophantic of commentators could not ignore the fact
that protests against the Prince's visit sparked off riots in the city.[92]
Matters improved little as he progressed around India. Ruth Watson
noted that, although his visit to Ajmere passed off peacefully, 'there
were no very large crowds to see the Prince and very little cheering
from the crowd – really the British Tommies . . . were the only people
who cheered the Prince enthusiastically.' Ruth went on to 'wonder
whether his coming to India at this time can do any good . . . it must
be trying for him to know that in so many places where he goes, the
population is either hostile or indifferent.'[93]

The nationalist attack on imperial ritual strengthened British determination to assert their authority symbolically. In 1925, while a
Collector at Karia, Reginald Maxwell used the visit of the Governor
to his district to 'make the Non-Cooperators – who are still fairly
strong in this district – look foolish. . . . I wanted to make a really big
splash . . . the streets were packed and the utmost enthusiasm was
shown. Everything went off with a swing as though no such thing
as Non-Cooperation had ever been heard of.'[94] Indeed, ritual
remained an important part of any civil servant's duties throughout
the 1930s. W. H. Samurez Smith, a subdivisional officer in Bengal,
mentions attending a King's Birthday Parade, a meeting to congratu-
late the King on his escape from an attempted assassination, a meeting to collect for the King's Memorial Fund, a public function of the
Constitutional League, a sports display associated with visits from
superior officers, and Coronation Day celebrations, in the course of
one year between 1936 and 1937.[95] Nevertheless, Indian nationalism indelibly altered Raj ceremonial. Indians no longer used the
language of loyalty and deference in their addresses. Even among
the British an ironic tone crept in. Reginald Maxwell's description of
his participation in the celebration of the King's Birthday in 1926
contrasts with Herbert Maynard's awed description of his experience
of a durbar in 1888, quoted above. At the parade ground he 'rolled
down the intervening sand bank and proceeded at a dignified pace to

where the DSP was awaiting me. He whirled his sword rapidly round his head, cutting off a whisker at each stroke, after the manner of his kind, I, in return slapped myself in the face and knocked my hat off.'[96] Even allowing for the differences in the age and experience of the two men it is clear that much of the mystery of Raj ceremonial had dissolved.

The implementation, in 1937, of the Government of India Act of 1935 weakened the foundations of Raj ceremonial even further. In Bombay the British found it increasingly difficult to persuade Congress Ministers to attend British ceremonial functions such as the departure or arrival of a Governor, urged as they were by Gandhi to reject imperial ritual as a symbolic power base. A compromise was generally reached whereby Indian Ministers would be formally presented to the official and then leave while the rest of the ceremony continued. Their behaviour confirmed that 'the high dignity, awe and respect earlier attached to the office of the Viceroy or of the Governor were noticeably on the decline.'[97] The hostility of Indian nationalists and the uncertain state of international affairs, combined with the financial state of the Empire, militated against grand display. For these reasons plans to celebrate the coronation of Edward VIII and then George VI, in a fourth imperial assemblage which was talked of between 1936 and 1938, were abandoned.[98] But ceremonial in itself had not ceased to be effective, for example the visits of Congress officials to towns and cities were celebrated using the British ceremonial format.[99] It was ceremonial performed by the British which had come to seem increasingly hollow. As the power behind the façade of splendour drained away, the figure of the sahib was left bereft of the force which gave it symbolic resonance.

The bureaucratic body

The front-stage ceremonial of the Raj had always been complemented by intense bureaucratic activity behind the scenes. In the days of the pre-1857 durbar British Residents attempted to impose regularity on the unpredictable activity of the Indian courts by negotiating the choreography of the durbars in lengthy private meetings between the various participants. Durbar lists were drawn up detailing those entitled to attend in order of precedence, based on land revenue payments and income tax returns. The *munshis*, who the British initially relied upon as mediators, were gradually reduced to the position of 'functionaries within the bureaucracy of the British Residency'.[100] Post 1857, those who in Britain advocated an autocratic centralized administration as a creative force in society, found in India a space in which to put these ideas into practice.[101] The 'negative' liberalism of the utilitarians, who saw the state as a neutral administrator of the law, was supplanted by a 'positive' liberalism which envisaged a more active role for the state.[102] While the extravagant splendour of ceremony placed greater emphasis on the representative of the crown, the Viceroy, as a symbol of 'authority, justice and unity', greater power in real terms was invested in the administration. The late nineteenth-century imperial assemblages were the products of weeks of intricate organization to ensure the smooth ritual expression of power. Two distinct spheres, of front-stage ceremonial and backstage bureaucracy, came to characterize the activities of the Indian Government between 1858 and 1947.

After 1858 the project of modernizing India was driven forward with new energy by an Indian Civil Service which B. B. Misra describes as developing towards bureaucratic despotism. In line with increased state intervention in Britain the Government, in its thirst for knowledge about India, set about collecting statistics on every conceivable subject, from land-holding patterns to caste, by means of censuses, surveys and racial anthropology. Increasingly interventionist government legislation (e.g. tenancy legislation) focused on regulating relations between individuals. New government departments (e.g. Forestry, Public Works, Education), employing experts, intervened in Indian life. In the principalities Residents took effective control and, where the rajahs were under-age, direct control through the Court of Wards.[103] Communications improved with the construction of roads and railways and the development of the postal and telegraph services. Between 1900 and 1914 the national efficiency movement within Britain created enthusiasm for the ideal of an efficient bureaucracy, which further reinforced the legitimacy of British colonial rule: 'it seemed axiomatic that an advanced, "efficient" nation or race was entitled to control, or even if need be to crush, an inferior race, which blocked its interests, which were ultimately those of civilization itself.'[104]

This interventionist, modernizing aspect of British rule seems difficult to reconcile with the archaism of the ritual representation of power, but the fact that archaic public ceremony and bureaucratic efficiency reached the peak of their intensity over the same period between 1890 and 1914 indicates the extent to which they worked in conjunction with each other. Ceremony, as the site where the government recognized the importance of its Indian allies, carried the political weight of reconciliation. It also ameliorated the effects of rapid change by creating a sense of continuity with the past. The obverse of ceremonial was the aggressive backstage activity of the bureaucracy, which was presented as bringing India forward into the modern world of civilization. By separating out the activities of representation and administration the British were able to bring into play parallel but conflicting justifications for their presence in India and to operate on two, often contradictory, levels. On the one hand, ceremony represented the British as an ancient and superior power while, on the other, the efficiency of the administration was presented as bringing progress.

Throughout the last half of the nineteenth century civil servants, began to feel the effects of bureaucratization. As the administrative hierarchy lengthened and became more complex, the powers of the lower levels of the chain of administration were reduced. The district officer's ability to exercise discretion and personal authority was consistently eroded as his position became more and more that of an impersonal administrator of thoroughly codified regulations.[105] A huge demand for reports emanated from the government secretariats as the process of gathering information gained momentum, and district officers found themselves increasingly burdened by paperwork. Alfred Lyall, who joined the service in 1856, observed this process with regret: 'I feel now positive pain when I look over the histories of the young civilians and officers who distinguished themselves in the old days of intrigue and fighting.... Now every reform tends to decrease civilians to mere magistrates and revenue officers.'[106] The old hands' resentment of the trend towards bureaucratization found expression in their condemnation of the competition-wallah. It was contemptuously pronounced that the best the middle classes could produce was a weakly bureaucrat who, with his 'energies worn out and exhausted by excessive and premature toil over books',[107] would suit this new desk-bound service.

Indeed, newcomers to the service found themselves initiated into a monotonous, time-consuming, and sometimes lonely, daily routine of magisterial duties and office work, limited to the space of *cutcherry* (office or courthouse) and bungalow, where their bodies were regimented by office hours, the rules of administration, and the need for good time-keeping and self-discipline. Walter Lawrence, assistant commissioner at Lahore in 1880, explained to his father, after having been in India for only a few months, that the pressure of work had even interrupted his dietary routine: 'I breakfast at 10.30 and don't eat anything till 7.30. This now 5.30 and I have been hard at work since 7.30 A.M. so my life is not a bed of roses and my dreams of Oriental luxury and repose have been rudely awakened.'[108] The burden of paperwork from morning till night so marked a civilian's life that it became a staple of ICS humour. Bureaucracy's stultifying effect was satirized in trivial literature and the newspapers. *The Delhi Sketchbook* of 1854 depicts a startled official confronted by a ridiculously long list of monthly returns, while another clerk staggers in under a pile of files (see plate 15). The comedy even extended to ICS dinner invitations, on which a civilian would frequently be pictured virtually buried under stacks of files.[109]

While the sphere of representation reduced the body of the sahib to a symbol of British authority, the sphere of administration seemed to many contemporaries to reduce civil servants to mere cogs in the vast colonial administrative machine. Bureaucratization disciplined the body through the regimentation of time and space, holding the British in the grip of the same mechanism of power by which they sought to discipline and control the subject population.[110] But civil servants were not simply the passive tools of a monolithic government, they participated enthusiastically in the process of disciplinization. In response to the denigration of the competition-wallah as a

Executive — "Holloa Baboo what the deuce is that:"
Head Baboo — "By masters leave Sir, it is the listee of the additional monthlee returns Sir, required by the new system Sir, master had plantee of work to do Sir, but he now hab bery much more plentee Sir."

Plate 15 An official buried by paper work. 'The D.P. works revised and improved.'

'myopic secretary', the bureaucratic body was celebrated through the development of a work ethic in which self-discipline became a valued personal quality, a benefit of civilization, which the British sought to instil in their subordinates. John Beames was proud that he had introduced hard regular work to the natives in his office.

> It was . . . only by the most punctuality and strictness that so much work could be got through . . . . When once you establish a dastûr (a custom or fixed routine) with natives they are allright. . . . they make themselves into machines and work admirably. There were never any arrears in the Cuttack office during the four years of my incumbency, and this was due not to any superior merit or cleverness on my part but simply to the introduction of a regular routine of work.[111]

For many civilians the pomp of ceremonial and the social life of the station and the Club were the backdrop to the 'real business of their lives' which was the hard grind of administering a vast country.[112] The bureaucrat maligned by the detractors of the competition system was transformed into a virtuous public servant who cramped his body over a desk for hours on end in the name of public duty. The bodily discomforts of the civilian's life, working long hours at tedious paperwork in the heat of India, enabled the re-working of the civilian into a bureaucratic but nevertheless heroic figure.

> There was hard work but it seemed worth doing; it was always concerned with people's lives. In the hot weather – when, as you shaved naked in the early light, the sweat dripped off your elbows and each drop vanished as it hit the brick floor of the bathroom – there was a feeling that you were in the front line; it was a braced, tense life in which there was the continual pleasure of responsible decision.[113]

The burden placed on the physique of the civilian by the heat and the hard work provided a justification for the substructure of servants who attended to his every bodily need. The body servants who dressed and bathed the Anglo-Indian official, going so far as to even roll on his socks for him; the entourage of cook, sweeper, water-carrier and so on who served him at home and while touring the district, were justified as a necessary support to the physical needs of an administrator of so vast and demanding a country as India.

It was the physical limitations of the official which acted as a catalyst for administrative reform. By the end of the century, the sense that the ICS would soon literally collapse under its burden of paper persuaded Curzon that reform was essential. Just as questions of importance sank into the 'quagmire' of red tape, so the civilians themselves were sinking into it as well, unable physically to withstand the demands of the job. Before any decision could be made each file passed from hand to hand, commented upon at increasing length according to the place of the official within the hierarchy. Curzon succeeded, despite making himself unpopular in the process, in reducing the number of memos circulated and in encouraging officials to reach decisions by talking to each other.[114]

The inhabited bureaucratic body of the civilian was a counter to the depersonalized symbolic body of the civilian which was brought into play during ceremonial. Reginald Maxwell in his office photograph, dressed in his English suit, sola topi on his lap, surrounded by his office staff, is the embodiment of the bureaucratic sahib (see plate 11). Despite the reduction in personal power, the personality of the official remained an important aspect of his role. At work in the court, the office or out in the fields the civilian exercised tangible power over the lives of Indians, and British rule was made manifest in his person. W. H. Samurez Smith remarked 'There is of course a lot of drudgery routine work and signature-appending. But there is also a great deal of work where the personality of the S.D.O. counts, and where his ability to get other people to follow his lead is tremendously important.'[115] It was this personalized aspect of the work, and the occasions when they were able to cut through the red tape and make decisions on the spot, which enabled civilians to reconcile themselves to the tedious grind of listening to cases in the courts, surveying land distribution and writing up the judgements and reports in the early mornings and evenings. Even after 1919 when the bureaucracy ceased to function as the government of India,[116] and after 1935 when power was surrendered to Indian Ministers, the civilians out in the districts still saw themselves as doing the real work of ruling the country on the ground.

Prestige and physical violence

Whether acting as a symbolic representative of the values of the British government in India, or in his office or *cutcherry*, exercising power and authority on the ground, the British administrator was expected to maintain that 'credible performance of haughtiness and mastery' which was necessary to sustain domination.[117] This performance, summed up by the term 'prestige', was manufactured and reinforced by bodily display to the extent that the British saw even a private shooting expedition or a casual cricket practice as an enactment of the superior physical and moral qualities of their race in front of an Indian audience. The concept of prestige supplied the British official with a detailed transcript for appropriate behaviour in the public domain. Looking back on his days as a Ceylon civilian, Leonard Woolf remarked on the unreal 'theatricality' produced by this sense that colonials were 'always...playing a part, acting upon...the stage [of] imperialism'.[118] Newcomers to India found that they could simply step into an established role, supported by the props of their official position: white skin; a supposedly manly Anglo-Saxon physique; British clothing, including the distinctive sola topi; and an authoritative manner and tone of voice.[119] In his memoirs John Beames described the process of inhabiting the role of the sahib. On arrival at his first posting in the Punjab, he was dumped unceremoniously by the mail cart 'by the roadside...at four in the morning'. No one showed any inclination to offer assistance. 'The position was new to me, but I had noted the respect paid to Elliot [a civilian friend of his]...and knew that I was entitled to the same here. So I announced myself in Hindustani as the new Assistant Sahib, and sternly demanded that someone should go with me to show me the way. This at once produced the effect desired.'[120] By taking on the authoritative manner and tone of voice of the sahib, Beames cloaked himself in a mantle of prestige which elicited Indian deference.

In the everyday running of the country, civil servants relied heavily upon 'that calm confidence which betrays no sign of misgiving, and the very quietude that indicates a consciousness of strength'.[121] Even in the face of Indian protest against British rule during the twentieth century, prestige was regarded as 'the European's safeguard in India. Funk is fatal to prestige.'[122] Women were expected to play their part in keeping up a brave front, and within Anglo-Indian literature it was those women who displayed masculine courage in the face of Indian insubordination, who adopted the sahib's air of invincibility in the public sphere, who were portrayed as a credit to the British race.[123] Looking back, Philip Mason, a civil servant from 1929 until Independence, found it 'hard to convey the authoritarian atmosphere of India, the expectation that anyone would do whatever you told him'.[124] Prestige continued to work so effectively in British officials' day-to-day dealings with Indians that, even when Indian terrorism was at its height, it did not occur to most of them that an Indian might attack them.

Prestige, manufactured at the level of face-to-face interaction, relied heavily on a deferential response on the part of Indians. Hence the British channelled a great deal of energy into imposing 'Indian' codes of behaviour on Indians. 'Once the British had defined something as an Indian custom, or traditional dress, or the proper form of salutation, any deviation from it was defined as rebellion and an act to be punished.'[125] In 1871 two schoolboys were expelled from their school for failing to salaam the Commissioner of Assam. A circular was then issued urging schoolmasters to attend to the inculcation of manners in their students. The ridicule this circular attracted in the Indian newspaper *Som Prokash* prompted irate letters to *The Englishman* from Anglo-Indians deploring the want of gentlemanly manners among Indians.[126] The British reaction to the 'Assam salaam case' reveals the almost pathological fear of insolence which colonists are said by Peter Gay to exhibit.[127] This stemmed from their awareness that 'Deferential attitudes [can] become a manner, one side of a habitual double-faced outlook, a form of self-presentation... [which] often covered a deep-rooted sense of grievance.'[128] An example of such deference offered without sincerity is provided by Lutfullah, who on seeing two Englishmen 'felt inclined to accost them; but thought myself too young... I raised my hand, however, to my forehead, in token of salutation, without uttering the Sacred sentence, "As salámun alaikum," to which my mind whispered none were entitled except true believers.'[129] British sensitivity to the slightest hint of a challenge to their dignity or authority meant that they frequently met any act which suggested insolence with physical violence. A book on British relations with Indians claimed that 'It is but too common an outrage to assault respectable residents of this country because when passing on the road they have not dismounted from their horses in token of their inferiority.'[130] It was in these circumstances that the belief in racial superiority, enshrined in the idea of prestige, mutated from arrogance into physical violence.

Certain groups in Anglo-Indian society were notorious for physical aggression. Blanchard, revealing the class prejudices of the Anglo-Indian elite, claimed that the worst offenders were 'Englishmen of a low class, who are apt to be arrogant on account of their white skins – the only gentility to which they can lay claim.'[131] Planters and soldiers were renowned for their violence towards coolies and regimental servants.[132] As the nineteenth century progressed, Indian outrage over their violent treatment at the hands of the British became increasingly vocal. In 1893 Ram Gopal Sanyal published a *Record of Criminal Cases as between Europeans and Natives for the Last Sixty Years* in which he detailed the failure of the British judicial system with regard to the protection of Indians from British violence. The book relates a large number of cases where, if they were found guilty at all, the Europeans received unjustifiably light sentences.[133] In 1905 questions were asked in the House of Commons which finally elicited an official response. Although an unreliable indicator of the real extent of inter-racial violence in India, the subsequent report confirmed the poor reputation of the army and planters. Out of the 199 cases of Europeans attacking natives reported in 1901, 146 were committed by members of the army, and a large number of incidents recorded in the return over the five years 1901–5 involved planters.[134] The assaults ranged from hitting and kicking to stabbing and rape, but the sentences for Europeans were uniformly light – confinement to barracks, a few days' imprisonment, forfeit of pay – in comparison to several months' to a year's rigorous imprisonment normally given out to Indians who attacked Europeans. Sanyal's complaints about the British system of justice were borne out by the report. The prejudice of the courts in favour of the British explains the level of Anglo-Indian protest in response to the Ilbert Bill in 1883, which would have given Indian judges the power to try cases involving Europeans. Later on in the century Curzon discovered that treating European attacks on Indians with leniency was seen by a great many of the British as essential to the maintenance of prestige. British soldiers could not be seen to be treated with the same severity as Indian offenders. Walter Lawrence, commenting on Curzon's attempts to have harsher sentences imposed on brutal soldiers, argued 'it is impossible to have an exactly equal law for Natives and Europeans.'[135]

During the last half of the nineteenth century the question of state violence became an issue of debate. It was asked whether a civilized government should still be sentencing criminals to whipping.[136] The public humiliation of whipping, abolished by Bentinck, was reintroduced in 1844, again abolished by the new Indian Penal Code in 1862, but reintroduced with the Whipping Bill of 1864. It was still in use as a quick and effective means of castigation in the twentieth century. Characterized by John Beames as particularly suitable for a 'simple race',[137] whipping was regarded as a short sharp punishment which sent the message home more effectively than a prison sentence. It had the added advantage that any appeal against the sentence was ineffective as the punishment was inflicted immediately. The majority of Anglo-Indians regarded whipping as a reasonable public-school punishment which many of them had themselves experienced in their youth. The use of whipping in India was therefore legitimized as an extension of a paternalistic attitude towards their subjects rather than as a sadistic and uncivilized use of force.

Although, as representatives of the government, civil servants wielded the power of state violence in public, in private they had a reputation for being far less likely to resort to violence. The need for civil servants to preserve the notion that they were respectable members of Anglo-Indian society, above the degradations of planters and the army, combined with the need to keep up prestige, the paternalistic rhetoric of the Raj, and the knowledge that they lived to a greater extent in the public eye, meant that brutal incidents such as the one detailed below were rarely reported.

> Mr G. Thornhill, a member of the Board of Revenue, was sent up a short time back as Commissioner to enquire into the conduct of a Junior Civil Servant in one of the North West districts of the Presidency. The charges proffered against the civilian were: 1, spitting in the face of a peon; 2, causing the public triangles to be brought to his house for the purpose of flogging his private servants; and 3, assaulting natives in an unbecoming way. Mr Thornhill in his report states that the charges have been admitted by the young Civilian, and that he has expressed the utmost contrition for his misconduct, solemnly promising to refrain from such conduct in future. He was suspended for three months and will then 'be appointed only as an Assistant Collector, and placed under the immediate supervision of some Collector.'[138]

Rather than describing the civilian's behaviour as brutal or inhumane the newspaper described it as unbecoming. This was the crux of the matter when it came to British aggression towards Indians. A correspondent to *The Englishman* in 1865, who complained of having seen a Judge 'in a public place, within a few yards of Government House, violently abusing his syce, and in a fit of rage, severely thrashing him with his riding whip',[139] was perturbed more than anything else by the public nature of the act. According to the rhetoric of imperialism the British ruled India by virtue of their specifically English ability to administer justice. Public displays of random violence on the part of respectable members of the British community undermined one of the substructures of prestige. A quick slap administered to a servant or the whipping of a recalcitrant bullock-cart driver might be regarded as reasonable, even as amusing examples of British spirit,[140] but uncontrolled fits of rage in public, or violence which resulted in severe harm or death for the victim, were condemned.[141]

Particular sites and situations tended to act as flashpoints where conflict and violence were more likely to erupt. One of the most notorious sites of conflict, where the contradictions implicit in the ideology of prestige came to the fore, was the railway carriage. The British were immensely proud of the railway system, which they represented as a vehicle of civilization in India.[142] The railway carriage was converted into yet another site for the display of prestige. Europeans in their first-class carriages travelled in a self-contained sphere of comfort: each carriage had its own bathroom and the luxury of Indian trains was in sharp contrast to the more utilitarian ones at home.[143] This reflected the added weight which imperialism gave to the expression of what in Britain were differences in social class. While in Britain members of the upper middle classes might choose to save money on train tickets, in India Europeans who travelled in anything less than comfort were seen as letting the side down. When Edmund Cox first arrived in India he travelled 'intermediate'.

> My brother, when I arrived at Bankipur the next morning, was horror-struck at seeing me in that class. It was impressed upon me that a European in India is a 'sahib,' and a member of the ruling race, and must not lower his position by travelling in anything less than second-class, and that it is only permissible to take a second-class ticket when your financial position absolutely prohibits the luxury of a first.[144]

Edmund Cox's lesson in Indian train travel reveals the drawbacks to the modernization process of which the British were so proud, for it also carried the risk of introducing unwanted democratization. The railway station and the train were weak points in the careful wall of separation that the British had built around their bodies. From the beginning, anxieties about contact with the Indian population were expressed. A correspondent to *The Englishman* in the 1870s was concerned about ladies 'being jostled by half-naked coolies' on the platform at Howrah.[145] As rail became the established mode of transport, some segregation was put into place. Every station had separate dining-rooms for Hindus, Muslims, and for Europeans. Even the water-carriers supplied different water to the different passengers. Many towns had separate stations, one for the Indian town, and one for the European station or cantonment. The trains were divided into first- and second-class mail trains, which ran on time, and tardy third-class and goods trains. On some lines there were carriages reserved for Europeans only,[146] but on the other lines Europeans quite frequently found Indians travelling with them. The result was that those Indians who did attempt to travel first class often found themselves in the humiliating position of being thrown out of the compartment, either by brute force or by the stationmaster. Even the most respectable of civilians was guilty of this kind of behaviour,[147] despite the fact that 'Notes for officers proceeding to India' reminded them that 'Indians are fully entitled to travel in first-class carriages if they pay the fare.... You are not entitled to demand to see their tickets. Indians often bring strange things into the compartment but anything about which you can really complain is rare. In no case must violence be resorted to.'[148] The railway carriage, a travelling symbol of British civilization, was frequently transformed into the site of extreme acts of British incivility.

Whenever the reasons for the British objection to Indian travelling companions were discussed, the claim that Indians and the British were *physically* incompatible was consistently used to justify separation. A distaste for bodily proximity with Indians was thus revealed. Edmund Hull explained the problem.

> Many of the natives are addicted to practices which make them anything but agreeable *compagnons de voyage* in close quarters. In the first place, they lubricate the body with oil, sometimes cocoanut, but often castor or margosa oil; the two latter kinds having a most fœtid and, to a European, a most disgusting and nauseating smell. Secondly, being often fat, the natives perspire very freely, which they can hardly be blamed for, but which intensifies the effect of the anointment.

He went on to detail the British objection to the Indian habit of chewing betel on the grounds of the 'copious red expectoration' and hideously stained mouth to which it gave rise. Thirdly, he explained that 'their habit of eructating on all occasions, without the least attempt to restraint . . . is . . . surprising to an Englishman.' Hull finished by asking his reader to imagine travelling in a carriage with such companions at a temperature of eighty degrees and rested his case.[149] Trevelyan went so far as to suggest that such was 'the incompatibility of manners that English ladies could not use the railway at all if native gentlemen were in the constant habit of travelling in the same compartment.'[150] Such discussions reveal racism articulated at the level of a physical revulsion to difference. It was this that led Edmund Candler to 'look upon racial incompatibility as something chemical or psychological, apart from reason, which is only called up among the supports of our self-respect in a losing battle'.[151] This physical aversion saddened Philip Mason on his arrival in India. On his first train journey he enjoyed a conversation with an Indian newspaper editor but 'when he went, his hair left on the window-pane where he had leaned a thick smear of some greasy substance, at which I looked with distaste, reflecting how often it is little things that keep people apart.'[152] Undoubtedly Indians were disgusted by aspects of British bodily behaviour, but the balance of power meant that Indian etiquette manuals advised Indians not about the disgusting quirks of the British but about how to accommodate to British tastes. Indian gentlemen who were permitted to travel in the same carriage as a European were cautioned that they should abstain from practices which might offend such as chewing betel, smoking a hookah and removing clothing from the upper part of the body.[153]

Gandhi's concept of *satyagraha*, or passive resistance, employed in the non-cooperation and civil disobedience movements, was admirably suited to act as a protest against a form of rule which relied heavily on Indian deference. Even more powerful was Gandhi's transformation of the despised Indian body into a site of resistance. Indeed, Gandhi used his own body as a potent weapon. 'Out of . . . its rhythms, vulnerabilities and strengths, he created high drama. Gandhi imprisoned, struck by a British *lathi*, fasting, silent, walking across dusty plains, brought down by three bullets – his tiny physical frame grew to fill an immense imaginative space, becoming the screen on which the misdemeanours of the entire British Empire were humiliatingly enacted.'[154] The bodies of his followers, clothed in *khadi* and a Gandhi cap, acted equally powerfully as statements of Indian resistance. They might continue to show respect to British officials, but their bodies clearly stated that they were neither deferential nor submissive.

As Indian nationalism grew in force the mass of ordinary Indians joined this refusal to respond to the British with deference. While he was Assistant Magistrate and Collector at Gaya in 1939, Ian Mac-Donald described how during a nationalist protest 'there were some ugly scenes' at the railway station. 'I and a police sub-inspector had just to stand and watch the happenings. Every time I appeared on any platform, the crowd gave vent to cries of "Angrezi raj nash ho!" – Down with English rule. But actually they were only excited and not really very violent.'[155] MacDonald's experience contrasts markedly with that of John Beames, quoted above, who found an authoritarian manner quickly elicited Indian deference. In the 1920s John Rivett-Carnac found that he could overawe crowds of protesting nationalists 'if I went down myself, making quite an impossible figure in full uniform with a helmet and a revolver on each side and riding boots'.[156] A sola topi and a haughty manner were no longer enough, however: Rivett-Carnac needed the additional prop of a revolver in his belt, and resorted to hitting leading members of the crowd. By the 1920s force was clearly a necessary adjunct to the impressive presence of the British official.

The British need to resort to force was illustrated most dramatically by the Jallianwalla Bagh massacre at Amritsar in 1919, when General Dyer ordered his troops to open fire on protesters. The ensuing unrest in the Punjab was brutally suppressed. Aeroplanes were used to strafe and bomb rioters at Gujranwala, public whippings were frequent, and in Amritsar Indians were made to crawl along the street where a female mission doctor had been attacked.[157] In its vindictiveness the British response went far beyond the need to suppress disorder. Its brutality destroyed the British reputation for justice and decency, two of the principles which underpinned the legitimization of their rule. Prestige, as a mechanism by which to distract attention from the fact that British authority rested on the potential use of state force, was now useless. On the other hand, the public outcry which followed Amritsar made it difficult for the government to suppress protest with violence. This meant that two of the mainstays of British rule – prestige and force – were becoming increasingly difficult to implement, severely weakening the power of the Raj. It wasn't until 1942 and the Quit India movement that the government used the circumstances of war to impose their rule upon India with levels of violence which equalled Amritsar. However, by 1942 it was increasingly clear that the British no longer ruled by prestige and that they could continue to sustain rule by force for only a short time.

5

The Social Body

Throughout the nineteenth century a distinctive Anglo-Indian culture developed, marked by continuity rather than change. By the twentieth century the Anglo-Indian body appeared to have been fossilized. Medical and racial notions of appropriate behaviour united with the official discourse of prestige to create a domestic regime of keeping up appearances which demonstrated racial difference as well as class position and status. The Anglo-Indian official and his wife within the home were moulded into appropriate representatives of racial superiority. However, prestige was an outdated and less useful concept after 1914, and as political pressure towards Indian independence intensified, the British were called upon to incorporate Indians into their social sphere. The slower pace of change on the cultural level meant that they were only partially successful in their response. As the twentieth century progressed the archaic and outdated nature of the Anglo-Indian body became increasingly apparent.

Social life and conformity

During the latter half of the nineteenth century the process of anglicization worked itself out to a logical end. The ban on the East was reinforced, while the anglicized bodily practices of the 1830s and 1840s were reified and preserved in virtually fossilized form. Initially developed as a distancing mechanism to separate Briton from Indian, the anglicized Anglo-Indian body increasingly came to serve as an active principle demarcating class as well as racial boundaries. This was in response to the pressure exerted on Anglo-Indian officialdom by the growth of the British community in India from the 1850s. The expansion of the bureaucracy brought the number of officials in the all-India services up to about 3,500, only a quarter of whom were actually employed in the ICS. With the increase in the numbers of British troops deployed in India after the Mutiny, army officers also made up a sizeable proportion of the Anglo-Indian community. In addition, the numbers of unofficial British residents in India were rising, with the whole European population, including women, numbering some 156,000 by 1921.[1] The ICS therefore became increasingly overwhelmed, representing only a tiny proportion of the British community in India. Anglo-Indian officialdom reacted by placing fresh emphasis on the grandeur of the high-ranking official's lifestyle, much in the style of the nabob.

The efforts of the official community to represent themselves as an aristocratic elite were always in danger of being neutralized by the fact that India provided all members of the British community with the opportunity to adopt a lifestyle which would have been above their means in Europe. Everyone of 'the middle and lower classes of Europeans in India' tended to give himself airs and consider 'himself a "Sahib" or gentleman'.[2] The social pretensions of the rest of the growing European community encouraged the officials to demarcate the barriers which secured their position as an elite more clearly. G. O. Trevelyan noted the regrettable decline in hospitality for which the Anglo-Indians had once been renowned, due to the fact that 'there are so many Europeans about of questionable position and most unquestionable breeding that it is necessary to know something of a man besides the colour of his skin before admitting him into the bosom of a family.'[3] Even within the charmed circle of officialdom the threat posed to social exclusivity by the increasing numbers, as well as concerns about the social background of competition men, encouraged officials to cling to and elaborate upon social rituals. The result was the distinctive imperial lifestyle which is associated in the popular imagination with the Raj.

In the early nineteenth century there was nothing very remarkable about the social life of the British in India. It was simply the lifestyle of the gentry which early Company officials had brought with them and replicated in another setting. What is remarkable is that the style of Anglo-Indian socializing changed so little. During the nineteenth century the larger inland stations, such as Cawnpore or Allahabad, developed as social centres in their own right, where everyone in the district would gather together for gaiety over the Christmas week. The number and size of hill stations, as well as the numbers visiting them during the hot weather, also rose. But the social calendar of the Anglo-Indian in the 1930s was filled, just as it would have been throughout most of the nineteenth century, with balls, theatricals, fancy-dress parties, picnics, fêtes and horse races, with a little more emphasis in the twentieth century on sporting activities such as gymkhanas or polo.[4] Set against changing patterns of socializing in Britain, the fixed nature of Anglo-Indian social life became increasingly effective as a signifier of the official community's position as a form of aristocracy.

Martin Wiener argues that, during the latter half of the nineteenth century, both the entrepreneurial and professional sections of the British middle classes developed a 'gentrified' bourgeois culture which looked to a myth of rural England as the foundation of the moral character of the nation.[5] Wiener attributes Britain's industrial decline to this idealization of country over town, of rural idyll over industrial progress, which meant that businessmen sent their sons to public schools where they would be educated as country gentlemen rather than entrepreneurs. The number of Victorian country houses built or improved during the latter half of the century testify to the rising middle classes' desire to replicate the country-house living of the gentry.[6] Eric Hobsbawm qualifies this argument by suggesting that the bourgeoisie, rather than being feudalized, simply hijacked certain aristocratic habits which complemented their culture. David Cannadine has also traced the development of a plutocracy which gradually invaded and displaced patrician society.[7] 'The test of aristocratic values now increasingly became a profligate and expensive style of life which required above all *money*', and those members of the genuine landed nobility who lacked the means to keep up with the new trend-setters simply faded into the background.[8] At the same time the lifestyle of the middle class, as opposed to that of the new plutocracy, was becoming more distinct, more independent and less grandiose. British urban middle-class leisure shifted its focus towards domestic relaxation rather than conspicuous display.

Due to its condition of stasis Anglo-Indian social life at the end of the century now mirrored that of the new metropolitan plutocracy. The Anglo-Indian official's self-conscious combination of office work with hunting and shooting holidays echoed the lifestyle of this distinctive section of the metropolitan upper middle class, which was made up of industrialists, wealthy merchants and city businessmen.[9] Although the majority of recruits to the services from 1858 onwards were drawn from the solidly middle-class families of clergymen or professionals, the photographs which the Anglo-Indians took of themselves posing as hunters (see plate 12), and the *shikar* trophies which decorated almost every Anglo-Indian bungalow, mess and club, reinforced the image of the civil servant as the country gentleman.[10] Similarly, in the Indian Army, the 'undistinguished middle class professional' backgrounds of the officers were ignored. 'It was tacitly assumed that none of us had chosen to serve in India for purely economic reasons, but simply because it offered better opportunities... for indulging one's sporting instincts and leading the gentlemanly life. When every three years or so we went home on leave it was supposed that we spent the time exercising the family hunters, dry-fly fishing or stalking in Scotland. Nobody really believed this but the fiction was upheld.'[11] A complementary image of Britain was constructed in the Anglo-Indian imagination as the rustic idyll of the landed gentry, with Home described as a land of 'green fields,... waving corn and rustling leaves,... smooth lawns and scented meadows;... pleasant manors,... tall houses and smiling countryside'.[12] Anglo-Indians' projection of themselves as paternal aristocrats played down the bureaucratic, interventionist side of government in India. While they might be responsible for bringing the technology and efficiency of the modern world to India, the British liked to present themselves as doing so through the medium of the 'ancient aristocratic paternalist patterns of... rural England'.[13]

By resembling the social life of the leisured classes, for whom socializing was a public act which established status while providing pleasure, the social life of the Anglo-Indians cast an aura of tradition and nobility over Anglo-Indian officialdom.[14] The projection of themselves as aristocrats drew attention to the Indian government's continuing reliance on the 'principle of innate, inherited superiority' as a justification for British rule. This echoed the metropolitan aristocracy's assumption that their superiority justified their political dominance. Benedict Anderson goes so far as to argue that 'the existence of late colonial empires even served to *shore up* domestic aristocratic bastions, since they appeared to confirm on a global, modern stage antique conceptions of power and privilege.'[15] By the end of the First World War, however, the aristocratic hold on political power in the metropole finally began to crumble in the face of 'full-scale democracy'.[16] The extravagance of the pre-war lifestyle of the rich was not revived. In contrast, post-war Anglo-India continued to rely on a justification for power which was quickly becoming outmoded, and to maintain a social life which began to appear archaic to newcomers. Those arriving in India after 1919 found that Anglo-Indian society appeared to have been petrified in the nineteenth century. Even in the 1930s A. I. Bowman found that, at ICS week in Lucknow, 'Everything carried an aura of the great days of the Raj, when the stamp of Victorian upper-class society was set on the British in India.'[17] The old-fashioned nature of Anglo-Indian social life lent it a certain glamour: 'where else could quite ordinary, middle-class people with not very much money indulge in racing, the sport of kings; polo, only for the very rich; balls, receptions, literally the pomp and ceremonies of this wicked world?'[18]

India therefore continued throughout the twentieth century to provide members of the middle classes and the declining gentry with the opportunity to rise to a level of social prominence, and to adopt a lifestyle, which they would have found unattainable in Britain. Although the curtailment of civilians' incomes meant that households now rarely reached the impressive size of Fanny Parks's fifty-seven (see Appendix), an average family might still employ thirteen or fourteen servants.[19] This was out of all proportion to the number of servants an ordinary civilian would have been used to at home, especially after the First World War when they became scarce and a British household used to five servants now had to manage with two.[20] Even railway officials in India in the 1910s could afford a lifestyle which resembled that of the leisured classes of the nineteenth century. In plate 10 Jim Bourne, a railway engineer, is pictured with his wife, Hilda, four of their fourteen servants, as well as two railway peons and four railway-trolley coolies, who did odd jobs for the household when they were off duty. The number of servants which a household could command was central to its claim to social significance. Just as in the days of the nabob, servants functioned as objects of conspicuous consumption, reflecting the social importance of their master and mistress, especially those which appeared in public alongside the Anglo-Indian. At Simla 'each household of any standing had its own particular jampanee-livery; only those attached to the Viceregal establishment were officially allowed to wear the imperial scarlet, but many of the others sported elaborate combinations of "purple and emerald with light blue trimmings", of "bright yellow tunics and claret coloured caps".'[21]

The fact that in India a railway official could afford the staff to suit a country gentleman meant that the official elite had to struggle constantly to maintain their social position. In the artificial society of Anglo-India, where the usual social regulators of birth and rank were subsumed beneath official position, the most effective way of maintaining social dominance was to emphasize the code of precedence which governed social relations. While prestige regulated British relations with the Indian population, precedence regulated social relations between the British themselves. The position of every official and military officer was detailed in a graded list known as the 'warrant of precedence'. Women took their social position from that of their husband's or father's place in the official hierarchy. The hierarchical ordering of British India was frequently likened to the caste system of Indian society, with the civil servants, known as the 'heaven born', occupying a social position equivalent to that of the Brahmins.[22] Within the services an internal hierarchy ranged from the Indian Medical Service and the Indian Police to Education and Railways.[23] The military considered themselves on a par with the civilians but in practice they tended to be ranked second. Below the official class came the professionals and businessmen, divided into the heads of large firms and box-wallahs, and then the planters, who divided into the upper ranks of tea and indigo, and the lower ranks of jute and sugar.[24] The ICS preferred to keep to themselves, but they would have mixed socially with all these levels of Anglo-Indian society to a certain extent, depending on where they were stationed and whether isolation meant that there were no alternative groups with which to socialize.[25] Those considered below them were generally made to feel their position. J. D. Gordon, a barrister in an up-country station, wrote with some bitterness of the way in which precedence functioned:

> In England there is a nasty radical notion prevalent that men must be taken on their individual merits, but here we look at matters differently. If a man is in the Civil Service he *must* be a gentleman; if in the army the odds are in his favour; if, however, he is in the railway he must be a cad. The police, as directly connected with the Civil Service, are not beyond the chance of salvation. Where barristers, merchants, and such like uncovenanted scum are to go, deponent sayeth not. These little distinctions can be so charmingly emphasized in the precedence arrangements of big dinner parties.[26]

If barristers felt they were treated badly, the domiciled whites, the Eurasian community, the British Other Ranks and missionaries, all considered to be on a par with the lower castes, were either ignored or patronized by the rest of the Anglo-Indian community.[27]

While in Britain the protocol of precedence was usually managed unobtrusively, in Anglo-India it dominated proceedings. The frequent comparisons made with the caste system were perhaps an attempt to justify a level of class consciousness which would probably have been seen as petty in Britain. By presenting themselves as the top half of a highly structured social system the British asserted their credibility as rulers of India, while implying that the special conditions of India demanded particularly intricate social division. While the rigid etiquette of the nineteenth century was gradually falling into disuse in

Britain, new arrivals in India were surprised to find that calling, a 'curious survival of English country life', was still in place in India well into the 1930s.[28] Attention to precedence transformed Anglo-Indian social events into elaborate enactments of social ranking, which served to confirm and assert the hierarchy which governed social relations in British India. The dinner party in particular was transformed into a central symbolic rite within Anglo-Indian social life.

The pressure on the official community to distinguish themselves from the rest of the European community led to the further tightening of the codes governing food consumption which had developed as part of the process of anglicization. As has already been observed, what you ate, and when and how you ate it, were seen as absolutely central to the definition of who you were in British India. The development of a hierarchy of foods begun in the second quarter of the nineteenth century continued to establish itself as the dominant pattern. This is well illustrated by John Beames's detailed account of what he and his wife ate while living in the districts around 1869–1870, which gives a picture of what most Anglo-Indians living in the *mofussil* would have subsisted on throughout the last half of the nineteenth, and well into the twentieth century.

> Our *chotà hàziri*, or little breakfast, was at five-thirty to six, and consisted of tea, eggs boiled or poached, toast and fruit.... Breakfast at eleven consisted of fried or broiled fish, a dish or two of meat – generally fowl cutlets, hashes and stews, or cold meat and salad followed by curry and rice and dessert. We drank either bottled beer – the universal Bass – or claret.... Between four and five there was tea and cakes,... Dinner at half past seven or eight consisted of soup, and entrée, roast fowls or ducks, occasionally mutton, and in cold weather once or twice beef, an entremet of game or a savoury, and sweets. We drank either beer or claret.... We did not indulge much in 'tinned' things, believing them to be unwholesome and thinking them often very nasty. But by many people in India they are considered very great luxuries.[29]

From Beames's account we can see that traces of Indian influence were still to be found in patterns of food consumption. *Chota haziri* was an Indian meal designed to accommodate to the early rising which the climate encouraged. The large breakfast, called 'brunch' or 'tiffin', was also strongly influenced by India. It included Indian food, normally in the shape of a curry, and was a more substantial meal, taken earlier than the British luncheon. This too was an adjustment to the Indian daily routine of early rising, exercise, a bath followed by breakfast and work. India continued to be a powerful presence in Anglo-Indian food culture during the morning, both in the form of the food itself and when it was consumed. As the day progressed Anglo-Indian eating patterns took on a more British cast. In the metropole, the lengthening of office hours and the postponement of dinner to the evening, combined with increased tea-drinking, encouraged the habit of taking tea in the afternoon from the 1840s onwards.[30] This practice became firmly fixed in the Anglo-Indian routine as an important British ritual when specially baked British cakes and biscuits, such as currant loaf, macaroons and rich chocolate cake, would be served.[31] From tea time onwards the food consumed acted as a reminder of home and of the Britishness of the meal's participants. Dinner, consumed at the same hour as in Britain, functioned as the defining meal of the day, when the Anglo-Indians tried their best to reproduce in alien surroundings the style current among the urban bourgeoisie in Britain. Indian food, 'The molten curries and florid oriental compositions of the olden time', which in the 1830s and 1840s had been relegated to the bottom of the hierarchy of dishes, were now altogether 'banished from our dinner tables; for although a well considered curry, or mulligatawni – capital things in their way, – are still frequently given at breakfast or luncheon, they no longer occupy a position in the dinner menu of establishments conducted according to the new regime.'[32] A review of Wyvern's *Culinary Jottings for Madras* in *The Calcutta Review* of 1879 argued that a cookery book for India 'to be really useful, should teach us, not how to prepare certain dishes peculiar to the country, but how best to produce, under the special circumstances of the country, the dishes approved by the taste of polite society at home'.[33] The menus of dinner parties detailed by John Laing in his diary in 1873, seen together (on page 158) with some seasonal menus from Mary Hooper's cookery book entitled *Little Dinners: How to Serve them with Elegance and Economy*, the third edition of which was published in 1878, which probably resemble average dinner-party menus of an inextravagant middle-class British household,[34] indicate the extent to which Anglo-Indians attempted to preserve their British eating habits at dinner time in India. Elisabeth Bruce, the daughter of Lord Elgin (Viceroy 1894–8) was astonished to find that while the heat had increased 'to a most trying degree', luncheon was 'roast beef and boiled puddings, like on a day temperature 0° at home'.[35] Faced with a meal of sausages, mash and suet pudding in 1929, Louise Ouwekerk remarked with surprised admiration, 'The English are a great nation; who else would have such faith in their national institutions as to order a meal like that in

Wilderness 28th Oct 1873	Alta Chambers 13th Dec 1873
Gravy Soup	Ox Tail Soup
Fillets of Fish Parsley Sauce	Stewed Eels
Breast Mutton Compôte	Mutton Egg Balls
Mutton Chicken Pie	Glazed Veal and Bacon
Italian Eggs	Roast Beef – Cauliflowers and
Lemon Custard Baked	Potatoes
	Thick Pan Cakes
	Anchovy Toast
	Baked Rice Pudding

JANUARY	OCTOBER
Calf's Tail Soup	Veal Broth
Turbot à la Reine	Fillets of Cod – Caper Sauce
Fillet of Beef – Roasted	Roast Rump Steak – Tomato
Artichokes	Sauce
Stewed Pheasant	Braised Partridges
Lemon Omelets – Chestnut	Custard Pudding
Cream	Raspberry Jelly[36]

the tropics?'[37] Consuming suet puddings in the heat made Anglo-Indians seem all the more archaic in the light of more adaptable twentieth-century eating patterns in the metropole. This perverse adherence to British food was one of the clearest indications Anglo-Indians gave that they were unwilling to adapt to India.

The attempt to produce authentic British dishes for the dinner table meant that Anglo-Indians still relied heavily on tinned food-stuffs.[38] The insistence on serving tinned British foods rather than fresh Indian ones persisted in the face of the fact that tinned foods often tasted 'nauseous'.[39] During the cold season many Anglo-Indians planted vegetable gardens, of which they were inordinately proud, as an alternative, and much tastier, source of British vege-tables.[40] The First World War temporarily reduced consumption of tinned food as it became extremely expensive, but in the 1930s cold-storage shops in large centres increased the ease with which European vegetables could be obtained.[41] Despite these efforts, Anglo-Indian food was monotonous, while its authenticity tended to be undermined by an underlying Indian flavour: 'Whatever the food, it always tasted the same. There was a strong flavour of spices in the simplest things. A crumb chop in everyone's house carried an insidious flavour of turmeric and powdered cinnamon, mixed with pepper.'[42] Even if the British element of the diet was unpalatable in the heat, at best tasteless and often dull, it was doggedly adhered to by the Anglo-Indians as a confirmation of their Britishness both symbolically and in substance. If you were what you ate it was important that the central meal of the day should at least approximate to British food.

The consumption of British food became an important element in prestige as it differentiated India's rulers from their subjects. The quality of the food was also an important consideration. Flora Annie Steel was of the opinion that much harm was done to the reputation of the British when the Lieutenant-Governor's camp bought only the common bazaar beef rather than specially fattened beef.[43] Although the centrality of British food in the Anglo-Indian diet served to create a sense of group solidarity in a foreign place, food was also used to differentiate status within the British community. The rules of precedence indicated the status of each guest; the food served, that of the host. Mrs Bell's fictional character, Esmé, learnt this to her cost when she served baked custard at a dinner party. She discovered to her horror that the offending pudding had '*no* official position whatsoever – it is *dâk* bungalow style!' and concluded that 'in India puddings have a social standing of their own.' At the same meal Esmé discovered that a Goanese cook (like a French cook in Britain) was an essential for any really status-conscious woman.[44]

The symbolism of the consumption of British food at dinner was reinforced by the gradual adoption of the practice of the upper classes in Britain of changing into evening dress for dinner, even when dining alone. Complaints were made – 'the very hue of the civilian "full-dress" is suggestive of dyspepsia in a hot climate, and quite incompatible with gaiety and merry-making' – but by the 1870s evening dress was dutifully donned for the evening meal.[45] The importance of evening dress as a symbol of Britishness meant that it was regarded as very important to adhere rigidly to British etiquette. E. J. Montgomery, Personal Assistant to the Resident at Mysore, wrote to his parents before they came on a visit: '*For goodness sake don't invent any form of evening dress. The dress worn here in the evening is the same as at home....* you may find it hot in cloth sometimes still it has just got to be worn one can't help it.'[46] Nevertheless, distinctively Anglo-Indian conventions did develop in response to the climate. In the hot weather, men in Bombay would don white dinner jackets and black trousers, while in Calcutta this was reversed. Everywhere in the heat the cummerbund was favoured over the waistcoat.[47] Even once the practice of dressing for dinner at home had begun to die out in Britain the Anglo-Indians clung to it.[48] Wearing evening dress drew attention to the leisured life of the Anglo-Indian official elite. Viola Bayley asserted that the practice simply 'suited our way of life .... We had no dinner to cook, no washing up to be done, and could therefore change into a long evening dress, perhaps too familiar to wear at parties any more but very becoming and a boost to feminine morale.'[49] Evening dress emphasized not only the Britishness of Anglo-Indians but their position as some of the last guardians of the aristocratic lifestyle.

The colonial, dressed for dinner even in the middle of the jungle, has become one of the most enduring images of the Raj. Many members of the ICS did indeed do their best to keep up standards, even while on tour. At breakfast in camp the Maxwells' table was set with care, including silverware and flowers (see plate 16). Mrs Dench claimed that 'Sadar [her head bearer], for one, would have been shocked if Will and I had appeared at table in riding-kit once the sun had gone down over the western ranges.'[50] The table rituals, especially surrounding the evening meal, were staged as much for the benefit of the audience of Indian servants, who the British turned into custodians of the tradition by virtue of the claim that they expected

Plate 16   A beautifully laid breakfast table in camp. 'Lyle – camp Jan 1915 Headload camp.'

it. The evening meal of British food, eaten in evening dress, was an enactment of the Anglo-Indian moral code, denoting one's allegiance to British values and one's membership of a superior race. For some, especially those leading isolated lives, the daily act of changing into evening dress acted like the donning of protective paraphernalia, functioning as a psychological support in alien and sometimes threatening surroundings.[51] Most importantly it was perceived as a guard against slipping into uncivilized habits. Even the drunkard, Mr Lackersteen, in *Burmese Days* is held upright by the 'breastplate' of his 'boiled shirt and *pique* waistcoat'.[52]

By the 1930s and 1940s the Anglo-Indian lifestyle appeared fossilized, an archaic relic of a lost era. It had hardened into a regimented and stable pattern, and appeared to be unaffected by the social and political changes of the twentieth century in the metropole and in India. Anglo-Indian life was governed by a restrictive set of social codes which maintained the rigid hierarchization of society. This is exemplified by the way in which food consumption developed into an extremely regulated and formalized aspect of Anglo-Indian life. Organized according to a preordained set of conventions, the dinner party took on the quality of Raj ceremonial in that protocol mattered more than the actor's intentions. Individual discretion where food choices were concerned were limited by the strict food code. The practices of eating thus became a powerful means of imposing conformity on the individual.[53]

Drawn from very similar social and educational backgrounds, new civil servants joined a tiny and exclusive society of officials in India. Each new influx of recruits – and their numbers each year were very small – tended to be rapidly socialized into the ways of Anglo-Indian officialdom where convention dominated the atmosphere, exerting enormous pressure on officials and their wives. The consequence was a remarkably homogeneous shared official habitus which acted as a protection against the new, thereby ensuring the survival of the anachronistic social patterns of Anglo-India.[54] Two of the most observant novelists of colonial life were quick to realize this. George Orwell described British Burma as 'a stifling, stultifying world in which to live. . . . Your opinion on every subject of any conceivable importance is dictated for you by the pukka sahibs' code.'[55] While, in Ronny Heaslop, E. M. Forster drew a portrait of a man moulded by the pressure to conform who has so completely become 'a sahib . . . one of us' that he no longer questions his assumptions, particularly with regard to his role as a ruler in India.[56] Adela Quested's vision of her future life married to Ronny describes the power of the continuity of the daily round to shape its participants.

In front, like a shutter, fell a vision of her married life. She and Ronny would look in to the Club like this every evening, then drive home to dress; they would see the Lesleys and the Callendars and the Turtons and the Burtons, and invite them and be invited by them, while the true India slid by unnoticed.... the menu was: Julienne soup full of bullety bottled peas, pseudo-cottage bread, fish full of branching bones, pretending to be plaice, more bottled peas with the cutlets, trifle, sardines on toast: the menu of Anglo-India. A dish might be added or subtracted as one rose and fell in the official scale, the peas might rattle less or more, the sardines and the vermouth be imported by a different firm, but the tradition remained: the food of exiles, cooked by servants who did not understand it. Adela thought of the young men and women who had come out before her, P.-and-O.-ful after P.-and-O.-ful, and had been set down to the same food and the same ideas, and been snubbed in the same good-humoured way until they kept to the accredited themes and began to snub others. 'I should never get like that,' she thought,... all the same, she knew that she had come up against something that was both insidious and tough, and against which she needed allies.[57]

Perhaps the most important site which daily reinforced collective identity was the club. A visit to the club before going home for the evening meal took over from the evening drive, which previously occupied the hours between five o'clock and sundown. Army officers had always had the mess, where wives, families and sepoys were left behind. In the latter half of the nineteenth century the club provided a similar venue for civilians, where a sense of solidarity between men of the same rank was fostered. In the Presidency towns a number were already well-established, like the Bengal club and the United Services Club in Calcutta, but in the later years of the nineteenth century clubs began to spring up in the smaller stations. In some places isolation and the tiny numbers of Europeans meant that class barriers were softened and planters and officials might share the same club, but in larger stations the civil service, the military and the unofficial community tended to separate out into their own institutions. The club provided a venue where specific groups of Anglo-Indians could relax together, stretch out in a planter's chair, cement social ties, play sports together, swap gossip or talk 'shop'. It was also the place where newcomers were initiated into the social code, or those who had been observed to stray from the narrow Anglo-Indian social path were chastised in a friendly manner for letting standards slip.[58]

One space in Anglo-India where the pressure to conform could temporarily be escaped was on tour. Most civil servants made a tour of their district in the cold weather and forestry officers spent large amounts of their time in camp out in the wilds. Here, the British were still on show and made an effort to keep up standards, carting boxes of china, silver and glass tableware around with them, but some of the social pressures were relaxed: 'Our evenings in camp were quiet and uneventful. . . . we lay in long camp chairs before a wood fire and read books from the library in Bombay or magazines from home.'[59] J. J. Cotton (ICS) can be seen relaxing in plate 17 in just this fashion in a typical Anglo-Indian pose: feet up on the rests of his chair, cigar in his mouth, book in hand. Not everyone changed for dinner in the jungle. Florence Meikljohn, wife of a forestry officer, generally dined in her khaki slacks when they were living in a tent.[60] It was out on tour where women began to liberate themselves from the restrictions of uncomfortable formal clothing.[61] J. B. Christopherson's plea for rational dress for women, published in 1930, was by then somewhat redundant as the trousers with puttees, tunic and mosquito boots which he recommended were already chosen by most wives accompanying their husbands up-country.[62] Out on tour in the 1930s Carol Hyde revelled in a 'long sleeved, open necked

Plate 17 A typical Anglo-Indian pose. 'Sompalle: Camp in Temple. 19 August 1900.'

short khaki frock; wide brimmed double felt hat; bare legs, socks and "sensible" shoes!!'[63]

Such changes in women's dress were considered by contemporaries to symbolize the general freeing up of British society during the 1920s and 1930s, a reflection of the development of a more collect-ivist and democratic polity. Women in British India reaped the ben-efits of these changes. The high boned collar, shoe-length dress and well-stiffened corset of the Edwardian period which 'nearly induced apoplexy' in the heat were thrown off in favour of cotton dresses during the day with 'only the sketchiest of underclothes under [neath]'.[64] It took some time for stockings to be discarded, but by the Second World War these too were no longer considered essential day-wear. A sign that India was becoming westernized were the smart and expensive dress shops which began to appear in the Presi-dency towns.[65] Men were slower to reap the beneficial effects of the changing metropolitan dress code. Shorts came into use during the twentieth century and were incorporated into the uniform of the military and the police but the civilian, although he might wear them on tour, was still expected to cut a smart figure in the office. Viola Bayley thought it terrible to see the men 'in a temperature of about 110° setting off to office in coat, shirt and tie. The advent of the bush-shirt brought some sanity, and by the end of the war, bush-shirts were permitted even in civilian offices.'[66]

Even though the clothing of the twentieth century gave the Anglo-Indian body the appearance of liberation, essentially it continued to be restrained by the highly structured, rule bound and regimented nature of Anglo-Indian society, which enforced a high degree of conformity upon its members. Britishness was the leading principle defining the Anglo-Indian body. However, the definition of British-ness which the Anglo-Indians worked with was an archaic one which reflected the paradoxes of the colonial experience. Many of the symbols they used to indicate their Britishness were peculiar to themselves: tinned foodstuffs, the tropical suit, the sola topi and polo. This marked out their lifestyle as distinctively Anglo-Indian, or as Anthony King expresses it, as a 'third colonial culture' which reinterpreted and redeployed British culture according to the require-ments of the specific colonial situation. The European food con-sumed at the dinner party in evening dress, the exaggerated emphasis placed on the social rituals of calling, and the etiquette of precedence, combined with the fact that the continuity of these practices made them seem archaic in the face of metropolitan change, all contributed towards the construction of the Anglo-Indian official as a caricature of a member of the British upper classes. What made the Anglo-Indians appear more British than their compatriots in the metropole was their embodiment of an idea of Britishness which belonged to the nineteenth century. This left the Anglo-Indians with a body which was as socially outdated and archaic as it was politically out of touch.

The fragility of domestic space

After the horrors of the Mutiny the British were eager to distance themselves from the Indian population. The new cantonments and stations, the new police and railway settlements, built all over India after 1857, were sited in clearly demarcated areas well away from the Indian town and each other.[67] This desire to achieve spatial separation of the races was given additional impetus by a new awareness of the importance of sanitation. Stimulated by the Crimean war and campaigners such as Florence Nightingale who highlighted the importance of sanitation, as well as concerns over the appallingly high death rate among European soldiers, a Royal Commission on the Sanitary State of the Army in India was set up.[68] Its report, published in 1863, found that living conditions in the Indian army contributed to the spread of disease. As a consequence barracks were re-sited, and drainage, conservancy, water-supplies and ventilation were improved. In addition, soldiers were discouraged from sampling prostitutes and Indian foods in the bazaar. These measures led to a significant change for the better in death rates. This forced the British to acknowledge that they could no longer blame the poor state of their health on the exacting climate of India, and to recognize that ill-health could also result from their own collective negligence. As the term 'hygiene' expanded to cover the idea of public as well as personal health, the medical gaze shifted to the community rather than the individual. This sharpened the racial dimension of the late nineteenth-century discussion of disease as attention was quickly directed towards the threat to Anglo-Indian health posed by the lack of hygienic behaviour among the Indian social body. According to the Reverend J. Cole the Indian population were 'ignorant of the fact that fevers are sure to rage in every district where the pure air, the pure water, and the daily bread that God has given to us are spoiled; they do not yet know that if the laws of health be disregarded they will be asserted and avenged.'[69]

Fear of infection by the Indian population could trigger a hysterical reaction, as in the case of the response to the arrival of the bubonic plague in Bombay in 1896. Rather than simply representing a public health problem, Rajnarayan Chandavarkar argues 'the plague...became the focus of the most terrible anxieties which India evoked in the British imagination. India appeared to be a land of potential sometimes hidden dangers, political and corporeal, moral and cultural.'[70] Draconian measures were imposed on the Indian population in Bombay in a fruitless attempt to eradicate the disease. Indian resistance was both evasive and violent, with the murder of two British officials by terrorists in Poona. The panic only subsided when the plague spread to the Punjab where the British, unable to enforce harsh measures, became aware that plague was a disease of poverty, posing no great threat to themselves.

Fear of infection highlighted the problems associated with the openness of the Anglo-Indian private sphere. Rather than neutralizing the threat of the Indian population by implementing a coordinated public health policy, the British favoured the less politically risky and less expensive solution of racial segregation combined with the application of the principles of sanitation learnt by the Indian army within British settlements.[71] Bungalows were divided by wide streets and surrounded by large compounds which separated them from their neighbours (see plate 7). The servants' quarters were sited well away from the bungalow on the edge of the compound.[72] Sanitation was added to the civil servant's medical catalogue of precautions with a new chapter on 'Conservancy' inserted into the Anglo-Indian's medical bible, W. J. Moore's *A Manual of Family Medicine*.[73] Numerous books offering advice on the sanitary construction of the bungalow and the application of principles of public hygiene to civilian life began to appear.[74] Their general conclusion was that 'The real danger to life in the tropics, arises more from the neglect of the ordinary laws of health, and the non-observance of recognized sanitary precautions, than from any specific form of disease peculiar to those latitudes.'[75] The hygienic 'value of fresh air, pure water, and efficient drainage' was tacked on to the early nineteenth-century tropical regimen of a temperate diet, regular and moderate exercise, early retirement to bed and early rising, sleep in a well-ventilated room; hot, cold and lukewarm baths, and clothing which protected the wearer from the sun and temperature changes.[76]

The rise in awareness of the need for sanitation increased the power of the medical and official discourses to direct behaviour within the domestic sphere. Numerous household manuals of advice for the woman newly arrived in the tropics argued that it was imperative not only for the health but also for the *prestige* of the entire community that European principles of sanitation should be applied within the household. The openness of the Anglo-Indian home to the gaze of Indian visitors as well as servants meant that official ideology viewed the bungalow as an additional site where the virtues of the British race could be displayed.[77] The responsibility for sustaining the performance of prestige within the home was placed on women's shoulders as this was seen to be their realm. Novelist Eva Bell reminded women that the servants acted as important mediators between the British and the rest of the Indian population: 'What they say of us in our compounds to-day, the district will say of us to-morrow. So it is worth while to try and make oneself known at one's *best* in one's own household. It seems to me that if we fail in our intercourse with native servants the very foundation stone of our dealings with natives is ill-laid.'[78] J. E. Dawson reiterated this point in *The Calcutta Review*, arguing that the Indian would form an opinion of British 'moral standards and beliefs... from the inter-pretations he reads in our lives'.[79] The discourse of prestige re-inforced medical advice, giving additional weight to the pressure towards conformity created by the Anglo-Indian social routine. Thus, pressure was brought to bear on the official's wife to mould herself into a suitable representative of British superiority.

The link made between civilization and cultures where individuals took responsibility for their health gave moral resonance to the achievement of strict sanitary standards within the bungalow. Flora Annie Steel and G. Gardiner, authors of *The Complete Indian House-keeper and Cook*, admonished their readers that 'A good mistress in India will try to set a good example to her servants in routine, method and tidiness.'[80] Housewives in India, like those in Britain, were instructed to begin an inspection parade immediately after breakfast.[81] First the kitchen, the cook, the day's provisions and the cooking pots were scrutinized. Steel and Gardiner were extremely critical of those mistresses who preferred not to interfere with the dirty habits of servants as long as they could serve a presentable dinner, but many mistresses found the principles of hygiene difficult to apply in the kitchen. After several years in India, Monica Camp-bell-Martin wrote with despair 'I could not be in the kitchen all day and... As soon as I left, I knew the cook would once again be sitting on the floor.'[82] Next on the inspection round was the storeroom, which was opened and the day's supplies of food and cloths doled out to the servants. The butler's accounts were then checked over on the verandah, often a source of conflict as it was customary for servants to supplement their income by overcharging their employers for supplies. A regular inspection of the servants' personal quarters was also recommended.[83] According to the evidence of women's letters and diaries, many followed the daily routine set out for them in the handbooks, especially Steel and Gardiner's, which women mention using as a guide well into the twentieth century.[84] In fact Anglo-Indian women, uncertain in strange surroundings, probably followed the advice of household manuals far more closely than women in the metropole, particularly as strict routines were a means of controlling the alien servants, whose presence in the home could be disconcerting.[85] This meant that within India the concerns of the medical discourse and of the government were able to reach further into the private sphere than was possible in Britain, acting as immensely powerful tools for the regulation of Anglo-Indian behaviour. The weight of conformity was thus intensified within the colonial context.[86] The discipline of routine and the regimentation of time and space was imposed on the memsahib in the bungalow, just as it was brought to bear on the sahib in his office. An image of the ideal female counterpart to the official was generated, who legitimized British rule by bringing to India western civilization's virtues of cleanliness and order.

If the bungalow was seen within the official discourse as a site for the display of British prestige, for its inhabitants it was 'an extended form of personal space', 'a culturally determined radius' or 'territorial unit' within which they were able to cultivate and protect their own culture.[87] Immense efforts were made to create a homely and distinctively British feel in the bungalow interior. Anglo-Indian housewives had poor materials and conditions to work with: open-plan and often old bungalows; second-hand, old-fashioned furniture acquired at auctions; constant moves and breakages; a climate which warped furniture and encouraged the growth of mould; and insects, especially white ants, which chewed their way through furniture, books, carpets, pictures, and even the thatch on the roof. Yet, despite these obstacles, with the help of chintz-covered sofas, curtains, rugs, pictures and photographs, many managed to evoke Home, thus creating a domestic atmosphere which confirmed the identity of the bodies which inhabited it as British and provided 'a pleasant contrast to the bamboo and jungle huts, the dirty native houses that formed the main environment of our lives'.[88] The interior was complemented by the surrounding garden in which 'great efforts were made to grow English flowers, which generally looked rather sickly in the Indian climate'.[89]

The private sphere as a refuge from India was, however, fragile. Just as disease threatened to invade the home from without, so too did India percolate into the environment of the bungalow, threatening its capacity to act as a 'relatively if not completely closed' physical space which confirmed and reinforced racial segregation.[90] King points out that for most people a limited integration of India was acceptable. India made its presence felt in the bungalow in the shape of 'a hundred terrible little Indian, Kashmir, and Burmese tables, stools and screens', the mementos, souvenirs and *shikar* trophies collected in various parts of the subcontinent.[91] In H. H. Davies' drawing-room a collection of oriental bric-a-brac takes pride of place in the centre of the room (see plate 18). These knick-knacks told the tale of a successful career or celebrated the sporting prowess of their owner. Even a view of the Indian town, or the sounds of India in the distance, could be interpreted as picturesque.[92]

Most of India's intrusions were less controllable as they took the form of an assault on the senses. The British preferred an acoustic field of silence to envelop the bungalow. Mulk Raj Anand described how the 'White Sahibs (really red), . . . lived and moved and had their being, in a seemingly grim, awe-inspiring silence, only broken now and then by an occasional pink Memsahib's call for the "Arderly" or the "Bera".'[93] This silence was difficult to maintain in the face of Indian habits. Rumer and Jon Godden remembered with nostalgia

Plate 18 An Anglo-Indian drawing-room with a curtained doorway and Indian bric-a-brac. 'My drawing-room.'

'all day and most of the night the tympany of the bazaar: a chatter like sparrows, street cries, a woman wailing, a baby's cry' which penetrated their childhood home in Narayangunj.[94] Hilda Bourne remembered the sound of tom-toms being played 'in the distance all the time' in Belgaum,[95] and drumming could often be heard far into the night. This was both vaguely menacing and irritating as the timing clashed with the British perception of the night as a period of silence in preparation for the more important activities of the day. In Ceylon the British sense of order was so disturbed by the Ceylonese practice of drumming and singing into the early hours that a police ordinance of 1865 gave the police powers to fine or imprison unauthorized disrupters of the night-time peace, including drummers.[96] More pervasive even than the sounds were the smells of India. Although certain flowers and trees and the smell of the earth in the evening or after rainfall were often romanticized, India also had many undesirable olfactory experiences to offer. When Mrs Hall moved to the Sind plain in the 1930s she was plagued by a stench which during the night 'seeped in from outside and filled the room'.[97] During the monsoon the outdoors invaded the bungalow's interior in the more tangible form of a variety of insects, amphibians and small rodents.

The struggle to create a symbolically British space around and within the bungalow was often defeated. For some the intrusion of India into the home created an impression of living constantly under siege, a feeling which could provoke insecurity, fear and anger. Monica Clough related how her mother 'in her fight to keep her own integrity was slightly hostile to Indian artefacts. There wasn't in her house anything that was made in India, no rugs or saris draped about the place and she was also spared the ghastly shikari trophies because my father was one of the first conservationists.'[98] The constant presence of Indian servants compounded the tensions caused by the sense of unease which this infiltration of India into the bungalow created. Indian servants tended to heighten awareness of the fragility of personal space in India. Isabella Stuart found that the servants eroded her sense of ownership or belonging by the way in which they negated her presence as soon as she left a room. She wrote to her brother:

> I don't like them [the servants] when I'm alone. I think in India I wd always have the feeling the moment I leave the room the house is not mine. There is such an Hotel feeling if I were going up just now to fetch my desk I'm sure a man wd rush in extinguish the light and stop the punkah, for instance.[99]

The recognition of microbes made the problem of Indian servants in the home even more acute. Despite Anglo-Indian medicine's resistance to the germ theory of disease, during the 1890s the notion of the etiological specificity of the causes of disease, as well as awareness of the various parasites and bacteria which caused malaria, cholera, dysentery and typhoid, gradually filtered into the medical discussion.[100] The recognition of microbes transformed cleansing practices into a battle with the invisible where every 'nook and cranny had to be scoured ... to remove a presence at once infinitesimal and dangerous'.[101] Women used disinfectants liberally and saw to it that vegetables and salad were thoroughly washed in potassium permanganate before consumption. By the twentieth century flies were recognized as carriers of disease, and bungalows were regularly sprayed with insecticide while fly-screens were fitted across windows and doorways. Supervision of the milking of the cow and the boiling of both the milk and the water used by the household was integrated into the memsahib's daily routine.

Anxiety about Indian dirt in general was particularized onto individual servants as potential carriers of deadly germs into the household on their bodies. Andrew Balfour, writing in 1921, advised that 'where possible it is a wise precaution to have native servants medically examined before engaging them.'[102] Just as in Europe, where the working man's hands were regarded with particular dread as 'culprits' in the transmission of microbes between people, the hands of servants were regarded with particular distaste.[103] During a cholera scare in the 1930s Margery Hall made her ayah scrub her hands with Dettol before she started work, while she personally disinfected the dishes before and after meals and used disinfectant liberally throughout the compound, particularly in the servants' latrines.[104] The person of the sweeper, due to the nature of his work, was regarded with particular suspicion, and while in the bathroom he was not supposed to touch the basins or the bath.[105] Many women did not allow the sweeper to enter the bungalow and Mrs Taylor recalled that although her sweeper came into the house to sweep she would never have allowed him 'to touch anything to do with the table'.[106] These restrictions on the sweeper were motivated not only by hygienic concerns but also by anxiety that the British would lower themselves in the eyes of the Indian community if they allowed themselves to be polluted by contact with an outcaste.[107]

Renuka Ray, the wife of an Indian ICS officer, found the memsahibs' obsession with cleanliness annoying, if not insulting: 'They were so immersed in keeping everything hygienic and clean in their homes. Every day they changed all the *jharans* [dusters]. They always had their servants use gloves before they served at table and things like that which irritated me.'[108] The practices of Anglo-Indian housekeeping were annoying because they were far more than a manifestation of worries about health. As Mary Douglas argues, cleaning practices are not simply a response to the presence of pathogens. Douglas observes that dirt is not an objective category but rather it is matter which is perceived as being out of place. Seen from this perspective an attempt to achieve a state of cleanliness is a positive, even creative, attempt to maintain a recognized system or order of things.[109] The Anglo-Indian housewife's concern with cleanliness can therefore be seen as an attempt to impose a European system of order onto her alien surroundings. Mrs Clough, who grew up on a tea plantation in the early twentieth century, perceived the need for cleanliness as a response to the threat of India:

> And another thing I think where you can see the threatened feeling the British had was an absolute obsession with hygiene. 'Don't touch that dear it's been in the bazaar'. 'Let me wash your annas before we put them in the Church collection because you don't know where they've been.' And this insistence, it was quite necessary from a health point of view, but I think it was also a way of expressing a deep anxiety about the whole Indian scene....I think it was a rationalization of deeper fears myself.[110]

Dane Kennedy suggests that the paraphernalia of protective clothing, the sola topi, spine pads and flannel underwear, gave psychological reassurance to the British in an environment where they felt dislocated. In the same way, it can be argued that the daily routine of inspection and chastisement of the servants, even if it was relatively ineffective, gave reassurance to Anglo-Indian women.[111] The difficulty of carving out an inviolable space meant that the Anglo-Indians were constantly engaged in a struggle to assert their Britishness through their surroundings.

The frequent disregard of her definition of order by the servants, combined with the circumstances of the climate, conspired against the memsahib to frustrate her desire to impose order and cleanliness. While many of the advice books urged women to treat the servants as a ready-made, full-time, philanthropic project, most memsahibs regarded them less as a philanthropic project than an unwelcome and irritating intrusion into their lives.[112] Anglo-Indian women were renowned for limiting their knowledge of India to the 'cantonments, a suspicion of prices, . . . a list of stores, and an utter ignorance of the natives',[113] and the knowledge of an Indian language to kitchen

Hindi. A haughty manner was often employed which, as Dane Kennedy suggests, 'served as a psychological substitute for the physical separation of the races, an attempt at emotional disengagement from the indigenous peoples encountered in daily life'.[114] The public nature of Anglo-Indian private life allowed the overriding concern with the maintenance of prestige to limit the extent to which the intrusion of India into the home could be controlled. The strain of living in the public eye, combined with the struggle to limit India's invasion of the domestic space, created tensions which took their toll on the memsahib. Novelists frequently describe the profound and often negative effect India had upon women. In Sara Duncan's *The Simple Adventures of a Memsahib*, the heroine, a young English girl, is transformed by the trials and tribulations of Indian housing, servants and climate.[115] By the end of the novel:

> Mrs. Browne has become a memsahib, graduated, qualified, sophisticated. That was inevitable...She has lost her pretty colour – that always goes first, and has gained a shadowy ring under each eye – that always comes afterwards. She is thinner than she was and has acquired nerves and some petulance.... To make up, she dresses her hair more elaborately, and crowns it with a little bonnet which is somewhat extravagantly 'chic'. She has fallen into a way of crossing her knees in a low chair that would horrify her Aunt Plovtree, and a whole set of little feminine Anglo-Indian poses have come to her naturally. There is a shade of assertion about her chin that was not there in England, and her eyes – ah, the pity of this! – have looked too straight into life to lower themselves as readily as they did before.[116]

India's effect was seen to be both moral and physical.[117] The hardening of her character was reflected in the bold and bitter postures of her body. India is portrayed as masculinizing, eradicating the grace and charm of the feminine ideal from the female body. Mrs Browne has acquired the 'unmistakable air of the woman who has become accustomed to living out East'.[118] Mrs Hall explains this as the product of a combination of superiority and being well-groomed. While the aggravation of dealing with Indian servants hardened the memsahib, her freedom from household tasks meant that she had plenty of time to spend on herself, which gave her the hardness of the confident aristocrat. It was this figure, moulded by the requirements of prestige within the domestic sphere, with a superior distanced air and a hardened manner and body, which came to epitomize the memsahib.

Prestige in the bathroom

The openness of the bungalow gave the official discourse of prestige greater weight within the home, creating pressure on the memsahib to uphold British standards of cleanliness and order within the colonies. The pressure to keep up standards did not stop here. In his medical manual, A. E. Grant reminded Anglo-Indians 'If there is one thing in which the British dweller in India should set a constant good example, it is in this matter of scrupulous cleanliness in person *and surroundings*, even at the cost of considerable trouble and a little expense.'[119]

In Europe bourgeois 'refinement and sentimentality was located not only on the boundaries between the household and the wider community (producing the privatization of the household); but also on the boundaries between one individual and another – personal and body privacy.'[120] Personal cleanliness was thus a major force in the formation of the European bourgeois private sphere. As the gaze shifted from the cleanliness of clothing and externals to the most secret and intimate parts of the body, bathing became an increasingly private occupation, withdrawn first into the home and then into the bathroom. The latter developed into an intensely private space from which others were excluded. Within the middle classes this process was aided by the employment of new technology such as plumbing, which made it possible to dispense with servants. Georges Vigarello concludes that 'the history of cleanliness consists in the last analysis, of one dominant theme: the establishment, in western society, of a self-sufficient physical sphere...to the point of exclusivity of the gaze of others.'[121]

This was not the case in India. Here the development of a private sphere marked by clear boundaries which reflected a greater level of individual privacy, and a focus on the self as a private individual, was less pronounced. Like other areas in the bungalow, the bathroom remained curiously open to the Indian gaze. This was not because Anglo-Indians were less advanced than their compatriots in Britain in terms of cleanliness. In fact, there is a good case for arguing that throughout the period 1800–1947 the British in India remained well in advance of the metropole in terms of bodily cleanliness. In the 1870s George Hunter commented that 'in tropical climates the daily bath has long been a regular institution, but it is only within the last few years that it has been generally practised in England.'[122] On arrival in Britain at the beginning of the First World War the young Godden sisters 'even as children...noticed the unwashedness of

English people's skins and clothes'.[123] While, for the Edwardians, 'Daily baths were by no means taken for granted',[124] it was common for their compatriots in India to take two baths a day whereupon they would change all their clothes. Despite the significantly greater importance placed on personal cleanliness in British India, the Anglo-Indian bathroom failed to follow the European example in that it did not develop into a private space.

One explanation for this lies in the backwardness of Anglo-Indian bathroom equipment. In Calcutta in the 1870s privileged members of the Anglo-Indian community were able to connect their bathrooms to a sewerage system, and judging from an advertisement in *The Englishman* for the latest sanitary fittings 'embracing all the latest improvements...now being used in London, Liverpool and Glasgow' they were able to furnish their bathrooms in some style. Even so, Government House, Calcutta was not fitted with a bathroom with running water until 1905, the last year of Curzon's vice-royalty.[125] Flush toilets reached Simla just before the First World War, and the residents of New Delhi rejoiced in 'running water and pull-the-plugs' in the 1930s,[126] but even in the 1940s the majority of Anglo-Indians still had the kind of bathroom John Masters describes.

> A *ghuslkhana* corresponds in function to a bathroom, but it is a profound misconception to think of white porcelain, taps, or water sanitation. The *ghuslkhana* is small and square and has a hole in the outer wall to let out water and let in snakes. One corner, around that outlet, is fenced in by a low parapet the height of a single brick. In this enclosure sits an oval zinc tub. Outside the parapet is a slatted wooden board to stand on, and a wooden towel horse. Ranged along the inner wall are a deal table holding an enamel basin, a soap-dish, and a jug; a chamber pot; a packet of Bromo hanging from a nail; and a wooden thing on four legs whose proper name may possibly be 'toilet', but which was never called anything but 'the thunderbox'....When a sahib wishes to use [the thunderbox]...he shuts both doors and, when he has finished, opens the outer door, shouts, 'Mehtar!' into the empty air, and forgets all about it.[127]

William Hart pointed out that in India 'servants...stand for what is represented by water pipes and by sanitary systems at home.'[128] But the reliance on servants to empty and clean the thunderbox and to bring in and empty out the bath water, made a mockery of the bathroom as a private space. The job of the sweeper made this servant in particular privy to his master's or mistress's most intimate bodily functions: '[The sweeper] knew more about the state of the household's health than the people concerned did themselves...and he was quite liable to spread it round the compound that the mem-sahib was going to have a baby before she had really grasped the fact herself.'[129]

The British in India were also slow to abandon body servants, who continued to attend them in the bath- and bedroom in order to help them to dress and undress, and to pour water, scrub backs, and provide massages. There had always been those who found such attentions distasteful but surprise, and the dislike of such intimate contact with servants, increased as twentieth-century sensibilities made such behaviour seem archaic, recalling the decadence of the nabob. Rosamund Lawrence arrived in India in 1914 and found that she had to send her ayah away while dressing: 'to have the dear old woman patiently holding out my chemise till I am ready for it, or expecting to draw on my stockings, is more than I can bear.'[130] Norman Watney recalled that 'I found this highly repulsive . . . and after two days of being a tailor's dummy I told my bearer to desist.'[131] Such attentions disturbed a newly developed sense of personal space and bodily privacy. Nevertheless, John Masters was wrong in thinking that his first District Magistrate in the early 1930s, who sat on his bed while his bearer rolled his socks on, was a relic from a lost Victorian age. Many Anglo-Indians quickly adapted to body servants and retained their services even in the 1940s. Radclyffe Sidebottom recalled that the inconvenience of servants was easily neutralized by ignoring their presence: 'My wife would have the bath first and the ayah would dress her. I would go in and have my bath and my personal servant would bring in a drink and give it to me in the bathroom and my wife and I would carry on a conversation as if the two servants in the room weren't there.'[132]

Even if they were ignored, the presence of servants was vital to the strategy of prestige which the British deployed in India. Here lies the fundamental explanation for the lack of privacy in the Anglo-Indian bathroom. If the surroundings of the bathroom were less than glam-orous, the very act of taking two or three baths a day as well as changing all one's clothing was in itself sufficiently magnificent behaviour to merit witnesses. John Morris, an officer with the Gur-khas in the 1920s, commented that the changing of 'one's under-clothing several times a day. . . . was a hygienic necessity in the humid plains, but in places such as Lansdowne, which had a European climate for much of the year, it was an affectation.'[133] But it was an affectation which colonials could well afford as the *dhobi* took on the burden of the voluminous amounts of washing which in Britain would have fallen on the housewife and her maid.[134] Such extrava-gance was only effective if it had an audience.

Although the British considered Indian sanitary habits to be deplorable they were still stung by their status as polluters in the eyes of Hindus, who were renowned for washing themselves after coming into contact with a European.[135] The British were therefore particularly concerned that tales of their personal fastidiousness should reach a wider Indian public. Lack of privacy was an indispensable concomitant of prestige. The peculiar failure to mark off the bath-and bedroom as a self-contained private sphere signalled the abandonment of their middle-class sensibilities by the British in India in exchange for a more aristocratic mode of self-perception which both permitted the gaze of outsiders to intrude and also relied more heavily on this gaze as an affirmation of the importance of the self. This was an effective means of maintaining prestige, but one which further contributed to the archaism of the Anglo-Indian body in the changing context of twentieth-century British society.

Degeneration and the regulation of sexuality

By the latter half of the nineteenth century doctors had reached the firm conclusion that Europeans were unable to acclimatize to the tropics. Although a temperate lifestyle and a constitution resistant to the effects of the heat could prolong health in the tropics, it could not prevent the adverse effects of 'long continued' heat on the European body.[136] George Hunter concluded that 'high courage, indeed, and pride of race, together with better food and sanitary arrangements, may enable them to endure where others would succumb; yet with all their physical superiority, they cannot really settle down.'[137] The medical discussion asserted that a prolonged sojourn in the tropics brought about a change in the bodily substance of the European. In particular the quality of the blood was said to alter, with the consequence that tropical anaemia generally set in, leaving the individual fatigued, listless and susceptible to disease.[138] Newspapers abounded with advertisements for medicines such as Holloway's Pills; Wilkinson's Essence or Fluid Extract of Red Jamaica Sarsparilla, The Grand Alternative Indian Tonic; Dr E. J. Lazarus's Essence of Hemidesmus, and Clarke's World Famed Blood Mixture, all of which purported to purify or restore the blood.[139] Medical pronouncements on the inevitability of tropical anaemia resonated with danger as, in the nineteenth century, 'blood' was synonymous with 'race'.[140] The deterioration of European blood in India therefore signalled the deterioration of the British race. D. H. Cullimore predicted, apocalyptically, that if the European remained in India he underwent 'racial deterioration' and he 'or, at all events, his children, assumes many of the mental, moral, and physical traits of the half-caste, and even of the native himself.'[141]

The fate of the Portuguese had always acted as a warning to the British. In 1880 Jemima Allen described how she had 'declined a New Year's dinner given by people of the name of Vernede...a most rummy lot', whose blue blood had 'grown rather black in its downward flow'.[142] Nor did the fate of the Aryans bode well for the British of the nineteenth century.

> When it is...proposed that the Englishman shall inure himself to the climate of India by bravely exposing himself to it, the work of generations is attempted to be effected at once; a work which, by the time it was thoroughly complete in the constitutions of his few surviving descendants, would have simply *re-transformed* them into Asiatics, stewed and torrefied under the same skies which have gradually concocted the Indian. By that time they would probably have become in no way superior to him; since the haughty Englishman has now to acknowledge with him the same Iranian or *Indo*-atlantic stock.[143]

The famed degeneracy of the nabob, who one rather hysterical commentator claimed had 'passed into a lower order of being', was also revived as a warning.[144]

Different temperaments or constitutions were supposed to be able to withstand the degenerative effects of the heat better than others, but women's constitutions in particular were characterized as vulnerable.[145] This was confirmed by the damaging effect the climate was said to have on the reproductive capacity of British women. George Hunter asserted 'European women transplanted to a hot climate are peculiarly liable to menstrual derangement and uterine diseases.'[146] William Moore advised all those with menstrual or uterine disorders, or who were chlorotic, anaemic or sallow, not to travel to India. Personal experience seemed to confirm the doctor's warnings. Reginald Maxwell, pleased to hear that his wife and baby were getting on well back in Britain, commented 'Of course it is getting on for two years since you were in India, and it all shows how much more normally things behave when you are not in a state of Indianization, and how wrong it is ever to have babies in this awful country or to keep them there.'[147] If the impairment of reproduction was not enough, the impossibility of Europeans surviving in India over several generations without losing their European characteristics was confirmed by the physical deterioration of European children brought up in a tropical climate. It was a commonplace that European children born and raised in India were pale, flabby and listless as a result of nervous systems over-stimulated by the heat and internal organs suffering from depression and congestion.[148] In the 1870s William Fayrer set out to test this assertion by studying the children of the Female European Orphan Asylum in Calcutta. Although he found that with 'proper hygienic conditions and careful physical training' children could thrive in the plains of India, he could not quite believe his own evidence and concluded that the 'deceitfulness, vanity and indisposition to study' he detected in the orphans was the product of 'an indefinable constitutional weakness' or, in other words, physical and moral degeneration.[149]

Anglo-Indian fears of rapid deterioration over a few generations were echoed and intensified by British eugenicist fears of racial deterioration due to the selectively falling birth-rate, which indicated that the best middle-class stock was gradually dying out while the working class was on the increase.[150] By the 1890s the growing influence of eugenics had constructed individual bodies as indicators of a society's capacity for national progress.[151] The degeneration of the individual body was interpreted as a sign of a more general process of the degeneration of the society as a whole. This tendency to treat the individual body as a barometer of social morality meant that the neglect of any of those practices which distinguished the colonizer from the colonized, or in fact any deviation from the pattern of expected behaviour, was regarded by colonial societies with great disfavour.[152] Thus, the focus of the medical, racial and official discourse on the body and behaviour of the individual became intense, adding to the pressure towards conformity.

Women, as the sex most likely to succumb to the climate, came under particular surveillance. Indolence on the part of European women, reminiscent as it was of the behaviour of Indian women in the *zenana*, and of Eurasians, who were renowned for their laziness, was seen as a sign of sinking into a racially degenerate state. Major Leigh Hunt and Alexander Kenny used the vehicle of their handbook to attack Anglo-Indian women who allowed themselves to sink into a state of debility, who gave in to the climate, breakfasted in bed, and only moved from bed to sofa in a dressing-gown to read 'literary trash', who stimulated their jaded appetites by snacking on 'highly seasoned and harmful' food, and who tried to energize themselves by taking nips of alcohol.[153] The pleasure-seeking, superficial and unrefined atmosphere of Anglo-Indian society was said to have a particularly bad effect on young girls. Denied the domestic, intellectual or religious spheres which offered a girl at home occupation and fulfilment, it was argued that the young British girl in India found it difficult to sustain self-discipline while the 'emotional, pleasure-loving side of her nature' became over-developed.[154] Alfred Lyall, in accord with this analysis of the effects of India on young girls, wrote to his sister that he was 'making vigorous attempts to keep [his daughter] from falling into the third rate flirty ways of the Indian girl'.[155] Once married, Anglo-Indian women, separated from their husbands during the hot weather and thrown together with young military men on leave in the Hills, gained a reputation for indulging in affairs.

The fast young woman and the adulterous wife were largely a literary creation, disseminated by newspapers, like *The Civil and Military Gazette*, which fed on gossip. This was Rudyard Kipling's paper, and he did much to create these stereotypes in *Plain Tales from the Hills* (1888).[156] On the other hand some members of British society did provide fuel for tales of Anglo-Indian immorality. Lord Lytton and his entourage were notorious for their Bohemian love affairs. Although Lytton probably did not go beyond flirting with pretty ladies in public his Military Secretary, George Villiers, was renowned for having got himself into a 'scrape' with a married woman, which became the talk of all India. However at the same time Lytton complained to Lady Salisbury from Simla that society there was 'grievously good'.[157] Twentieth-century comment is as contradictory, with some remarking on the 'very low...standards of behaviour, or morals,...in India' where there were no parents or relatives to say '"Stop behaving like that"'.[158] While others refute the claims, arguing that 'We seemed to lead a life of exemplary rectitude, to the point of stuffiness by modern standards.'[159] Anglo-Indian society was probably no more nor less moral than middle-class society in Britain. The tiny size and close-knit nature of the community simply meant that gossip could circulate more easily. Certainly Indian servants were renowned as transmitters of gossip from one Anglo-Indian household to another.[160] In fact much of the criticism of Anglo-Indian immorality was generated within the metropole where 'a constituency ready to be stirred by...scandals' among the aristocracy existed in the form of the increasingly vocal lower-middle and respectable working classes, who were in the process of developing an ideology of respectability opposed to the scandalous behaviour of the British elite.[161] The social life of the rich, which the Anglo-Indians mirrored, was strongly associated in Britain with low moral standards. A reputation for lax morals can therefore be seen as the cost of the image, which Anglo-Indian society liked to project of itself, as an aristocracy in India.

The recommended cure for the indolent Anglo-Indian wife was 'the sight of a woman of sound sense going cheerfully about her household duties, and making light of the petty discomforts of tropical life'.[162] The fear of degeneration was thus used to intensify the pressure on Anglo-Indian women to conform to the stipulated household routine. The medical discourse further intensified the rule-bound nature of Anglo-Indian society by creating the idea within the minds of the Victorian and Edwardian generations of Anglo-Indians that if they kept to the rules of civilized life they would be able to withstand the threat of India. Anxiety about the internal process of bodily decay was gradually alleviated as the focus shifted towards maintaining a moral lifestyle as the key to survival. The evidence of nearly a century of British rule in India by hardy, moral Englishmen gave the Anglo-Indians greater confidence. G. O. Trevelyan argued that 'The earliest settlers were indolent, dissipated, grasping, almost orientals in their way of life, and almost heathens in the matter of religion. But each generation of their successors is more simple, more hardy, more Christian than the last.'[163] The conclusion was drawn that as long as India never became a settler colony, children were sent home at the age of seven, 'individual settlers continue[d] to return to their own country and to yield their place to newcomers charged with nobler ideas',[164] and those living in India followed the prescriptions of the official, medical, racial and moral discourses, Anglo-Indians could survive India without ill effects. Survival was thus predicated on conformity to social etiquette. Confident supporters of colonialism claimed the British would succeed where their predecessors had failed, and the 'strong Saxon hand and the cool Saxon brain' would enable them to 'grasp the mighty prize that fell from [the] enervated' grip of the Mussulman and the Portuguese.[165]

The emphasis placed on leading a moral and conformist life meant that sexual incontinence and the degeneration brought about by miscegenation was increasingly identified as the real threat to the British race. From the 1880s a great deal of attention was directed towards the regulation of Anglo-Indian sexuality. This was in part a reflection of the growing strength of the moral crusade within Britain, where anxieties associated with the extension of the franchise, the decline of national vigour and the future of Ireland and the Empire were deflected onto the sphere of sexuality by virtue of the deep-seated 'belief that the roots of social stability lay in individual and public morality'.[166] For the Anglo-Indians, sharing metropolitan anxieties, and faced with the rise of Indian nationalism, moral purity was added to the list of British virtues which justified their rule in

India. Sexual restraint thus became integrated into the concept of prestige.

The properly circumstanced Victorian man, leading a temperate life, was supposed to be able to gradually transform and restrain his libido.[167] Those seeking to regulate Anglo-Indian sexuality were faced by the problem that sexual restraint was believed to be much more difficult to achieve in the tropics. The heat had long been renowned for stimulating the sexual organs and desires.[168] The theme of the sexual licentiousness of Indians ran through writing on India from the comments of the Abbé Dubois in 1817, who identified the Hindu religion as the source of sexual wantonness, to George MacMunn's fascination in the 1930s with the link between sex and murder in the cult of the goddess Kali.[169] The sexual stimulation which the European experienced in the tropics was often interpreted as yet another indication of his internal physical and moral degeneration. Perversely the climate, especially in moist, malarious regions, was also thought to drain the vigour required to satisfy these inflamed desires, bringing the manliness of the European in India into question.[170] This might be addressed by one of the medicines for 'Weak Men' advertised in the newspapers,[171] but the reduced potency of the European in India was less worrying than the idea that the sexual profligacy which the climate encouraged would undermine British claims to moral superiority.

The moral element of prestige meant that it was seen as imperative that British behaviour in India should in no way bring the morality of the British race into question in the eyes of the subject population. Predictably the behaviour of the lower classes of European in India gave rise to the most anxiety. A furore during Curzon's viceroyalty over the debauched lives of white barmaids demonstrated the British fear of revealing the more sordid aspects of European life to the gaze of the Indian population.[172] Official disapproval was even greater when sexuality appeared likely to lead to a more fundamental breakdown of the boundary between colonizer and colonized. Hence the hostile official reaction to the marriages of white women to Indian Rajahs as these unions subverted both class (the women were often working-class) and racial hierarchies.[173] Such marriages were particularly disturbing in the context of the post-Mutiny horror of the violation of white women by Indian men, which Anglo-Indian trivial literature kept alive throughout the latter half of the nineteenth century and which was revived at times of stress such as when the campaign against the Ilbert Bill sparked the spread of unlikely tales of women assaulted by their Indian servants.[174] Inter-racial sexual relations offended something which went far deeper than sexual morality, 'that is … racial morality'.[175] A preference for brown skin was regarded not only as a betrayal of race but also as a perversion of natural instincts. For this reason, when the practice of concubinage in the colonies came to the attention of moral reformers in Britain in 1909, Lord Crewe, Secretary of State for the Colonies, issued a circular which reminded officials that the authority of the government was thereby brought into question and warned that they were likely to be disciplined if found to be consorting with native women.[176] Within India, outside the short stories of Kipling and a few novels where British officials fall in love and marry Indian women, and a few exceptional and covert cases, the Indian mistress was generally regarded as having long since been abandoned.[177]

In fact the comments of civilians from the twentieth century suggest that Indian civil servants led chaste lives. Douglas Stanton-Ife recalled:

> because of the fact that the Raj was so personal because one had no private life I didn't dare do so because I thought this was bound to get round in the bazaar … Looking back now I think I could have had perhaps, without doing very much harm to the Raj, rather more fun than I did have. But I mean this was one of the sacrifices that I thought I was making for the Raj.[178]

Another civilian remarked that the district officer, 'living as he did under constant public inspection, particularly when he was on tour or in camp, he had of necessity to be something of an anchorite or possibly even a stylite.'[179] The consciousness of oneself as an embodiment of a superior race, plus the fear of disclosure, seem to have prevented many civilians from exploring the sexual potential of the Indian population. As Ronald Hyam asserts, 'physical aloofness' characterized relations between civil servants and the Indian population from the 1860s onwards. Civil servants were well aware that the slightest sexual dalliance on the part of a representative of the imperial power would not only bring about personal shame but would also damage the substructure supporting government.

What was defined as a threat to prestige was nevertheless contingent. The British purity movement's campaign against the Contagious Diseases Acts revealed the extent of sexual activity among the British army in India, but despite their best efforts they were only able to achieve a short-lived victory in India between 1889 and 1895.[180] The discontinuation of compulsory examination of the Indian prostitutes who served the British army during this period resulted in an increase in the cases of venereal disease among the soldiers. As a result 'lock hospitals', where prostitutes were virtually held prisoner in order to undergo compulsory examination and treatment, were covertly reinstated, and the Indian Government's regulation and, by implication, tacit approval of prostitution, continued.[181] It was not in the interests of the British government to worry about racial mixing, social purity or the moral reputation of Anglo-India when the health of British soldiers was at stake.

In addition, the Empire and especially India, was often constructed as a world where men might escape the cloying constraints of domesticity and live out their masculinity free of feminine control.[182] India was defined as a man's country, 'a pitiless country which straightens the back and strings up the nerves and muscles; where men learn to endure hardness, and carry their lives in their hands with cheerful unconcern.'[183] This meant that India took on the form in many people's imaginations of a place where they could break out of the constraints of the metropole. This might include sexual adventure. The writings of Richard Burton, as well as numerous authors of trivial literature, constructed India as a land seething with sexual potential. Hyam's evidence would suggest that the Empire did provide men, especially members of the army, with greater sexual opportunity than Europe, particularly for the exploration of alternative sexualities.[184]

Outside the army, and for the majority of civil servants, the sexual world of India simply formed a remote backdrop to their respectable lives, fascinating but also repellent. Pockets where sexual intimacy with the native population was possible existed, but on the peripheries of the Raj. On the social periphery, planters were said to take native companions well into the twentieth century. The fact that they led isolated lives probably facilitated the continuation of the practice.[185] On the geographical periphery, civil servants appear to have engaged in liaisons with native women. The practice of keeping mistresses was well established in Burma, while Leonard Woolf, in Ceylon, casually mentions spending the night with the niece of one of his clerks.[186] Archibald Bowman mentions his 'native girlfriend' in his letters from the Lushai Hills, where he was stationed on loan to the army from the ICS during the Second World War.[187] The comments of G. P. Stewart suggest that Assam was an area where native mistresses were commonplace even in the 1930s. He relates how when, in 1931, he went to Mokokchung, in Assam:

> I relieved Lloyd Rees, Rees, a young officer of the Indian Police, a Welshman. He had taken to himself a Naga wife, following the not uncommon practice. It was a proper Naga marriage, he paying the

customary bride-price and following all Naga custom. When he got his orders of transfer he duly divorced his wife, again according to Naga custom and paying whatever the customary compensation was for divorcing a wife. All was done with the full knowledge and approval of the local people, and no ill-feelings prevailed. In fact, the opposite.[188]

The remoteness of Assam from the rest of India, and within Assam of Europeans from each other, may have made it easier for British officials to keep native mistresses there. The fact that in Assam the British were living among a tribal people, who tended to be viewed more romantically than ordinary Indians, possibly made a native mistress more acceptable. The continuation of the practice may also be explicable due to differences within the indigenous societies themselves. Burmese, Ceylonese and Assamese societies were, possibly, less protective of their lower-status women and more open to racial mixing. On the British side, it would seem that sexual restraint among civilians was far less the product of a strict morality and far more the result of effective social monitoring of behaviour. As soon as this was relaxed Anglo-Indian men were willing to redefine the boundaries between the races. The presence and disapproval of European women is also strongly indicated as a deterrent by the fact that, as soon as British women left for the Hills, men in Calcutta would take out Eurasian girls.[189] India presented the British with a series of climatic, sexual and moral challenges which, according to the official discourse, had to be overcome in order to demonstrate their fitness for rule. It was therefore seen as essential that the official discourse should impose sexual conformity of behaviour upon its representatives in order to preserve prestige.

Race and sociability

In 1909 the Hobhouse Commission discovered that many of the old grievances on the part of respectable Indians, such as being kept waiting without a chair, and an arrogant and insulting manner on the part of the official, were still damaging the relationship between ruler and ruled.[190] Pandit Madan Mohan Malaviya summed up the relations between the British and the Indians in the bald statement that 'The real obstacle to a freer intercourse with the people is the deplorable feeling which European officers generally have that Indians belong to a subject race and are an inferior people.'[191] The bodies of Indian gentlemen were still the main battleground over which the struggle to maintain prestige on one side and deference on the other raged. A pleader and journalist in Nagpur complained that an Assistant Commissioner had required him to remove his shoes, forcing him to apply for a declaration that his dress was proper.[192] This was despite the fact that the 1854 Bengal Resolution, which allowed native gentlemen to appear before Englishmen wearing European boots or shoes, was extended to all of India in 1874. A plea to the Lieutenant-Governor of Bengal from a number of Indian gentlemen, requesting that *pugris* might be abandoned in favour of caps which could be doffed in durbars, courts or whenever going before an English official, was met with similar levels of hostility. Indian gentlemen were reminded, in the reply, that it was presumptuous of them to assume that they could understand British dress codes: 'The memorialists are much mistaken if they imagine that in wearing brimless caps they are imitating European customs. No European of respectability would appear in public in such caps and they cannot therefore claim as they do to associate its adoption with "Western Culture".'[193] The hostility of the British reaction stemmed from the fact that by fostering westernization they found that they had created a powerful challenge to their own rule. Well-versed in British rhetoric, the Indian elite were able to turn the language and assumptions of the British against them and to argue in British terms for the equality of Indians as well as their political right to independence. By constructing their bodies as convincing reflections of the sahib they blurred the distinction between colonizer and colonized while making manifest a cultural allegiance which opened the possibility of the Indian making a political claim to equality. The Indian body refashioned in the image of the sahib in a British suit, and often more immaculate than the British official, threatened to neutralize the symbolic power of the Anglo-Indian body. The westernized Indian laid claim to the possession of the inner qualities which the outer map of the British body was supposed to reveal. The Anglo-Indians' reaction was to interpret the adoption of western manners as nothing more than a veneer concealing the lesser moral and cultural capabilities of the Indian race, and to close ranks. Reginald Maxwell's comment that 'it is ... when they become westernized that one doesn't feel at home with them' is typical of the British response.[194] Harcourt Butler recognized the injustice and contradictory nature of the British attitude: 'I must say I think it hard that a man whom we have induced to undergo a western education, leave India and go back to England, to sever all the old ties, and who comes back cultivated and more or less refined should be tabooed in society.'[195]

The British preferred those Indians who affirmed the paternal role of the civil servant, thereby confirming the British official's superior position as not only legitimate but also benevolent. Most favoured were the simple, honest villagers for whose good most civil servants out in the districts really felt they were working. As nationalism grew in strength this preference for the simple people was heightened. Reginald Maxwell enjoyed chatting to 'a group of the local notables ...nice, simple, hospitable people who are totally untouched by political agitation so long as they are understood and treated politely and feel that their position is recognized.'[196] A hard-working life out in the districts with ordinary Indians fitted better with the ideal image civilians had of themselves as feudal lords and heroic bureaucrats. According to Andrew Fraser:

> Nothing is more delightful than such work as this, to march for a month or two on end through the villages of a District or Division or Province, bringing the Government into contact with the people...; seeing the people in their own homes; ascertaining their circumstances, and especially their troubles and calamities; and seeking quietly, in personal contact with them, to improve their condition and to secure their easily won gratitude and affection.[197]

Fraser emphasizes the 'human warmth, in a mutually assenting relationship' which paternalism suggests.[198] In this way the reality of the paternal relationship, which as Howard Newby points out is in fact structured around a dialectic 'of autocracy and obligation, cruelty and kindness, oppression and benevolence, exploitation and protection', was disguised.[199] A similar strategy was employed with increasing frequency with household servants. British memoirs and reminiscences of the twentieth century often mention the 'affectionate relationship [which]...grew up between the bearer and his sahib', and the close bond between the mistress and her loyal *ayah*.[200] In this way the British drew attention away from the tensions inherent in the colonial situation as well as from the brutality and violence which was also present in their relationship with Indian servants and villagers.

At the end of the First World War the British were forced to adjust to new political and economic circumstances which fostered greater inter-racial competition in the public sphere. It was no longer as easy for them to ignore and reject westernized Indians. The accelerated indianization of the services and, to a more limited extent, the army, as well as the principle of dyarchy introduced in 1919, meant that Anglo-Indian officials found themselves having to cooperate with Indian colleagues and politicians. In business successful Indian entrepreneurs posed a threat to the virtual monopoly of the British.[201]

Both in business and the administration the British relied upon 'personal relationships and trust' maintained through socializing.[202] If the British were to rise to the challenge of inter-racial competition, they needed to incorporate their Indian competitors into their social circles. Business circles were extremely resistant to indianization, to their cost,[203] but within the administration more commitment was shown towards integrating Indians into Anglo-Indian networks of power. Dorothy Middleton recalled how her father, the Governor of the Central Provinces between 1927 and 1932, successfully incorporated his Indian ministers into his government and built good relationships with them over dinner at his house.[204] Efforts were made to accommodate to Indian habits. Philip Ray remembered that curry was served at a small ceremony at Government House in Lahore where Indians were present.[205] In response to the political situation created by the new constitution of 1935 the Viceroy reminded the Governor of Bombay that he 'attach[ed] the utmost importance to breaking down the social barrier'.[206] Plate 19 shows the Governor of Sind making an informal visit to the home of the Indian Collector of Hyderabad, whose daughter breaks the social ice a little by standing hand in hand with her mother and Lady Graham, the Governor's wife. At long last the ICS appeared to be making a concerted effort to implement Malcolm's *Instructions*, which although they were written in 1821, were still being issued to new recruits in the 1930s as part of the *Civil Service Manual*.

For the British the sharing of food was central to cementing social and political bonds. The breaking of religious food taboos on the part of the Indians in order to eat with the British was therefore regarded as a sign of real friendship as well as a triumph over insulting and superstitious religious codes. Henry Lawrence was delighted when one of his greatest friends, G. K. Gokhale,

> ... defied outcasting by inviting Henry to dine in Poona, the very home of orthodoxy. Two other Brahmin rebels joined them. They were Mr R. P. Paranjpe, senior Wrangler at Cambridge, and Mokshagundam Vishvesivaraya, later Premier of Mysore. They sat on the ground, ate with their fingers, and were served by the wife and daughters of the host. Henry considers this the greatest compliment he has ever received.[207]

A willingness on both sides to work around cultural differences meant that problems with conflicting bodily norms could be overcome. Reginald Maxwell found that caste Hindus were prepared to eat with a European as long as the food was vegetarian.[208] His Muslim district superintendent (DSP) was willing to dine with the family 'provided that nothing ... contains any product of the pig and

Plate 19   The Gholaps' daughter breaks the ice between British and Indian. 'His Excellency and Lady Graham visit the Collector of Hyderabad and his family (Mr and Mrs N. T. Gholap) informally at their home.'

that the meat has been killed according to Mahomedan rites.' He added 'I don't think the DSP really likes our meals, but he is fairly used to them and anyhow likes being invited!'[209] Mildred Archer organized parties in the garden with Brahmin cooks so that caste restrictions were not violated and invited the women to tea, 'which seemed to be something you could get away with'.[210] The Goddens would invite the orthodox Mr Bannerjee, Divisional Collector of Narayangunj, to come for coffee after dinner as he could not dine with them.[211] An accommodation could therefore be reached which suited both sides, although the onus was upon the Indians to adapt to British customs.

Even if food taboos could be worked around, Reginald Maxwell noted that 'With caste Hindus, the meal is a sort of religious ceremony, and I don't think they talk at all, though many of the old rules are very much relaxed in these days.'[212] It rather defeated the aim of cementing social and political relationships with Indians over dinner if they were unused, or unwilling, to converse. While the political situation impelled the British to create more fluid and open relationships with Indians, the problems of bodily incompatibility, which were in their turn bound up with racial prejudice, hindered the development of amicable relations. Here we can see the needs of the political sphere coming into conflict with the cultural sphere. Developments in the latter were taking place at a much slower pace and acted as a drag on change. While working as Political Agent in Cambay State Maxwell was frustrated by the way in which 'No one made the slightest attempt at conversation unless directly addressed by me.'[213] Gordon Ray, similarly noted in his diary, after attending a farewell dinner for one of his Magistrates:

> these parties are heavy going – very little conversation – in fact I had to do most of the talking. Indians are strange at such functions – so terribly solemn – no party spirit at all – very little light conversation and never a smile or a joke. They just sit at table, eating rapidly; without uttering a word. I did all I could to liven things up, but it was pretty exhausting.[214]

Conversational lulls could be pre-empted by careful organization. Reginald Maxwell described how at the Gidneys' mixed dinner party 'round games and competitions' had been organized, 'which helped to keep things going'.[215]

Indian attitudes towards women's role in the public sphere were a second hurdle to the development of an inter-racial social life. In 1905 Bhudev Mukhopadhyay, an assistant inspector of schools, noted that among Indians who had been to Europe there was a 'new fashion of going out with one's wife',[216] but even during the Second World War Philip Ray never met the wife of an Indian lawyer friend of his with whom he used to dine in the garden.[217] As a result of indianization in the services Indians were gradually beginning to be admitted to some British clubs, but the British deeply resented the fact that the Indians tended not to bring their wives. However, often unable to speak English and unwilling to drink or dance, they would have felt uncomfortable. Raj Chatterji, a former executive with Imperial Tobacco, recalled that

> apart from people like my mother, who was a very keen bridge-player and played tennis, I can't remember more than about two Indian women who regularly attended the club. The British would bring their womenfolk sometimes; but then they said 'It's more or less a men's club as far as we're concerned, because Indians are not here with their wives.' So their more intimate parties were always held either at the Delhi Club or in their own homes.[218]

This was a good excuse, then, for the British to preserve racial exclusivity. The only way to build up social links with the majority of Indian women was to organize purdah parties or to engage in philanthropic work.[219] Previously considered outside the scope of the memsahib, as it would have involved too great an amount of contact with the Indian population, philanthropic work became an important pursuit for many Anglo-Indian women. Dora Skrine, wife of the Resident for the Madras States, is a good example. She was involved in a Ladies' club, the YWCA and running a group of girl guides.[220]

Conflicting ideas of appropriate deportment meant that for the most part socializing with Indians was limited to tennis or bridge. Louise Ouwekerk found that tennis was one of the few activities where Indians and the British were able to meet freely. She had her own court in the garden where guests could play without the difficulty of club membership.[221] Ouwekerk was interested in meeting Indians from all walks of life, but the tennis party commemorated in plate 20 suggests a more typical scene. Taken in Jaipur in the 1890s the photograph shows a mixed group of British men and women and Indian gentlemen, some still holding their tennis rackets. The Indians are described as local dignitaries and may have been associated with the princely court. It is suggestive of the preference

Plate 20 Tennis broke down racial barriers. 'Tennis party including Col. Irwin, and Mrs Jacob and local dignitaries, Jaipur.'

among the British for upper-class Indians – especially those from, or associated with, noble or princely families. This class prejudice even cut across racial prejudices at times. When Clarmont Skrine made the mistake of booking himself a second-class berth on the voyage back to India, he preferred to wangle a place at dinner in the first class, where he dined with the Diwan to the Maharaja of Travancore and the Secretary to the Maharajah of Kasim Bazar, than to dine with his second-class white companions who failed to change for dinner.[222] By the 1930s tennis parties, some of the less exclusive clubs and horse-racing provided venues where the upper levels of Anglo-Indian society mingled freely with the upper echelons of Indian society.[223] As in the early days of British rule, when the British and the Indians would meet at a cockfight or *nautch*, the boundaries between the British and the Indians were reformulated to allow for a level of inter-racial mixing acceptable to both sides.

The limitations on acceptable sites and activities did mean that ultimately Indians were not properly integrated into Anglo-Indian social life. Indian members of the ICS rarely felt properly integrated. Rajeshwar Dayal, an Indian civil servant, recalled that during ICS week 'At the most, we received invitations to tea and tennis from the British seniors.... We were never invited to stay with them. But we were invited to stay with the Indian ministers and senior officials. The Indians seemed to have parallel functions going on, so it was a rather peculiar situation.'[224] He also recalled that, at balls at Government House, the Indians and the British would occupy different sides of the room, neither side asking the other to dance.[225] On a more personal level friendly working relationships might be established between colleagues such as that between W. H. Samurez Smith and the Subdivisional Police officer, Hazifuddin, who he found to be 'a nice young Mohammedan . . . and I think we shall get on very well together. (It is vital to the efficiency of the administration that we should).'[226] But on the whole these remained professional rather than personal friendships.[227] Ultimately the majority of the British were uninterested in anything more than this. The sentiments of W. O. Horne, defending the policy of banning Indian members from the club before the First World War, would have been echoed by a great many Anglo-Indians right up until 1947:

The life and work of the majority of the members required them daily, and in an increasing degree, to mix with their Indian fellow-subjects, not only in work or business, but also socially, from Government House downwards, and it was surely not asking too much that a man might have, after his day's work, a place where he could for an hour or two take his ease in the society of men of his own race, and those whose habits and customs were the same as his own.[228]

From the Indian perspective full integration into British social circles posed its own set of problems. Keen to invade British circles of power, Indian congressmen were constantly reminded by Gandhi's nativism of the power of a boldly Indian body to subvert British authority. Full adaptation to British customs and habits therefore posed them with a dilemma.

During the first half of the twentieth century the barriers between the races did begin to break down. The lines around the body of the Anglo-Indian were redrawn, allowing for greater openness to intimate social contact with the Indian body. But, by this time, the structures of imperialism had hardened to the point where it was extremely difficult to overcome them: 'The position of ruler and ruled always vitiated personal relationships.'[229] This was made worse by conflicting definitions of friendship. 'The better disposed Indians and the better disposed Europeans wanted to be, but were afraid to be, friends. The Indians were afraid that, if the barriers were down, they would be misunderstood and perhaps snubbed. The Europeans were afraid that they would be taken advantage of. In both cases the fears probably had some foundation in actual experience.'[230] The Indian expectation that friendship meant using your influence to assist your friend smelt of overt corruption to the British.[231] Philip Ray explained that it was fear of these kinds of expectations which made the British seem rather stand-offish. 'You always had to be terribly careful, it was necessary to have in the back of your mind that an Indian friend might try to manipulate the situation' or trade on a friendship with a European with other Indians.[232] In order to prevent corruption, British officials had not been allowed to accept gifts from Indians since the days of Cornwallis. This caused the embarrassing situation for G. P. Stewart that he had to formally apply to the government for permission to accept the wedding presents given to him by his 'well-to-do Indian friends'.[233] Such regulations made overt a level of distrust which would put a strain on any friendship. The Second World War and the influx of people with different attitudes broke down barriers further, but up until 1947 the structural problems of colonialism and racial prejudice, combined with the very slow pace of change of the bodily norms surrounding contact with others, proved an immense barrier to friendly interracial relations.

Epilogue: The Dissolution of the Anglo-Indian Body, 1939–1947

When war broke out in Europe the British in India responded in the only way they knew how – by keeping up prestige. The news of the fall of France was greeted in Simla by the response that things should carry on as normal. Accordingly, the viceregal garden party planned for that afternoon went ahead, and the British sipped tea and ate ices while the band played. 'Lord Linlithgow had decided that we should show the natives of India that the imperial machine was still in being and the rulers of the Empire were confident of victory.'[1] Indianization of the services and the army, as well as the Indian nationalist movement, had begun to undermine the British body as a symbol of power, but the British continued to believe that their physical presence and haughty manner were sufficient to demonstrate British superiority and elicit deference from their Indian subjects. For the period of what might be termed 'the phoney war in India' this policy appeared to work. Initially India felt extremely remote from the war: 'It's very hard to realise there is a war on up here. We go on just the same as we have done for years and the same minor problems crop up as we have in peace.'[2] Then the Japanese attacked Pearl Harbor and marched into Malaya and Burma. India was suddenly very close to the war.

The British defeat in South-East Asia had a tremendous impact on the Raj, fatally damaging British prestige. The fall of Singapore in February 1942 to a much smaller Japanese force and the capture of most of the British and Indian troops stationed there severely undermined British claims to military prowess. During the Japanese advance into Burma the British army were routed. As trains carrying sick and wounded soldiers from the front began to pass through northern India the extent of the physical defeat of the British became clear to the Indians. Many of the soldiers were sick with malaria and dysentery, most 'had nothing but their boots and the pair of shorts they were wearing' and some had been crucified or hanged by the Japanese before being rescued. All bore witness to the physical humiliation of the British by the Japanese.[3] Indian labourers also began to return from the front 'with sores on their feet and many lurid stories to tell of the British retreat'.[4] Among some sections of Indian society the Japanese were seen to have superseded the British as a new race of supermen.[5] John Griffiths 'felt that although respected as an individual Englishman, I was considered to belong to a race whose virtue had gone out of it.'[6]

Added to the shame of defeat was the disreputable way in which the British had been seen to abandon their subjects. In Burma most of the civilians were said to have 'cleared off in cars with their own possessions leaving other people to fend for themselves'.[7] According to Archibald Bowman, 'That the British deserted the Malays will be remembered and held against them, the Dutch who stayed behind in Java are better liked.'[8] At least 10,000 of the estimated 400,000 Indians who fled from Burma died on the road. It was even rumoured that there were two routes out of Burma, an easier one for the whites and a more arduous one for the natives. Thus, the British defeat dealt a blow to the patriarchal justification of imperialism which cast the British as the defenders of the humble. Aware of the damage it would inflict upon their reputation, the Indian government censored press reports dealing with officials' abandonment of Indians in Rangoon. Also censored were reports of British incompetence or panic.[9] The inefficiency and inability of the British to cope with the soldiers and refugees at the front, as well as the panic which set in, especially with the threat of Japanese air raids, undermined the image of self-assurance which was an important facet of prestige. Penderel Moon was 'really rather appalled' by the fact that 'In March most Englishmen in Lahore seemed to have quite lost their balance.'[10]

The Quit India movement of 1942 revealed the extent to which British authority was undermined by the war. Bihar was one of the areas where lawlessness was worst, and the British almost lost control. Here price rises associated with the war, the requisitioning of private property and the evacuation of entire villages to make way for military installations, plus the sense that the war was illegitimate, produced a high level of discontent. The populace were further emboldened by the Japanese defeat, which exposed the fact that the British were not as omnipotent as they claimed. In combination these factors 'overcame engrained motives of fear and deference to colonial authority'.[11] The most powerful indication that Indian deference was breaking down were the murders of two army officers and two pilots during the unrest. 'These incidents were . . . open attacks on the physical presence of colonial rule and constituted, one may argue, a final violent assault on colonial hegemony.'[12]

The British responded to the Quit India riots with a savagery which they had not displayed since Amritsar. Public whippings, indiscriminate acts of violence and the use of firearms against demonstrators imprinted the power of the colonial state on the bodies of its subjects. The use of such force thoroughly discredited the legitimacy of the British position in India as they were seen to have acted outside the restraints of the law which they were supposedly there to uphold. In the face of such oppression the rhetoric which constructed the Allies' war as a battle for democracy rang hollow in the ears of Indian nationalists.[13] The demoralization with, or lack of support for, the colonial regime demonstrated by the lower levels of the administration, the police and even the wealthy landowners during the Quit India riots left the British without the vital support structure of their rule. After 1942 it therefore became clear that they were almost entirely reliant on the army to maintain their position as rulers.[14] Prestige as a physical expression of power was revealed as a façade propped up by the physical violence of the army.

British disregard for the law appeared to be matched by disregard for the well-being of their subjects. The British preparations for a possible Japanese invasion of eastern India, which included requisitioning of boats and the stationing of large numbers of Allied soldiers in the area, was blamed for the 'chronic shortages of food, and other essentials like cooking fuels, cloth, and medicines'.[15] These shortages culminated in the Bengal famine of 1943, resulting in the death of up to three million people. Wavell concluded that the 'damage to our reputation here . . . is incalculable'.[16] Amid the misfortunes of the Indian populace the behaviour of some of the Allied troops made matters worse. American troops were a particular problem. Gordon Ray thought them 'a wild undisciplined lot'. He discovered they had been indulging in night shooting, which involved driving 'slowly down the country roads, after night fall, shooting blindly to right and to left at each suspicious object they see'. The matter came to light when they accidentally shot an 'unfortunate village woman squatting in a ditch answering the call of nature'.[17] Incidents like this revealed a contempt for the Indian population which treated them as subhuman. Indian campaigners for independence turned them to their advantage to discredit the Raj. Sanjoy Bhattacharya concludes that 'There can be no doubt that the stationing of an enormous Allied army in India adversely affected the standing of the colonial state.'[18]

American troops, better equipped and better paid than the British troops, with their free and easy ways, were blamed for eroding the values and proprieties which preserved the Anglo-Indian body as a symbol of prestige. Passing a hotel in Calcutta, Eugenie Fraser was shocked to see a naked American officer talking to a bearer.[19] It was said by some Indians that it was the spectacle of American soldiers that lost the British the Raj.[20] For Eugenie Fraser, 'More amazing than anything else was the scene of an American playing tennis with one of the bearers – a scene to send shudders through the British Raj.'[21] In fact many of the servicemen – both British and American – who came out to India during the war showed a disregard for racial segregation. Often politically left-wing, without a stake in the system and convinced that independence should and would be granted to India, they showed no regard for Anglo-Indian racial proprieties. Douglas Dickens, a typical example of the left-wing wartime service-man, used to take time off from the RAF at a club with no colour bar. Here army personnel socialized with the Women's Army Corps girls, many of whom were Eurasian.[22] Indians found the newly commis-sioned officers eager to meet them on equal terms in their own homes, and to try out Indian customs. D. K. Palit remembered them as willing to 'eat with their fingers, wear Indian clothes, learn Hindi and something about our music'.[23] Sir J. Herbert hoped to turn the openness to Indians of the newcomers to the government's advantage. He commented to Linlithgow that 'The modern educated British soldier seems readily to make friends with middle class Indians, and I hope by various means to bring them together more. Through such contacts Indians may be made to realise that we are not as bad as some politicians make out.'[24] According to Kushwant Singh, 'a lot of the bitterness in the Indians' mind was taken away by the presence of these people, because they were keener to make friends with Indians than mix with their own lot.'[25]

Indianization of the Civil Service was already well-established by 1939, but within the Army it was much less advanced. By the end of the war, however, the number of Indian officers had increased from 'one in every eleven to one in every five.'[26] John Masters described how 'One day I looked up to find a tall young Indian standing in my office.... The young man said his name was Dutt, and that he had been posted as our medical officer. This was a shock, as in those days all King's Commissioned officers in a Gurkha battalion were Brit-ish.'[27] All King's Commissioned officers had club membership rights, so consequently the Indian membership of the clubs increased.

Social barriers within the British community in India were also broken down as planters and 'junior tycoons from the great merchant houses of Calcutta and Bombay' were recruited as officers.[28] The war broke down many of the boundaries erected around the Anglo-Indian body and eroded the principles of distance and arrogance which made up so much of prestige. A final symbolic blow was given to prestige by the arrival of Louis Mountbatten, who immediately widened the social and political world of Indian government by throwing open the doors of Viceroy's House to Indians 'who would never have found their way here before'.[29] Determined that he would find a solution to the intractable problems of Indian independence, Mountbatten also made it clear that he and his wife would visit Indian leaders in their homes without staff and protocol.[30]

Throughout the entire period of British rule in India the British sought to maintain their authority over Indians by reinforcing the bodily differences between ruler and ruled. In this way racism was generated on the site of the body. An exaggerated notion of the British body as Anglo-Saxon was juxtaposed against that of a variety of Indian bodies, all trapped by their biological inheritance in an inferior position on the scale of humankind. This view of the body was integral to the concept of prestige, which relied heavily on a belief in, and the physical display of, British difference and, by implication, superiority. The influx of newcomers, over whom the Anglo-Indians were unable to exert the pressure to conform, exposed the archaic nature of this concept of the British body. Once racial boundaries were broken down and the Anglo-Indians were forced to accept Indians – who often dressed and behaved like them – into their social circles and into positions of political and military authority, the foundation of bodily difference upon which prestige rested was severely shaken.

Anglo-Indian arrogance was now frequently met with hostility rather than the deference which it relied upon as a confirmation of its efficacy. Small actions on the part of the Indians demonstrated that they were no longer overawed by the physical presence of the British. During the festival of Holi, when coloured dyes are squirted over everyone, 'Jimmy Stewart, . . . travelling home from the head office through the bazaar, received a squirtful in the open window of his car and arrived home in a fury – his suit ruined by pink splashes. No one previously would have dared to throw dye over a European, but now attitudes appeared to be changing with the Indians growing bolder.'[31] The structure of British authority was in tatters at the end of the Second World War. 'Walking through the

Indian neighbourhoods of Calcutta in his uniform, [Eric Stokes] realised with "what cold hatred the politically conscious people (clerks etc.) regarded me".'[32] As the structure crumbled, so too did its symbols – the figures of the sahib and memsahib. Even the topi, once such a powerful symbol of British authority, began to disappear from the heads of Anglo-Indians. Mrs Winifred Brown was astonished to find on returning from a year's leave during the war that topis were no longer worn. The experience of the troops in Burma had shown that 'the taking of salt pills was all the precaution needed' against sunstroke.[33]

In the early nineteenth century the open and flexible British body adapted well to the political needs of rule in an Indian idiom. Between 1820 and 1857 changing bodily practice both stimulated and reinforced the direction of political change. In India the black suit of Victorian Britain took on additional resonance as the colour, not only of middle-class sobriety, decency and uprightness, but also of good government, political legitimacy and neutral administration of the law. The withdrawal into the body, which was the consequence of the process of anglicization, marked the beginnings of a bourgeois sensibility among Anglo-Indians. But even as they adopted middle-class codes of respectability the Anglo-Indians incorporated tropical suits, cheroots, 'Hindoostanee nights', sola topis and cholera belts into their definition of Britishness, creating a distinctive hybrid Anglo-Indian culture.

The body played a vital role at the centre of Anglo-Indian culture, interacting with the social, economic and political processes as an active site where norms and practices were generated. The Anglo-Indian preference for European foodstuffs stimulated trade in European goods.[34] Thus the body as the site of a map of tastes, where preferences are experienced and expressed, encouraged the growth of a hybrid colonial economy, while at the same time the emphasis on British food reinforced the process of the anglicization of the nabob. Similarly, under pressure from medical concerns and the scorn of their subjects, the British in India redefined what it meant to be clean. Anglo-Indian attitudes towards personal cleanliness expose 'a highly complex continuum stretching from the physical sensations verbalized by the individual to the public language of morality and aesthetics'.[35] In this way the corporeality of the individual is linked to the wider social structure of social relations and the ethics governing that society.

The incompleteness of the process of anglicization ensured that the Anglo-Indian body was never a mere reflection of the Victorian body in the metropole. Acknowledgement of the inertia which preserved aspects of the nabob's lifestyle within the domestic sphere of children and servants adds complexity to the standard periodization of Indian history by highlighting those aspects of the sahib's body which echoed that of the nabob. Rather than withdrawing into the privacy of bourgeois domesticity the Anglo-Indians continued to lead extraordinarily public lives. The lavish consumption of food and drink, the enduring importance of luxurious bodily practices, as well as the flamboyance of Anglo-Indian leisure pursuits were all reminiscent of the nabob and continued to construct the official's body as an aristocratic body in the Indian context. On the other hand, the rigid social routine, the exaggerated concern with etiquette, and the elaborate lengths to which the Anglo-Indians went in order to replicate British eating and clothing habits meant that the Anglo-Indians became almost caricatures of Britishness. The body of the sahib (and the memsahib) which emerged during the latter half of the century sought to project an image of itself within the Indian political context as at one and the same time an embodiment of British bourgeois values, a racially superior body, and an aristocratic body. The result was a fragmented body which reflected the difficulties surrounding the construction of a bourgeois body outside the context of a nation state as well as the contradictions and difficulties of the colonial situation.

The dramatic political and social events of the twentieth century called for a rapid adjustment to the new demands on the body of the Anglo-Indian official. The fixed and regimented nature of Anglo-Indian bodily norms meant, however, that on the cultural level change occurred at a much slower pace. Anglo-Indian culture in the twentieth century preserved an archaic concept of Britishness. The notion of the Anglo-Saxon imperial mission which infused British national identity with the notion of racial superiority was in the process of being abandoned in the metropole, where cultural rather than racial explanations for imperial rule were emphasized and support for self-government in the colonies was growing.[36] The concomitant notion of British masculinity, fed by the cult of athleticism within the public schools, was now 'associated...with a kind of militarism that was being brought into discredit by revulsion at the carnage of the First World War'.[37] Even the notion of the gentleman had shifted with the democratization of British society. The bodily concepts of the majority of old-hands were therefore outmoded and out of step with the political and social events leading up to Indian independence. A greater understanding of the cultural factors which triggered and hindered social and political change in British India is thus achieved by the study of the body. The chronology of bodily change within British India suggests that an analysis of the body must allow for an interplay between different influences on it as well as for the differential impact of these influences. This would suggest that further research on the development of the modern bourgeois body, even within Europe, should search for the contradictory aspects of the process as well as areas where the dominant discourses prove less effective, and for conceptualizations of the body which remain constant.

Financially unable to lead the glamorous life of the leisured classes that they were used to in India, retired Anglo-Indians sunk into insignificance after 1947, a fate which most returned Anglo-Indians before them had shared. Regarded as bores by those without colonial experiences they tended to stick together. Certain parts of London, and towns like Edinburgh, Cheltenham and Tunbridge Wells, were regarded as centres for retired Anglo-Indians.[38] Others escaped the fate of a gloomy retirement in Britain by seeking out a colonial life within Africa, or sought the more compatible colonial atmosphere of America and Australia. As early as 1873 the psychological problems which the loss of prestige caused were recognized by George Hunter, who warned that the retired Anglo-Indian was likely to suffer from 'mental morbidness'. 'As the illusion of their importance is dispelled their self-esteem is shocked, and they grow crotchety, peevish and irritable.'[39] In order to confirm their identity and sense of purpose the Anglo-Indians in Britain reversed their technique of creating little Englands in India and tended to create little Anglo-Indias in their British homes. They attempted to reproduce the distinctive curry and rice, and chutneys and pickles of Anglo-India, and collected around themselves the souvenirs of their past life in the form of Indian carved furniture, hunting trophies, cloths, rugs and photographs.[40] The Anglo-Indian's sense of loss and displacement in Britain forcefully demonstrates to what extent Anglo-India was a self-contained world which developed its own norms and fostered the construction of a distinctive Anglo-Indian body.

Appendix

A list of servants in a private family (taken from Fanny Parks, *Wanderings*, I, pp. 209–10).

Number		Wages, Rupees per month
1	A *khānsāmān*, or headman; a Musalman servant who purchases the provisions, makes the confectionery, and superintends the table	12
2	The *ābdār*, or water-cooler; cools the water, ices the wines, and attends them at table	8
3	The head *khidmutgār*; he takes charge of the plate-chest, and waits at table	7
4	A second *khidmutgār*, who waits at table	6
5	A *bārwarchi*, or cook	12
6	Mate *bārwarchi*, or cook	4
7	*Masalchî*; dishwasher and torchbearer	4
8	*Dhobee*, or washerman	8
9	*Istree wālā*, washerman for ironing	8
10	A *darzee*, or tailor	8
11	A second tailor	6
12	An *ayah*, or lady's maid	10
13	An underwoman	6
14	A *doriya*; a sweeper, who attends to the dogs	4
15	Sirdar-bearer, an Hindoo servant, the head of the bearers, and the keeper of the sahib's wardrobe; the keys of which are always carried in his kamarband, the folds of cloth around his waist	8
16	The mate bearer; assists as valet, and attends to the lamps	6

22	Six bearers to pull the pankhās, and dust the furniture &c.	24
23	A *gwālā*, or cowherd	4
24	A *bher-i-wālā*, or shepherd	5
25	A *murgh-i-wālā*, to take care of the fowls, wild-ducks, quail, rabbits, guinea-fowls and pigeons	4
26	A *mālee*, or gardener	5
27	A mate ditto	3
28	Another mate, or a cooly	2
29	A gram-grinder, generally a man who grinds the *chanā* for the horses	2
30	A coachman	10
38	Eight *sāises*, or grooms at 5 Rupees each for eight horses	40
46	Eight grass-cutters, at 3 Rupees each for the above	24
47	A *bhishti*, or water-carrier	5
48	A mate ditto	4
49	A *barha'i mistree*, a carpenter	8
50	Another carpenter	7
52	Two coolies to throw water on the tatties	4
54	Two *chankîdārs*, or watchmen	8
55	A *durwān*, or gate-keeper	4
57	Two *chuprāsîs*, or running footmen, to carry notes, and be in attendance on the verandah	10
57	Total Rupees per month	290

Notes

Introduction

1 Bagnall Papers (CSAS), p. 37; Thornhill Collection (OIOC), /14, 29 August 1868; Stock Papers (CSAS), p. 39; Wakefield, *Past Imperative*, pp. 8–9; Kaye, *Peregrine Pultuney*, II, p. 60.

2 Beames, *Memoirs*, p. 292.

3 'British public schools and British parents in India', *The Calcutta Review*, 10 (1848), p. 190.

4 Drewitt, *Bombay*, p. 72.

5 Maynard Collection (OIOC), /1, 22 November 1891.

6 [Henderson], *The Bengalee*, p. 217.

7 The term Anglo-Indian was used to describe the British in India until 1911, when people of mixed blood adopted the label for themselves instead of the term Eurasian. Due to the fact that it frequently occurs in the sources, the term Anglo-Indian is used throughout the book to refer to the British in India.

8 The conceptualization of the body also draws upon the work of Mary Douglas. See Douglas, 'Do dogs laugh?'; Douglas, *Natural Symbols*.

9 Bourdieu, *The Logic*, pp. 52–80; Honneth et al., 'The struggle for symbolic order', p. 42; Mahar, 'The basic theoretical position', p. 12.

10 Bourdieu, *The Logic*, p. 69.

11 J. B. Thompson, *Studies*, p. 55.

12 Mauss, 'Body techniques', pp. 104–5. For the development of anthropological work on the body see Blacking, *The Anthropology of the Body*; Benthall and Polhemus, *The Body*; Synnott, *The Body Social*; Lock, 'Cultivating the body'.

13 See Duden, *The Woman*, pp. 11–12.

14 Vigarello, *Concepts of Cleanliness*, pp. 93–104.

15 Ibid., p. 216; Darnton, *The Great Cat Massacre*, pp. 105–40; Perrot, *Fashioning*, pp. 30–2; Outram, *The Body*, p. 12.

16 See Budd, *The Sculpture Machine*.

17 Foucault, *Discipline*, p. 137. See also Burke, *Critical Essays*, pp. 1–2.

18 Ibid., pp. 138–45.
19 Shumway, *Michel Foucault*, p. 150.
20 Shilling, *The Body*, pp. 79–80. In his later work Foucault escapes some
of these criticisms. In his last works on sexuality he paid more attention
to the self. See Foucault, *The History of Sexuality*. 'The idea of "technologies of the self" enables Foucault to conceive of individuals as
active agents with the capacity to autonomously fashion their own
existences. This notion transcends the limitations of the etiolated view
of individuals as docile bodies that characterizes the middle phase of
Foucault's work.... The idea of technologies of the self enables Foucault to elaborate a theory of resistance – an "ethics of the self" – which
is situated in the interstices of power relations, at the level of individuals' daily practices.' McNay, *Foucault*, p. 7.
21 Outram, *The Body*, pp. 18–21.
22 With all its faults, Foucault's work cannot be dismissed. Much of its
value lies in the fact that he constantly challenges our assumptions and
questions what is assumed to be natural. For a discussion of the value of
Foucault's work to historians see Jones and Porter, *Reassessing Foucault*. Many of the problems with Foucault's work tend to be replicated
in sociologies of the body. See T. Turner, 'Review of *The Body and
Society*', p. 212. They remain caught in the trap of constructing the
relationship of the body with society from above without successfully
conceptualizing the body as at one and the same time a result of
collectively held norms and a force in the construction of these norms.
Recent sociology of the body has therefore simply spawned numerous
bodies (for example Bryan Turner presents us with four: the reproductive, regulated, restrained and representative) with resulting confusion
to the point where it is possible to ask, as Berthelot does, 'is there any
meaning in a sociology of the body?' Berthelot, 'Sociological discourse
and the body', p. 155. See Frank, 'Bringing bodies back in'; Frank, 'For
a sociology of the body'; Featherstone, 'The body in consumer culture';
O'Neill, *Five Bodies*; B. S. Turner, *The Body and Society*.
23 Elias, *The Civilizing Process*, pp. 263–513.
24 For example the fork, the handkerchief and the nightshirt erected a
barrier between one's own body and the bodies of others. They are
' "instrument[s] of civilization," a symbol of the transformation at work
in man: an "emotional wall" is beginning to arise between man and his
own body.' Fontaine, 'The civilizing process', p. 247.
25 For criticism of Elias see van Krieken, 'Violence, self-discipline and
modernity', p. 197; Kuzmics, 'Civilization, state and bourgeois society',
p. 517; Duerr, *Der Mythos vom Zivilisationsprozeß*.
26 Bogner, 'The structure of social processes', p. 390. See also Nistroj,
'Norbert Elias', p. 141.
27 Fontaine, 'The civilizing process', p. 246.
28 For the points of convergence and divergence between the two theories
see Featherstone, 'Norbert Elias', p. 203; Hunt, 'French history',
pp. 217–18; Hutton, 'The history of mentalities', p. 254.

29   For a discussion of the literature on the European body see Porter, 'The history of the body'. For work on India and the colonies which touches on the British body but for which it is not the main focus see Arnold, *Colonizing the Body*; Ballhatchet, *Race*; Cohn, 'Cloth, clothes and colonialism'; Ernst, *Mad Tales*; Foley et al., *Gender and Colonialism*; Hyam, *Empire and Sexuality*; Kennedy, *Islands of White*.

30   The officials tended to set the tone for the rest of respectable British India, and the study of the army would be complicated by military ideas of deportment and masculinity.

31   For a discussion of the way in which Britishness, or Englishness, was constructed through a dialogue with the notion of others see Colley, *Britons*; Young, *Colonial Desire*, pp. 1–6.

32   Scott, *The Raj Quartet*, p. 496. Nicholas Thomas affirms that much of colonial discourse probably impinged little on the colonized, directed as it was at itself and the metropole. Thomas, *Colonialism's Culture*, pp. 57–8.

33   Tarlo, *Clothing Matters*, p. 101.

Chapter 1 The Indianized Body

1   Thackeray, *Vanity Fair*, pp. 26–7.

2   'From the Hindi meaning a deputy, . . . was applied . . . to a delegate of the supreme chief, viz. to a Viceroy or chief Governor under the Great Mogul . . . From this use it became a title of rank without necessarily having any office attached.' Yule and Burnell, *Hobson-Jobson*, p. 295.

3   See Backscheider and Howard, *The Plays*; Raven, 'English popular literature', pp. 253–5.

4   Cited by *The Oxford English Dictionary* from the *New Monthly Magazine* (1834).

5   This term is used by Majeed, *Ungoverned Imaginings*, p. 22.

6   Marshall and Williams, *The Great Map*, pp. 160–1.

7   Leask, *British Romantic Writers*, p. 9.

8   William Jones cast Cornwallis in the role of Justinian, who ensured the rule of justice in ancient Greece and Rome, and N. T. Halhed likened the British acquisition of Bengali to the Roman study of Greek. Cohn, 'The command of language', pp. 295–6.

9   Majeed, *Ungoverned Imaginings*, pp. 22, 29–30.

10   This move backfired as the British, interpreting the rejection of Mughal authority as a recognition of their own paramountcy, eventually annexed Awadh. Fisher, 'The imperial coronation', p. 265.

11   Majeed, *Ungoverned Imaginings*, p. 6; Colley, *Britons*, p. 231. The nabobs' ruling style also owed something to that of the patricians of eighteenth-century Britain. See E. P. Thompson, 'Patrician society'.

12   Valentia, *Voyages*, I, pp. 235–6.

13   Anon., *Hartly House*, p. 20.

14   Campbell, *Excursions*, I, p. 140.

15 British willingness to adapt to Indian modes of communication is also illustrated by their announcement of a decision over a religious dispute at Kanchi in 1786 by means of a tom-tom, a traditional Tamil means of announcing state policy. Irschick, *Dialogue*, p. 22.

16 See Nilsson, *European Architecture*, pp. 118–19.

17 Stocqueler, *The Hand-book*, p. 257.

18 Elwood, *Narrative*, II, pp. 1–2.

19 Fanny Parks commented that some households also employed an *assaburdar* for show who carried a silver stick before you. Parks, *Wanderings*, I, p. 210. In contrast to her fifty-seven servants, a household in Britain with an income of over £20,000 would on average have employed twenty-two servants. See Gerard, *Country House Life*, p. 146.

20 Isaac, *The Transformation*, pp. 34–42.

21 Lt.-Col. Tredway-Clarke Papers (OIOC), pp. 18–19.

22 Williamson, *The East India Vade-Mecum*, I, p. 181.

23 See Archer, *Company Paintings*, pp. 61–2, 103.

24 For a discussion of this process see Mayer, 'Inventing village tradition'; Dirks, 'Castes of mind'.

25 C. A. Bayly, *Indian Society*, pp. 155–8.

26 Washbrook, 'Economic depression', p. 261.

27 See for example Eastwick, *Autobiography of Lutfulah*, pp. 34–5.

28 See Irschick, *Dialogue*, pp. 1–13.

29 C. A. Bayly, 'The origins of swadeshi', pp. 286–8.

30 Irschick, *Dialogue*, p. 74.

31 Valentia, *Voyages*, I, pp. 235–6.

32 Razzell, 'Social origins', p. 250; Cohn, 'Recruitment and training', p. 110. These works have been relied upon as there has been little recent research into the social background of covenanted civilians and Indian Army officers. See also MacKenzie, 'Essay and reflection' for the active role the Scots played in the Empire.

33 Razzell, 'Social origins', p. 250; Cohn, 'Recruitment and training', p. 110.

34 See Schumpeter, *Imperialism*, pp. 25, 85.

35 Stocqueler, *The Hand-book*, p. 96.

36 MacFarlan Collection (OIOC), /B, 24 January 1820.

37 Cordiner, *A Voyage*, pp. 104–5.

38 Spear, *The Nabobs*, p. 58.

39 James M. Holzman, cited by N. Bhattacharya, *Reading the Splendid Body*, p. 86.

40 Ross, *Status and Respectability*, p. 11; Maynard, *Fashioned*, pp. 42–3.

41 [Henderson], *The Bengalee*, p. 217.

42 See also D'Oyly, *The Europeans*, pl. iv; Atkinson, *Indian Spices*, pl. xxvi.

43 Schivelbusch, *Das Paradies*, p. 99.

44 [Henderson], *The Bengalee*, p. 374.

45 N. Bhattacharya, *Reading the Splendid Body*, p. 88.

46 Teltscher, *India Inscribed*, p. 162.

47   See Williamson, *The East India Vade-Mecum*, II, p. 2.
48   J. Johnson, *The Influence*, p. 464.
49   Reece, *The Medical Companion*, p. 104.
50   A group of men drawn largely from the Scottish and Irish intelligentsia. Many of them continued to pursue their medical careers successfully on their return to Britain, where they gained a measure of influence over the British profession of medicine. See Arnold, *Colonising the Body*, pp. 22–3; Crawford, *A History*.
51   Cited by Corbin, *The Foul*, p. 38.
52   Huggins, *Sketches*, p. 136.
53   See Marshall and Williams, *The Great Map*, pp. 129–38; Teltscher, *India Inscribed*, p. 114.
54   See Pfeiffer, *The Art*, p. 174.
55   Wallace, *A Voyage*, pp. 115–16.
56   Patterson, 'The medical practice', p. 41; Goodeve, 'A sketch', p. 125.
57   J. Johnson, *The Influence*, p. 5.
58   Ibid., p. 417.
59   V. Smith, 'Cleanliness', p. 136.
60   J. Johnson, *The Influence*, p. 418.
61   Ibid., p. 433.
62   V. Smith, 'Cleanliness', pp. 85, 87.
63   See C. A. Bayly, *Indian Society*, pp. 157–8.
64   J. Johnson, *The Influence*, p. 436. See also Reece, *The Medical Companion*, p. 103.
65   Medwin, *The Angler*, I, pp. 5–6.
66   Whorton, *Crusaders*, p. 70.
67   Fenton, *The Journal*, pp. 51–2. This was probably 'Hindoo Stuart' whose book *The Ladies' Monitor* is discussed later on in this chapter.
68   MacFarlan Collection (OIOC), /B, 1 August 1817 or 1818, p. 5.
69   Mr Sherwood noted in his diary 'We buy twelve small fowls for a rupee, three or four large roasting fowls for the same, a lean sheep for twelve annas, a quarter of fat mutton for a rupee.' This was paid for out of a salary of Rs 506 or £63 5s. a month. Darton, *The Life and Times*, pp. 273–4.
70   Cordiner, *A Voyage*, p. 110.
71   J. Burnett, *Plenty and Want*, p. 57.
72   Cordiner, *A Voyage*, p. 110.
73   *The Englishman*, 3 June 1834, p. 2.
74   Valentia, *Voyages*, I, p. 241.
75   Spilsbury Collection (OIOC), 1, October 1822.
76   See also D'Oyly, *Indian Sports*.
77   Dubois, *Description*, p. 116. See also Briggs, *Letters*, p. 32; Eastwick, *Autobiography of Lutfulah*, p. 235.
78   See Quennell, *Memoirs*, pp. 234, 240.
79   'A griffin is the Johnny Newcome of the East, one whose European manners and ideas stand out in ludicrous relief when contrasted with those, so essentially different in most respects, which appertain to the

new country of his sojourn.' A griffinage lasted one year. Bellew, *Memoirs*, I, p. 2. See also D'Oyly, *The Europeans*, pl. x; *Exotic Europeans*, pl. 83.

80 Williamson, *The East India Vade-Mecum*, I, p. 220.
81 Spilsbury Collection (OIOC) /1, October 1822.
82 Williamson, *The East India Vade-Mecum*, I, pp. 224–5.
83 Parks, *Wanderings*, I, p. 148.
84 Berridge and Edwards, *Opium*, p. 56; Milligan, *Pleasures and Pains*, p. 115.
85 Cited by Butler, *The Eldest Brother*, pp. 152, 230.
86 See Losty, *Calcutta*, pp. 57–8.
87 Williamson, *The East India Vade-Mecum*, I, p. 166.
88 Huggins, *Sketches*, p. 119.
89 Cited by Naidis, 'Evolution of the sahib', p. 432.
90 Doctor Solomon's *Guide to Health*, cited by F. B. Smith, 'Sexuality in Britain', pp. 26–7.
91 Long, 'A peep', p. 49.
92 Reproduced in C. A. Bayly, *The Raj*, p. 178.
93 Archer and Falk, *India Revealed*, p. 46.
94 For example Francesco Renaldi's painting *The Palmer Family* (1786) pays tribute to William Palmer's relationship with Bibi Faiz Bakhsh. Reproduced in Archer, *India and British Portraiture*, p. 282.
95 See Kirkpatrick Collection (OIOC), /18, 96, 96(2) 'Report of an examination instituted by direction of his excellency the most noble Governor-General, Fort St. George', 7 November 1801, Home Miscellaneous Vol. 464; Archer, *India and British Portraiture*, p. 361. See also Cotton, 'George Beechey'.
96 This mongrel tongue continued to develop throughout the period of British rule. See Kaye, *Peregrine Pultuney*, I, p. 5; Trevelyan, *The Competition Wallah*, pp. 22–3; Duncan, *The Simple Adventures*, p. 232; Westmacott Papers, p. 207.
97 See Barrell, *The Infection*, p. 16.
98 Ribeiro, *Fashion in the French Revolution*, p. 131.
99 Leask, *British Romantic Writers*, p. 7.
100 Ibid., p. 8.
101 See Marshall, *The Writings and Speeches*; Edwardes, *Warren Hastings*, pp. 166–7; Teltscher, *India Inscribed*, pp. 111–31, 169.
102 Huggins, *Sketches*, p. 61.
103 See Edwardes, *The Nabobs*, p. 14.
104 See Backscheider and Howard, *The Plays*.
105 N. Bhattacharya, *Reading the Splendid Body*, pp. 96–7.
106 Backscheider and Howard, *The Plays*, p. 38.
107 Frederick John Shore Collection (OIOC) /6–8, 23 November 1818.
108 N. Bhattacharya, *Reading the Splendid Body*, pp. 110–11.
109 Fenton, *The Journal*, p. 16.
110 See Marshall, 'The private fortune'; Feiling, *Warren Hastings*, pp. 208–9; Archer, *India and British Portraiture*, p. 94.

111   See Fisch, 'A solitary vindicator of the Hindus', p. 53.
112   [Stuart], *The Ladies' Monitor*, p. 27.
113   'When the next return of peace removes the war of sentiment from the breasts of our fair ladies, and leaves them at liberty to glance the eye once more to their old fountains of instruction on the continent; I expect they will follow the example of French ladies, in the adoption of the ancient robe, so recently revived in that country.' Ibid., p. 14.
114   Mercier, cited by Ribeiro, *Fashion in the French Revolution*, pp. 124–5.
115   Norbert Peabody describes this as a 'segmented mode of othering' working along horizontal and vertical axes of social difference, generating a multiplicity of Others. See Peabody, 'Tod's *Rajast'han*', pp. 189–90.
116   Sennett, *The Fall*, p. 186.
117   [Stuart], *The Ladies' Monitor*, p. 30.
118   See Marshall and Williams, *The Great Map*, p. 132; Morgan, *Manners*, pp. 52–8.
119   [Stuart], *The Ladies' Monitor*, pp. 44–5.
120   Ibid., p. 26.
121   Ibid., pp. 16–17.
122   Majeed, *Ungoverned Imaginings*, p. 85.
123   [Stuart], *The Ladies' Monitor*, pp. 36–7.
124   Williamson, *The East India Vade-Mecum*, I, p. 501.
125   Ribeiro, *The Dress Worn at Masquerades*, p. 223.
126   See C. A. Bayly, *The Raj*, p. 110.
127   Ribeiro, *The Dress Worn at Masquerades*, p. 233.
128   Archer, *India and British Portraiture*, p. 88; Losty, *Calcutta*, p. 48; Dyson, *A Various Universe*, pp. 126–7.
129   V. Smith, 'Cleanliness', p. 163.
130   J. Johnson, *The Influence*, p. 426.
131   Yule and Burnell, *Hobson-Jobson*, p. 65. When Tom Raw calls on his CO he finds him dressed in *pyjama* trousers, smoking a hookah. Charles D'Oyly, reproduced in Stanford, *Ladies in the Sun*, facing p. 36.
132   Williamson, *The East India Vade-Mecum*, I, p. 501.
133   Ibid., II, p. 115.
134   See Shrimpton, 'Dressing for a tropical climate', p. 65.
135   Parks, *Wanderings*, I, pp. 286, 393; II, p. 329. Turkish dress was adopted by a few strong-minded British women throughout the nineteenth century as a signifier of their independence. See Macleod, 'Cross-cultural cross-dressing'.
136   See the analysis of *Hartly House, Calcutta* in Teltscher, *India Inscribed*, pp. 134–8.
137   See Leppert, *The Sight of Sound*, p. 95.
138   Spear, *The Nabobs*, p. 22.
139   Heber, *Narrative*, I, p. 591. See also Jacquemont, *Letters*, I, p. 398.
140   Spear does acknowledge that Indian washing practices found their way back to Britain through the influence that they had on Anglo-

Indians but does not emphasize the importance of this process. Spear, *The Nabobs*, p. 147.

141 'New barracks for the artillery at St. Thomas's Mount authorised and baths to be erected at all European hospitals', Board's Collections, File no. 5282, F/4/232, OIOC, pp. 18, 23.

142 'Lunatic Hospital, favourable reports on the state and management of', Board's Collections, File no. 7831, F/4/340, OIOC; 'Report on Captain Jekyll's vapour bath', Board's Collections, File no. 54568, F/4/1373, OIOC.

143 Mahomed, *Shampooing*, pp. 11–12. See also Reece, *The Medical Guide*, p. 170. For more on Mahomed see Fisher, *The First Indian Author*.

144 J. Johnson, *The Influence*, p. 470.

145 Ibid. p. 15.

146 Ibid. p. 445.

147 Tennant, *Indian Recreations*, I, p. 101.

148 Bellew, *Memoirs*, I, pp. 251–2.

149 C. Grant, *Anglo-Indian Domestic Life*, p. 79. See also Stuart Papers (CSAS), 28 November 1855.

150 Bushman and Bushman, 'The early history of cleanliness', p. 1220.

151 Wright, *Clean and Decent*, p. 138.

152 Reece, *The Medical Companion*, pp. 219–20.

153 Bathroom equipment featured strongly in the inventories of the period. See 'Sale book of the effects of the late Surgeon Charles Simon', 9 February 1825, Madras Inventories 1831, L/AG/24/27/263, OIOC; 'Anstruther Cheape Esq. Inventory and Accounts', Madras Inventories 1834, L/AG/34/27/271, OIOC; 'Inventory of the estate of Capt. J. A. Hepworth, deceased', Bengal Inventories 1830, L/AG/34/27/95, OIOC; 'Estate of John Bennet Esq. H. C. Civil Service', Bengal Inventories 1836, L/AG/34/27/112, OIOC; 'A true and perfect inventory of all and singular the goods and chattels and rights and credits of Thomas Lawrence late an assistant surgeon in the Military Service', Bombay Inventories 1831, L/AG/34/27/394, OIOC.

154 For the introduction of bathrooms into the British middle-class house see Dixon and Muthesius, *Victorian Architecture*, pp. 16, 32, 63.

155 Vigarello, *Concepts of Cleanliness*, p. 174.

156 [Stuart], *The Ladies' Monitor*, p. 198.

157 Williamson, *The East India Vade-Mecum*, II, p. 191.

158 Parks, *Wanderings*, I, p. 136; II, p. 501.

159 C. Grant, *Anglo-Indian Domestic Life*, pp. 82–3.

160 The increasing popularity of steam baths in Britain probably also made hair-washing more popular. Fanny Parks mentions that washing the hair is 'most agreeably performed in a *hummam* [steam bath]. Parks, *Wanderings*, II, p. 501.

161 *The Englishman*, 1 and 7 January 1920. The use of 'shampoo' to mean liquid soap is first recorded in 1866.

162 Dubois, *Description*, p. 108.

163 [Crosthwaite], *Ensign*, p. 125.
164 Maxwell Papers (CSAS), Boxes XI and XII/2, 11 February 1926.
165 Research on cleanliness and its significance for the middle classes in Britain is lacking. Virginia Smith's Ph.D. thesis deals with the development of the notion within hygiene literature but fails to link the development of the norm with class distinction and the development of the middle classes in the same way as Manuel Frey has done so adequately for Germany. Frey, *Der reinliche Bürger*; V. Smith, 'Cleanliness'.
166 The term is not used in Bhabha's sense of the word, which sees hybridity as a means by which the colonized can subvert colonial authority. Bhabha, *The Location*, pp. 112–16.
167 'I am of the opinion that the word *transculturation* better expresses the different phases of the process of transition from one culture to another because this does not consist merely in acquiring another culture, which is what the English word *acculturation* really implies, but the process also necessarily involves the loss or uprooting of a previous culture, which could be defined as deculturation. In addition it carries the idea of the consequent creation of new cultural phenomena, which could be called neoculturation. In the end, as the school of Malinowski's followers maintains, the result of every union of cultures is similar to that of the reproductive process between individuals: the offspring always has something of both parents but is always different from each of them.' Ortiz, *Cuban Counterpoint*, pp. 102–3.

Chapter 2   The Anglicization of the Body

1 See Headrick, *The Tools of Empire*, pp. 22, 130–8.
2 Stokes, *The English Utilitarians*, p. 35.
3 Metcalf, *Ideologies*, p. 39.
4 Philips, *The Correspondence*, I, p. xxx.
5 Stokes, *The English Utilitarians*, pp. 51–2.
6 C. A. Bayly, *Indian Society*, p. 122.
7 Low, *Lion Rampant*, p. 18.
8 Cohn, 'The British in Benares', p. 189.
9 Postans, *Hints*, pp. 14–15.
10 Spry, *Modern India*, I, pp. 122, 124.
11 Malcolm, 'Memorandum', p. 50. See also Kerr, *A Few Words*, pp. 54, 83; Postans, *Hints*, p. 26.
12 Stocqueler, *The Hand-book*, p. 50.
13 Fisher, 'The Resident', p. 432.
14 Ibid., p. 423.
15 Drewitt, *Bombay*, p. 61.
16 Ibid., pp. 58–64.
17 Spear, *Twilight of the Mughuls*, pp. 167–81. See also Prior et al., 'Bad Language'.
18 'Circular letter restricting the intercourse between Natives of Rank at the different Courts and British officers and the sale of property by the

latter to the former', Board's Collections, File no. 59576, F/4/1511, OIOC.

19 Spry, *Modern India*, II, p. 247.
20 Majeed, *Ungoverned Imaginings*, pp. 143–5; Zastoupil, *John Stuart Mill*, pp. 8–39.
21 Journal of R. N. Cust, Vol. I, p. 75.
22 Bradley, *The Call to Seriousness*, pp. 100, 109.
23 See C. A. Bayly, *Indian Society*, pp. 165–7; Shore, *Notes*, I, p. 20; Journal of James Fenn Clark (OIOC) /c, Vol. II, pp. 9, 14.
24 George Latham Papers (OIOC), p. 115.
25 Huggins, *Sketches*, p. 79. See also George Latham Papers (OIOC), p. 148; 'Indian affairs', *The Englishman*, 31 December 1834, p. 837.
26 Shore, *Notes*, II, p. 503.
27 Mukherjee, '"Satan let loose upon Earth"', p. 95.
28 Shore, *Notes*, I, p. 525; G. W. Johnson, *The Stranger*, II, p. 157; 'English life in Bengal', *The Calcutta Review*, 33 (1859), pp. 312–13; Briggs, *Letters*, p. 60.
29 Lunt, *From Sepoy to Subedar*, p. 26.
30 Shore, *Notes*, I, p. 10.
31 Brodie, *The Devil Drives*, p. 74.
32 [Henderson], *The Bengalee*, p. 329.
33 See Archer, *Company Paintings*, p. 36.
34 Shore, *Notes*, II, p. 112.
35 Chaudhary, *Imperial Honeymoon*, pp. 427–8. Removal of the shoes was a gesture of respect within Indian culture.
36 Gilchrist, *The General East India Guide*; Briggs, *Letters*.
37 Postans, *Hints*; Kerr, *A Few Words*.
38 Malcolm, 'Memorandum', p. 51.
39 Kerr, *A Few Words*, pp. 66–7.
40 Briggs, *Letters*, pp. 51–2; Kerr, *A Few Words*, pp. 55–7.
41 Shore, *Notes*, II, p. 108.
42 Shore, *Notes*, II, p. 119. Although in fact the poor gained little power from the changes instituted in the Reform Act and the middle class did not fully wrest power from the landed families who continued to dominate parliament until the 1880s. Wood, *Nineteenth Century Britain*, pp. 85–6.
43 Thackeray, *The Newcomes*, pp. 84–5.
44 Quennell, *Memoirs*, p. 250; Dodwell, *The Nabobs*, p. 183.
45 'The English in India', *The Calcutta Review*, 1 (1844), p. 32.
46 Blomfield, *Lahore to Lucknow*, p. 15. This change was noticeable in other colonies as well. In the Cape black broadcloth dominated by the 1850s. Ross, *Status and Respectability*, p. 87.
47 Blanchard, *Yesterday and Today*, p. 27.
48 For a more detailed discussion of changes in the suit see Harvey, *Men in Black*, pp. 130–4; Byrde, *The Male Image*, pp. 80–7.
49 Victor Jacquemont, cited by Losty, *Calcutta*, p. 105.
50 Kaye, *Peregrine Pultuney*, II, pp. 29–30.

51   Stocqueler, *The Hand-book*, p. 238.
52   'The English in India', *The Calcutta Review*, 1 (1844), p. 27.
53   In Indian representations of the British they are very often marked out by their black top hats. See for example, 'Panorama of a durbar procession of Akbar II, Emperor of Delhi', reproduced in C. A. Bayly, *The Raj*, p. 179.
54   Lyall Collection (OIOC), /3, 30 March 1857.
55   Berners Papers (CSAS), 11 May, 28 March, 1854, pp. 33, 35–6.
56   E. Roberts, *The East India Voyager*, p. 31.
57   Finch, '"Hooked and buttoned together"', p. 343. See also Perrot, *Fashioning*, p. 93. Minnie Wood assured her mother back in Britain, 'Dearest Mama, I attend strictly to all your advice, and I never leave off my stays.' Vansittart, *From Minnie*, p. 52.
58   See for example Hockley, *The English in India*, I, pp. 306–7.
59   J. Statham, cited by Hawes, *Poor Relations*, p. 82. For the importance of usefully occupying one's time within the evangelical moral code see Bradley, *The Call to Seriousness*, p. 25.
60   Chapman, *Hindoo Female Education*, p. 28.
61   E. Roberts, *The East India Voyager*, pp. 22–4.
62   Becher, *Personal Reminiscences*, p. 66.
63   Elias, *The Civilizing Process*, pp. 445–56.
64   Records, File nos 6, 18, 113, 116, 139, L/F/10, OIOC.
65   Edwardes, *Bound to Exile*, p. 12.
66   'List of European British subjects residing in the districts mentioned within', Board's Collections, File no. 54788, F/4/1374, OIOC.
67   Williamson, *The East India Vade-Mecum*, I, p. 453.
68   W. D. Arnold, *Oakfield*, p. 91.
69   Stocqueler, *The Hand-book*, p. 204; Day, *Hints*, pp. 32–3.
70   C. A. Bayly, *Indian Society*, pp. 75–6.
71   Fontaine, 'The civilising process', p. 247.
72   Castle, *Masquerade*, pp. 333–41.
73   Duden, *The Woman*, p. 15; Perrot, *Fashioning*, pp. 30–2; Roche, *The Culture of Clothing*, p. 58. In the 1840s men wore corsets and padding beneath their suits which moulded their bodies into the fashionable hour-glass shape. Kidwell and Steel, *Men and Women*, pp. 126–9.
74   Frederick John Shore Collection (OIOC), /5, 10 July 1828. Shore took advantage of the fact that he lived in a remote area to ignore the general trend and continued to wear 'Hindostanee' dress even though 'people tried to bully me about it.' A regulation of 1830 banning the wearing of Indian dress on public occasions by Company officials was directed at Shore, who even wore his Hindostanee dress in court. Cohn, 'Cloth, clothes and colonialism', p. 310.
75   Emma Roberts, cited by Losty, *Calcutta*, p. 98; Hawes, *Poor Relations*, p. 79. George Johnson wrote of the Eurasians: 'Their love of tinsel, and their mistake of the florid and bombastical for the appropriate, appear in their dress, in their language, and even in their children's names.' G. W. Johnson, *The Stranger*, I, p. 183.

76 Fenton, *The Journal*, p. 82.

77 *The Friend of India*, 29 January 1846.

78 See Mollo, *The Indian Army*, pp. 17–29, 55; Alavi, 'North Indian military culture', p. 183; C. A. Bayly, *The Raj*, pp. 167, 172.

79 See Beames, *Memoirs*, p. 81.

80 E. Roberts, *Scenes and Characteristics*, I, pp. 73–4.

81 V. Smith, 'Physical puritanism', p. 184.

82 Day, *Hints*, pp. 32–3.

83 Stocqueler, *The Hand-book*, p. 206.

84 'The growth of French cuisine in England owed much to the large numbers of immigrant French chefs who settled here in the late eighteenth and early nineteenth centuries.' J. Burnett, *Plenty and Want*, p. 60.

85 See Elias, *The Civilizing Process*, I, p. 99.

86 J. Burnett, *Plenty and Want*, pp. 54–9.

87 G. W. Johnson, *The Stranger in India*, I, p. 164.

88 Shore, *Notes*, II, p. 130. See also C. Grant, *Anglo-Indian Domestic Life*, pp. 39–45.

89 Cited by Berg, 'Manufacturing the orient', p. 413; Charlotte Grant, 'The visual culture', pp. 125–6.

90 On the improvement of techniques for preserving food, see Bitting, *Appertizing*.

91 E. Roberts, *Scenes and Characteristics*, I, p. 75.

92 Cited by Yalland, *Traders and Nabobs*, p. 67.

93 Burton, *The Raj at Table*, p. 161; Kennedy, *The Magic Mountains*, pp. 107, 110; Hockings, 'British society', p. 338.

94 Later on in the century Thomas La Touche 'wish[ed] for a good English apple' despite the abundance of 'very good' mangoes, pineapples and plantains. La Touche Collection (OIOC), /1, 8 May 1882.

95 This analysis of the significance of food draws on Douglas, 'Deciphering a meal'; Barthes, 'Toward a psychology'.

96 Campbell-Martin, *Out in the Midday Sun*, p. 52.

97 For more on kedgeree and curry see Burton, *The Raj at Table*, pp. 83–4, 74–6.

98 See 'A profound essay on bones', *The Englishman*, 2 October 1834, p. 348.

99 Williamson, *The East India Vade-Mecum*, I, p. 499.

100 The cheroot came to India from the Spanish Americas via Spain, and from there to Java in the 1650s from where it spread westwards to Burma and India. See Goodman, *Tobacco*, p. 88.

101 Blanchard, *Yesterday and Today*, p. 27.

102 'The English in India – our social morality', *The Calcutta Review*, 1 (1844), pp. 321–2.

103 Williamson, *The East India Vade-Mecum*, I, p. 412.

104 Ibid., I, pp. 456–7.

105 Stocqueler, *The Hand-book*, p. 49.

106 Hawes, *Poor Relations*, p. 18; Ballhatchet, *Race*, p. 144. It would seem that the practice of keeping an Indian mistress survived longer

within the army than among the civilian officials. See Brodie, *The Devil Drives*, pp. 51–2; Kerr, *A Few Words*, p. 83; Postans, *Hints*, p. 84; Lunt *From Sepoy to Subedar*, p. 26.

107   Brodie, *The Devil Drives*, p. 51.

108   C. A. Bayly, *Indian Society*, pp. 145–6. See also Chatterjee, *Gender, Slavery and Law*, pp. 24–7, who argues that the mistress was in effect a slave.

109   Cited by Hawes, *Poor Relations*, p. 9.

110   Spear, *The Nabobs*, pp. 140–1.

111   See Knapman, *White Women in Fiji*, pp. 4–17, 137–43, 175. Stoler, 'Carnal knowledge', pp. 64–71.

112   Mason, *Victorian Sexuality*, pp. 285–6.

113   James Kirkpatrick (Resident at Hyderabad 1798–1805) sent his son and daughter home to be cared for by his father, while Brian Hodgson, Resident at Nepaul (1834–43) entrusted the care of his 'poor brown children' to his sister in Britain although he had evidently been urged to abandon them. Kirkpatrick Collection (OIOC), /96(2); Papers of Brian Houghton Hodgson and his wife, p. 61.

114   Edmonstone Papers.

115   Fowke Manuscripts (OIOC), /F3, 18, letter 13. See also Hawes, *Poor Relations*, p. 4.

116   Fowke Manuscripts (OIOC), /F3, letter 15, 26 November 1782, f. 34.

117   Darton, *The Life and Times*, p. 309.

118   See Williamson, *The East India Vade-Mecum*, II, p. 216; Bellew, *Memoirs*, p. 123; D. Arnold, 'European orphans' pp. 107–13; Hawes, *Poor Relations*, pp. 10–11.

119   Spilsbury Collection (OIOC), /1, 24 October 1813.

120   See Mason, *Victorian Sexuality*, pp. 125–6; Tosh, *A Man's Place*, pp. 130–2.

121   Parks, *Wanderings*, I, p. 161. These were all forms of enjoyment of which strict evangelicals notoriously disapproved.

122   W. D. Arnold, *Oakfield*, I, p. 16.

123   Ibid., I, p. 57.

124   See Darton, *The Life and Times*, p. 252.

125   Neill, *A History of Christianity*, pp. 169–72.

126   Frederick John Shore Collection (OIOC), /5, 14 July 1827, p. 30. See also Sleeman, *Rambles*, II, p. 253.

127   Arnold commented that it was seen as a moral duty for an officer of a regiment to go to church but 'not to fear God or the devil'. W. D. Arnold, *Oakfield*, I, p. 242.

128   Stocqueler, *The Hand-book*, pp. 225–6.

129   Williamson, *The East India Vade-Mecum*, I, pp. 116, 165. Stocqueler, *The Hand-book*, p. 226.

130   G. W. Johnson, *The Stranger*, I, p. 273. See also Beames, *Memoirs*, p. 83.

131   Lunt, *From Sepoy to Subedar*, p. 24.

132 Douglas, *Natural Symbols*, p. xxxii.
133 Lind, *An Essay on Diseases*, p. 171.
134 See for example Ainslie, *Medical, Geographical, and Agricultural Report*; Rankine, *Notes*; Irvine, *Some Account*. These medico-topographical surveys formed part of a larger body of texts which described and defined India, fixing it in the European mind. India was in this way brought within the sphere of European knowledge, and in many ways the collection of medical information was an end in itself in that it helped the British to define the country which they found themselves ruling. The extraordinary nature of disease in the tropics also helped to carve out a special place for Company physicians within the developing medical profession as experts in a specific branch of medicine. See D. Arnold, *Colonizing the Body*, p. 30.
135 Curtin, *Death by Migration*, p. 46.
136 Spry, *Modern India*, II, p. 30.
137 See for example Sherwood, *The History of Little Lucy*, p. 128.
138 See M. Harrison, *Climates and Constitutions*, p. 124.
139 W. Anderson, 'Climates of opinion'; Livingstone, 'Human acclimatisation', p. 388.
140 M. Harrison, *Public Health*, p. 47. For example John McCosh identified filthy habits, scanty clothing, bad diet and poor quality of drinking water as the causes of disease among the natives. McCosh, *Medical Advice*, pp. 116–36.
141 Spry, *Modern India*, II, p. 98. See also Boileau, *Personal Narrative*, p. 24.
142 'Few Europeans know anything of the native portion of great Indian cities, although they may live for months and years in their vicinity.' *Autobiography of an Indian Army Surgeon*, p. 194.
143 Rankine, *Notes*, p. 47.
144 'Calcutta, like most other oriental towns, contains two quarters – the well-built, cleanly-kept, broad-streeted European quarter, and the ill-built, filthy, narrow-passaged native town.' Knighton, *Tropical Sketches*, I, p. 146.
145 [Monkland], *Life in India*, II, p. 125.
146 A similar anglicization of the landscape occurred in the Cape, where Grahamstown was a miniature representation of England. Ross, *Status and Respectability*, p. 79.
147 Rankine, *Notes*, p. 51.
148 E. Roberts, *The East India Voyager*, p. 27.
149 D. Arnold, *Colonizing the Body*, p. 42.
150 See J. O. Walker to James McAdam, 'Reports on the climate of the Mahabaleshwar Hills', Board's Collections, File no. 53003, F/4/1337, OIOC, pp. 33, 90–114; see also 'Proceedings relating to the sanatorium at Cherranpoonjee in the Copya Hills', Board's Collections, File nos 56964 and 56965, F/4/1448 and F/4/1449, OIOC.
151 *The Friend of India*, 14 May 1846; 'School at Cherranpoonjee', *The Englishman*, 11 October 1834, p. 281.

152   *The Englishman*, 3 March 1834, p. 2.
153   'Capt. Gowan's suggestion for a convalescent hospital for European soldiers', Board's Collections, File no. 19634, F/4/724, OIOC.
154   Kennedy, *The Magic Mountains*, pp. 27–8.
155   'The Sick Room in India,' *The Calcutta Review*, 3 (1845), p. 81.
156   *Forbes East India and Colonial Guide*, p. 32.
157   Bruce Papers (CSAS), Vol. I, 1894, p. 72. See also Lyttleton, *How to Pack*, p. 19.
158   Renbourne, 'The history of the flannel binder', p. 217.
159   See Watson Collection (OIOC), /23, 21 May 1922; Westmacott Papers (OIOC), p. 79; Godden, *Two*, p. 94; Hogg, *Practical Remarks*, p. iii.
160   Chapman Papers (CSAS), p. 4.
161   Moore, *A Manual*, p. 645; Baden-Powell, *Indian Memories*, p. 184.
162   Renbourne, 'Life and death', pp. 207–8.
163   Parks, *Wanderings*, I, p. 286.
164   'On hats', *The Meerut Universal Magazine*, 2, 6 (1836), pp. 187–8. The article goes on to give advice on how to plant the topi on your head and how to lift it when saluting a lady. George Johnson, commenting on cricket in Calcutta, remarked that 'the field exhibits no peculiar feature to the eye of an English freshman, but the universally-worn white hats, with very broad brims, made of a vegetable pith, called sola, which is far lighter than cork, and an admirable non-conductor of heat.' G. W. Johnson, *The Stranger*, II, p. 62.
165   Jeffreys, *The British Army*, p. 14.
166   Ibid., pp. 55–69; 107–11.
167   See Lawrence, *Indian Embers*, p. 81; William Robert Millar, 'Indian letters, 1874–5', 25 February 1875.
168   Skrine Collection (OIOC), /1, 26 November 1912.
169   Louise Ouwekerk, a schoolteacher in Trivandrum in the 1920s, wrote of the 'Eurasians, poor pathetic scraps who wear topees in the pretence that they are real Europeans'. Ouwekerk Collection (OIOC), /60, 24 August 1929. Tarlo, *Clothing Matters*, p. 70.
170   Hull and Mair, *The European*, pp. 64–5.
171   Bruce Papers (CSAS), Vol. I. 1894, p. 33. See also Moore, *A Manual of Family Medicine*, p. 645.
172   Martin, *The Influence*; Birch, *The Management*; Goodeve, *Hints*; Green, and Green-Armytage, *Birch's Management*.
173   M. Harrison, *Public Health*, p. 53. For the dissatisfactions and disadvantages of the surgeon's position in India see Norman Chevers, 'Surgeons in India – past and present', *The Calcutta Review*, 23 (1854), pp. 217–54.
174   Kennedy, 'Climatic theories', p. 50.
175   For a discussion of the way in which regimen harmonized with a particular middle-class view of society in Britain see Cooter, 'The power of the body'.

Chapter 3   The Limits of Anglicization

1   See Castle, *Masquerade*, pp. 334–5.
2   Reproduced in Archer, *India and British Portraiture*, p. 136.
3   Darton, *The Life and Times*, p. 366.
4   For children's dress in Britain see Ewing, *Dress and Undress*, p. 53.
5   MacFarlan Collection (OIOC), Mary Ann MacFarlan's diary, June 1834, p. 6.
6   See Darton, *The Life and Times*, p. 365.
7   For the decline of wet-nurses in Britain see Lewis, *In the Family Way*, pp. 195, 209; Fildes, *Breasts*, p. 182; Fildes, *Wet Nursing*, p. 204.
8   For the relationship between the wet-nurse and her employer in Britain see A. Roberts, 'Mothers and babies', p. 286; Fildes, *Wet Nursing*, p. 194.
9   Darton, *The Life and Times*, p. 295.
10   Thornhill Collection (OIOC), /1, 25 November 1854.
11   See Lady, *The Englishwoman*, p. 97; Solomon, *The Indian Family Doctor*, pp. 327–30; Medical Practitioner, *A Domestic Guide*, pp. 71–5.
12   Yalland, *Boxwallahs*, p. 123.
13   A. Roberts, 'Mothers and babies', p. 292; Berridge and Edwards, *Opium*, pp. 97–104.
14   Spilsbury Collection (OIOC), /1 October 1821.
15   Berners Papers (CSAS), 9 December 1856, p. 117.
16   Gilchrist, *A Dictionary*, I, p. xxxii; Hunt and Kenny, *Tropical Trials*, p. 391.
17   Lutyens, *The Lyttons*, pp. 52, 89.
18   Lyall Collection (OIOC), /4, 15 July 1866.
19   A further contradiction was that while the British condemned infanticide, by employing a wet-nurse they implicitly condoned the neglect of the wet-nurse's own child, which generally died. Dyson, *A Various Universe*, pp. 174–5.
20   'Miscellaneous notes', *The Calcutta Review*, 1 (1844), p. 568.
21   Medical Practitioner, *A Domestic Guide*, p. 49.
22   Darton, *The Life and Times*, p. 300.
23   Sherwood, *The History of Little Henry*, p. 14.
24   Williamson, *The East India Vade-Mecum*, I, p. 341. These anxieties persisted well into the twentieth century. See Hart, *Everyday Life*, pp. 78–9; Diver, *The Englishwoman*, p. 36.
25   E. Roberts, *Scenes and Characteristics*, I, p. 333; See also Stuart Papers, (CSAS) 4 January 1855; Berners Papers (CSAS), 12 June 1854, p. 40; Chaudhuri, 'Memsahibs and motherhood', pp. 531–2.
26   C. Grant, *Anglo-Indian Domestic Life*, p. 114.
27   For childhood in India in the twentieth century see Allen, *Plain Tales*, pp. 21–36.
28   Berners Papers (CSAS), 18 June 1855, p. 77.

29 Cited in Allen, *Plain Tales*, p. 26.
30 Burnett, *The Secret Garden*, pp. 7, 26–7, 30. Mrs Sherwood has left a very good portrait of a wilful Anglo-Indian child in her description of Miss Louisa, see Darton, *The Life and Times*, pp. 365–6.
31 Lyall Collection (OIOC), /4, 5 January 1865, p. 95.
32 Lady, *The Englishwoman*, p. 99; Campbell, *Excursions*, pp. 256–7.
33 Becher, *Personal Reminiscences*, p. 90.
34 [Monkland], *The Nabob*, I, p. 90.
35 Girouard, *The Victorian Country House*, p. 28. For a discussion of the middle-class separation of public and private and the way in which this was reflected in the home see Davidoff and Hall, *Family Fortunes*, pp. 357–69, 375–80; Davidoff and Hall, 'The architecture of public and private life'. For the structural layout of the home see Barley, *The House and Home*; J. Burnett, *A Social History of Housing*, pp. 104–11. For the layout of the bungalow in India see Pott, *Old Bungalows*.
36 E. Roberts, *Scenes and Characteristics*, I, p. 319.
37 Ibid., pp. 319–22.
38 Berners Papers (CSAS), 6 April 1857, p. 126. See also Hull and Mair, *The European*, p. 131.
39 Thornhill Collection (OIOC), /12, March 1867 (Ellen).
40 Darton, *The Life and Times*, p. 367. See also Mitchell, *In India*, p. 80.
41 Berners Papers (CSAS), 21 October 1855, p. 92. See also 'The English in India – our social morality', *The Calcutta Review*, 1 (1844), p. 333; Sleeman, *Rambles*, II, p. 255.
42 Tytler, *An Englishwoman*, pp. 32–3.
43 Davidoff and Hall, *Family Fortunes*, pp. 388–96.
44 E. Roberts, *Scenes and Characteristics*, I, pp. 7–8.
45 Charlotte Canning, cited by Hibbert, *The Great Mutiny*, p. 27. Henry Bruce affirmed that this created a sense of unease: 'Servants are generally not far off, and though they are apt to be absent at the critical moment, you are more likely to be troubled by a vague sense of "somebody always there".' Bruce, *The Native Wife*, p. 18.
46 Meaning 'Is there anyone?' This system for calling servants led to old Anglo-Indians being labelled 'Qui hys'.
47 Shore, *Notes*, II, p. 513.
48 Frederick John Shore Collection (OIOC), /5, 23 December 1833.
49 Robbins, *The Servant's Hand*, p. 109.
50 Ross, *Status and Respectability*, pp. 80–1.
51 G. W. Johnson, *The Stranger*, I, p. 29. See also *English Homes*, I, p. 117.
52 E. Roberts, *The East India Voyager*, p. 32.
53 Isaac, *The Transformation of Virginia*, pp. 34–42.
54 The blurring of lines between family and servants was not unfamiliar in some households in Britain, for example the homes of farmers, where even into the nineteenth century the servants dined and whiled away their leisure hours in the company of the family.
55 Berners Papers (CSAS), 15 November 1854, p. 53.
56 Datta, 'The Europeans of Calcutta', p. 212.

57   Maxwell Papers (CSAS), Box XVII, 21 March 1926.
58   'You can do very little in one day in India, *for this cause* that you can hardly *do anything* for *yourself*, and whatever you must perform through the medium of a native is both loss of time and wreck of patience.' Fenton, *The Journal*, pp. 20–1.
59   Kaye, *Peregrine Pultuney*, II, p. 141.
60   Heber, *Narrative*, I, pp. 3–4.
61   Parks, *Wanderings*, I, p. 231; Graham, *Journal*, p. 2; Drewitt, *Bombay*, p. 78.
62   Darton, *The Life and Times*, p. 361.
63   Gilchrist, *Dialogues*, pp. 130–3. See also Carey, *Dialogues*.
64   See Cohn, 'The command of language'.
65   Shore, *Notes*, I, p. 11.
66   Lyall Collection (OIOC), /2, Good Friday 1858.
67   Carey, *Dialogues*, p. 25; Gilchrist, *Dialogues*, p. 154.
68   Cordiner, *A Voyage*, pp. 124–5.
69   'Chum' meant that they shared a house. Spilsbury Collection (OIOC), /1, July 1813.
70   Drewitt, *Bombay*, p. 72.
71   See for example the case of Mr Smith and his *dhaye* in *The Englishman*, 7 June 1834, p. 2.
72   Darton, *The Life and Times*, pp. 264–5.
73   Trevelyan, *The Competition Wallah*, p. 119. Other incidences of such treatment of the lower orders are given by Thomas Williamson, who advised that when dealing with *dandies* 'recourse to the manual' might sometimes be effectual although it should be handled with care. Williamson, *The East India Vade-Mecum*, II, p. 375; Henry Spry recounted how 'a sharp application of the back of a sword soon brought' his palankeen bearers 'to their senses' when they refused to travel further that day. Spry, *Modern India*, I, p. 52.
74   For incidences of physical abuse of servants in Britain see Gerard, *Country House Life*, p. 254; Horn, *The Rise and Fall*, pp. 118–21.
75   Later on Mrs Sherwood asserted that 'the English in India are universally kind masters.' Darton, *The Life and Times*, pp. 264–5. This may in part have been a transference of British attitudes, sharpened by racism in the colonial context. In Britain 'the master and servant laws ... extend[ed] to the master every assistance in disciplining and controlling servants who perversely refused to behave in a properly obedient fashion.' Tholfsen, *Working Class Radicalism*, p. 180.
76   In Britain the realization of a need to conciliate the lower classes, combined with an overall trend towards decreasing interpersonal violence, resulted in a decline in physical attacks on domestic servants as the nineteenth century progressed. See Gatrell, 'The decline of theft and violence'.
77   *The Englishman* was full of letters of complaint about the abolition of flogging. For example, 2 March 1835, p. 411; 4 March 1835, p. 431; 15 April 1835, p. 716; 30 April 1835, p. 818.

78 Stocqueler, *The Hand-book*, p. 198. George Parbury warned: 'Your treatment of your servants is worthy of attention. It is a common practice to beat and abuse them if they appear the least stupid or awkward. Do neither, but get rid of them as soon as you can.' Parbury, *Handbook*, p. 327.
79 Briggs, *Letters*, pp. 54–5.
80 Shore, *Notes*, II, p. 320.
81 C. A. Bayly, *Indian Society*, p. 134.
82 Cited by Mukherjee, ' "Satan let loose" ', p. 112.
83 Dawson, 'The imperial adventure hero', p. 49.
84 'A narrative of the late massacre at Segowlee', Letters and Papers Relating to the Indian Mutiny, ff. 49–51.
85 See C. A. Bayly, *Indian Society*, pp. 169–94.
86 Tytler, *An Englishwoman*, pp. 57–8; Parks, *Wanderings*, I, p. 76. Sleeman, *Rambles*, p. 3.
87 Cited by Dawson, 'The imperial adventure hero', p. 49. 'We have been so insulted and degraded in the eyes of natives by the violation and murder of our women, that nothing but extreme vengeance can restore our prestige.' Lyall Collection (OIOC), /3, 29 December 1857.
88 See Muir, *Records of the Intelligence Department*.
89 The revenge the British took was extremely brutal. Indians suspected of being rebels were hung and shot from cannon, often without proper trial.
90 'The story of Mrs Goldeney's escape' (OIOC), pp. 47–9.
91 Case, *Day by Day*, p. 124.
92 Rees, *A Personal Narrative*, p. 141.
93 Thornhill, *The Personal Adventures*, pp. 172, 174, 220; Case, *Day by Day*, pp. 61, 66–7.
94 Hibbert, *The Great Mutiny*, p. 164.
95 Cited by Robinson, *Angels of Albion*, p. 181. See also 'The story of Miss Sutherland', Letters and Papers Relating to the Indian Mutiny, f. 96.
96 See Metcalf, *The Aftermath*, which perhaps overstates the importance of the Mutiny.
97 Ibid., p. 324.
98 Wonnacott Collection (OIOC), /3, 5 August 1871; Beames *Memoirs*, p. 93.

Chapter 4   The Sahib as an Instrument of Rule

1 Even before the Mutiny it was clear that the life of the East India Company was limited, and the change was made to prevent the Directors' powers of patronage being transferred to the British government.
2 'Competition-wallah: Applied in modern Anglo-Indian colloquial to members of the Civil Service who have entered into it by the competitive system. ... The phrase was probably the invention of one of the older or Haileybury members of the same service. These latter, whose

nominations were due to interest, and who were bound together by the intimacies and *esprit de corps* of a common college, looked with some disfavour upon the Children of Innovation.' Yule and Burnell, *Hobson-Jobson*, p. 239.

3   Birdwood, *Competition*, p. 9.

4   *Papers Relating to the Selection and Training of Candidates*, p. 33.

5   J. Fergusson, L. R. Ashburne, E. W. Ravenscroft to the Secretary of State, August 1882, File no. 1480, L/P&J/6/81, OIOC.

6   'Précis of correspondence between the Secretary of State and the Government of India, Madras and Bombay as to physical robustness of civil servants', File no. 411, L/P&J/6/119, OIOC; 'Civil Service of India. First periodical examination of candidates selected', June 1883, File no. 1018, L/P&J/6/126, OIOC.

7   Lodwick, *John Bolt*, I, p. 3. The wildness of old Haileyburians is affirmed by the Records of the East India College. See for example 'Statement addressed to the Court of Directors by J. C. Colebrooke Sutherland, 24 November 1809, The Records, East India College, Haileybury, file no. 509, J/I/24, OIOC. See also Keene, *A Servant*, p. 2.

8   Metcalf, *The Aftermath*, pp. 250–2.

9   'Typical civilians', *The Englishman*, 22 February 1870, p. 2.

10   M. Monier-Williams, cited by Danvers, *Memorials*, p. 87.

11   Lodwick, *John Bolt*, I, p. 3.

12   Birdwood, *Competition*, p. 16.

13   See Gowan, 'The origins', pp. 18–19; B. B. Misra, *The Bureaucracy* p. 98.

14   Dewey, 'The education', p. 271; B. B. Misra, *The Bureaucracy*, pp. 102–3.

15   B. B. Misra, *The Bureaucracy*, p. 105.

16   Compton, 'Open competition', pp. 281–2.

17   Rubinstein, *Elites and the Wealthy*, pp. 187–97. In fact the sons of professionals and clergymen made up the majority of recruits. Sixty-seven per cent of recruits between 1858 and 1897 came from professional families, one quarter of recruits between 1854 and 1876 were from clergymen's families. Dewey, 'The education', p. 283; Compton, 'Open competition', pp. 281–3.

18   'The Indian Civil Service as a career for University men', *The Oxford and Cambridge Undergraduate's Journal*, 7 December 1882, p. 149.

19   From *The Times* in 'Covenanted civil service. Physical and mental efficiency of members selected by open competition', File no. 45, L/P&J/6/89, OIOC. See also 'Cram and crash', *Punch*, 25 December 1882, p. 292.

20   Young, 'Virtue domesticated', pp. 485–8.

21   Taylor, *Seeta*, I, p. 146.

22   Cassidy, *Social Intercourse*, p. 5.

23   Lorimer, *Colour, Class*, p. 107.

24   Birdwood, *Competition*, p. 10.

25   Bourdieu, 'Sport and social class', p. 826.

26   Brown, *Modern India*, p. 141.

27   This view was truly hegemonic in the sense that some sections of the Indian middle classes accepted this image of themselves. The late nineteenth-century Indian physical education movement identified intense study as a source of 'brain fever, and indigestion' as well as physical atrophy, which it sought to remedy through exercise. See Rosselli, 'The self-image of effeteness', p. 124.

28   B. B. Misra, *The Bureaucracy*, p. 110; Sinha, *Colonial Masculinity*, pp. 105–6.

29   Stocking, *Victorian Anthropology*, pp. 63–4.

30   Bates, 'Race, caste and tribe', p. 239. See also McKenzie, '"The laboratory of mankind"', p. 114; Pinney, 'Colonial anthropology'.

31   Beddoe, 'On the stature and bulk of man'; S. Bayly, 'Caste, and "race"', pp. 171–2; Szreter, *Fertility, Class and Gender*, p. 130; Searle, 'Eugenics and class' p. 234; Rich, *Race and Empire*, p. 18.

32   See Pick, *Faces of Degeneration*, pp. 176–221; Searle, *Eugenics and Politics*, pp. 20–7.

33   Pike, 'On the physical characteristics', pp. 156–8, 164, 168–9. In fact Pike, as an anti-German, was arguing that these qualities were inherited from the ancient Greeks and that the English were more closely related to the Celts than the Saxons. This does not alter the argument as he was trying to reallocate the origin of what were widely held to be Anglo-Saxon qualities. See also MacDougall, *Racial Myth*, pp. 92–3.

34   The extent to which nineteenth-century thought about character was infused with ideas about race is demonstrated by H. G. Keene's characterization of Wellington (born in Ireland): 'Wellington was distinctly Saxon, or Anglo-Norman, and he had naturally no Celtic sympathies.' Keene, *A Servant*, p. 40.

35   G. Jones, *Social Darwinism*, pp. 142–4.

36   Vogt, *Lectures on Man*, pp. 426–7.

37   Taylor, *Seeta*, I, pp. 143–5. For a discussion of the pseudo-science of physiognomy see Cowling, *The Artist*, pp. 8–39.

38   Rivett-Carnac, *Many Memories*, p. 75; Keene, *A Servant*, p. 71. See also Lytton Collection (OIOC), /18, Letters Despatched, 1876, Vol. I, 14 April 1876, and Charles MacGregor, who peppered his diary with comments on the physique of his companions. Trousdale, *War in Afghanistan*.

39   The Amendment made all homosexual acts illegal. Weeks, *Sex*, p. 103.

40   Tosh, *A Man's Place*, p. 151.

41   See Haley, *The Healthy Body*, pp. 123–40; Mangan, *Athleticism*, pp. 136–8.

42   Fowke Manuscripts (OIOC), /3, 26 November 1782, letter 15, f. 35.

43   See for example, Baden-Powell, *Pigsticking*; Braddon, *Thirty Years of Shikar*; Carpenter, *Hog Hunting*; Maconochie, *Life in the Indian Civil Service;* Brown, *Shikar Sketches*; Dunlop, *Hunting in the Himalaya*; Newall, *Scottish Moors and Indian Jungles*; *Sketches and Scenes in India*. Women joined in the hunting craze as well, see Tyacke, *How I Shot My Bears*.

44 Trevelyan, *The Competition Wallah*, p. 161.
45 Baden-Powell, *Pigsticking*, pp. 111–12.
46 For more detailed discussion of hunting see Bennett, 'Shikar and the Raj'; MacKenzie, *The Empire of Nature*; MacKenzie, 'Chivalry', pp. 98–114.
47 C. E. Buckland mocked a Bengali civilian who was known to have requested to be transferred from a station with 'excellent snipe shooting and a great opportunity for pig-sticking'. Cited by Sinha, *Colonial Masculinity*, p. 42.
48 Baden-Powell, *Pigsticking*, pp. 5–6.
49 'The competition system and the Indian Civil Service', *The Calcutta Review*, 40 (1864), p. 18. Reginald Maxwell found that after shooting his first panther he was 'regarded as a public benefactor by the village of Navalur'. Maxwell Papers (CSAS), Box XVII, 26 March 1907.
50 Perrin, *The Anglo-Indians*, p. 105. Prince Albert was also said to reveal his cowardly German nature in his unsportsmanlike love of shooting animals as they were driven past a platform. Weintraub, *Albert*, pp. 165–6. See Pandian, 'Gendered negotiations' for a discussion of the hierarchy of hunting among the British, and the tensions caused by skilful and manly hunting on the part of Indians.
51 For the cost of hunting in Britain see F. M. L. Thompson, *English Landed Society*, pp. 97, 138, 146.
52 Cowling, *The Artist*, pp. 161–3.
53 'The Indian Civil Service. *The Times* 1855', *The Calcutta Review*, 27 (1856), p. 358.
54 B. B. Misra, *The Bureaucracy*, pp. 283–4.
55 Ibid., p. 284.
56 Ibid., p. 291.
57 Hyde Papers (CSAS), ff. 119, 106.
58 Horne, *Work and Sport*, p. 280.
59 J. C. Scott, *Domination*, p. 12.
60 Edward Ward Walter Raleigh Papers (OIOC), pp. 29, 51.
61 Eden, *Up the Country*, p. 27.
62 Here I differ from Bernard Cohn who argues that the British misinterpreted the mystical aspects of the durbar and saw it simply as a symbol of a contractual relationship. Cohn, 'Representing authority', p. 169.
63 Fane, *Five Years*, p. 262.
64 Cohn, 'Representing authority', pp. 179–83. For a more detailed discussion of the British redefinition of their role in India see Inden, *Imagining India*, pp. 180–5.
65 Cohn, 'Representing authority', p. 208.
66 Bell, *Ritual Theory*, p. 211; Haynes, 'Imperial ritual', p. 497.
67 Maynard Collection (OIOC), /1, 22 February 1888.
68 Humphrey and Laidlow, *The Archetypal Actions*, p. 2. 'The formalization of ritual often appears to involve a distancing within actors of their private and social identities.' Bell, *Ritual Theory*, p. 216.
69 Nuckolls, 'The durbar incident', p. 530.

70 Maxwell Papers (CSAS), Box XVII, 24 November 1921.
71 Cohn, 'Representing authority', pp. 191, 196–7, 200, 208.
72 Cannadine, *Aspects of Aristocracy*, pp. 77–108; Cannadine, 'The context, performance and meaning', p. 120.
73 Trevithick, 'Some structural and sequential aspects', pp. 563, 567; Cannadine, *Aspects of Aristocracy*, p. 90.
74 Maynard Collection (OIOC), /1, 27 December, 1902.
75 'Reference paper, referred to the Secretary in the Political Department', 5 July 1880, File no. 922, L/P&J/6/16, OIOC.
76 'Minute by the Viceroy. State ceremonial and costume in India', 8 August 1879, File no. 922, L/P&J/6/16, OIOC.
77 Massy Collection, p. 18.
78 'Minute by the Viceroy. State ceremonial and costume in India', 8 August 1879, File no. 922, L/P&J/6/16, OIOC.
79 Cox, *My Thirty Years*, p. 13.
80 Haynes, 'Imperial ritual', p. 494.
81 See for example Cox, *My Thirty Years*, p. 13.
82 Haynes, *Rhetoric and Ritual*, p. 132.
83 Elsmie, *Thirty-five Years*, p. 102.
84 Haynes, *Rhetoric and Ritual*, p. 128.
85 'For [Curzon] . . . great ceremonials were "pages of history", "chapters in the ritual of state".' Cannadine, *Aspects of Aristocracy*, p. 83.
86 Cannadine, 'The context, performance and meaning', pp. 124, 126; Cannadine, *Aspects of Aristocracy*, p. 77.
87 Trevithick, 'Some structural and sequential aspects', pp. 575, 577.
88 Bell, *Ritual Theory*, p. 190.
89 Ibid., p. 194. Trevithick, 'Some structural and sequential aspects', pp. 561–2.
90 Haynes, 'Imperial ritual', pp. 500, 510.
91 Ibid., p. 518.
92 See for example *The Times of India*, 1, 2 and 4 December 1911; *The Leader*, 2, 5 and 6 December 1911; *The Leader*, 17, 21 November 1921, 19 March 1922.
93 Watson Collection (OIOC), /23, 29 November 1921. Mountbatten, who accompanied the Prince as his ADC, noted the lukewarm reception he received around India. Ziegler, *The Diaries*, pp. 199, 210–14, 224, 229, 237.
94 Maxwell Papers (CSAS), Box XVII, 23 November 1925.
95 W. H. S. Smith, *A Young Man's Country*, pp. 11, 17–19, 21, 69–72.
96 Maxwell Papers (CSAS), Box XVII, 7 June 1926.
97 B. B. Misra, *The Bureaucracy*, p. 347.
98 Cannadine, *Aspects of Aristocracy*, p. 90.
99 Haynes, 'Imperial ritual', p. 518.
100 Fisher, 'The Resident', pp. 420, 447; C. A. Bayly, *The Local Roots*, p. 41.
101 See Searle, *The Quest*, pp. 30–1.
102 Inden, *Imagining India*, pp. 180–4.

103 See Brown, *Modern India*, pp. 95, 101–2, 136; Bates, 'Race, caste and tribe', pp. 229–30.

104 Searle, *The Quest*, p. 96. See also Harris, *Private Lives*, pp. 12, 201–8.

105 B. B. Misra, *The Bureaucracy*, p. 91; Metcalf, *The Aftermath*, pp. 254–5.

106 Lyall Collection (OIOC), /4, 1 March 1863, p. 18.

107 Birdwood, *Competition*, p. 9.

108 Sir Walter Roper Lawrence Collection (OIOC), /10, 6 January 1880. See also Elsmie, *Thirty-five Years*, p. 46; Wilson, *After Five Years*, pp. 14–41; Hyde Papers (CSAS), 15 March 1933, p. 102; Braddon, *Thirty Years of Shikar*, pp. 147–8; W. H. S. Smith, *A Young Man's Country*, pp. 20, 27, 54, 62–3.

109 Knight Papers (CSAS), Miscellaneous documents, f. 19; A. B., *A Romance*, p. 2.

110 See Foucault, *Discipline*.

111 Beames, *Memoirs*, p. 225.

112 P. Mason, *A Shaft of Sunlight*, p. 102.

113 Ibid., pp. 103–4.

114 See Edwardes, *High Noon*, pp. 51–2, 80–2; Gilmour, *Curzon*, pp. 153–4, 160.

115 W. H. S. Smith, *A Young Man's Country*, p. 15.

116 B. B. Misra, *The Bureaucracy*, p. 389.

117 J. C. Scott, *Domination*, p. 11.

118 Woolf, *An Autobiography*, p. 143.

119 This discussion is based on Erving Goffman's definition of a 'front' as 'that part of an individual's performance which regularly functions in a general and fixed fashion to define the situation for those who observe the performance'. This is not meant to imply that the front of prestige was static: each individual not only contributed to its construction but also helped to change its shape. Goffman, *The Presentation of Self*, pp. 2, 34, 37.

120 Beames, *Memoirs*, pp. 94–5.

121 John Kaye, cited by Wurgaft, *The Imperial Imagination*, p. 96.

122 Hoey, *'Going East'*, p. 22.

123 Greenberger, *The British Image of India*, p. 29. See also N. Burke, 'The Raj', p. 14.

124 P. Mason, *A Shaft of Sunlight*, p. 97.

125 Cohn, 'Cloth, clothes and colonialism', pp. 347–8.

126 *The Englishman*, 25 April 1871, p. 2; *The Englishman*, 21 July 1871, p. 2.

127 Gay, *The Cultivation of Hatred*, p. 86.

128 Snell, 'Deferential bitterness', p. 165. J. C. Scott, *Weapons of the Weak*, pp. 284–9.

129 Eastwick, *Autobiography of Lutfulah*, pp. 41–2.

130 Cassidy, *Social Intercourse*, p. 3. Violence was a commonplace of most colonial societies. See Hansen, *Distant Companions*, p. 50.

131　Blanchard, *Yesterday and Today*, p. 152. For reports on Europeans assaulting their servants see *The Englishman*, 7, 14 January, 26 March, 18 May, 27 July, 8 September 1870; 23 March 1871.

132　On planters see, for example, Stobie, 'An incident of real life in Bengal', *The Fortnightly Review*, 17 (1887), 329–41. On the army see Julius, *Notes on Striking Natives*; Ex-Civilian, *Life in the Mofussil*, I, pp. 76–7.

133　Particularly outrageous is the case of Mr C. Webb, Agent of the India General Steam Navigation Company, who was fined Rs 100 for raping, and thereby causing the death of, a coolie woman. Sanyal, *Record of Criminal Cases*, pp. 25–40.

134　'Return showing the number of assaults committed by Europeans on natives and by natives on Europeans in the five years 1901–1905', File no. 3445, L/P&J/6/781, OIOC. For example: 'Assault by Mr A. L. Juckes, manager of the Sephinjiri tea garden, on a village postman, who was distributing letters among the coolies and so interrupting their work. The man is said to have been kicked and afterwards shut up for sometime in the garden office. The postman would not prosecute. Private Ryan, Royal Inniskilling Fusiliers, charged with striking a native sweeper. The assault was serious, three of the man's ribs were broken. Tried by district court-martial and acquitted.' Cases 7 and 175 for 1901.

135　Dilks, *Curzon*, I, pp. 198–200. For Lytton's attempts to impose harsher sentences on violent Europeans see Lutyens, *The Lyttons*, pp. 34–6.

136　See 'Corporal punishment in India'. Minute paper. File no. 10, L/P&J/6/16, OIOC; Cotton, Sir Henry, 'Corporal punishment in India', *The Humane Review*, 6 (1906), 215–21; Chakravati, Hiralal, 'Whipping in India', *The Humane Review*, 9 (1908), 172–82. For a description of such a punishment see Hunt and Harrison, *The District Officer*, p. 62.

137　Beames, *Memoirs*, p. 102.

138　'A civil servant in trouble', *The Englishman*, 5 November 1870.

139　*The Englishman*, 30 January, 1865.

140　See Maynard Collection (OIOC), /1, 1 May 1887. See also Sanyal, *Record of Criminal Cases*, p. 99.

141　Witness the horrified British reaction to the murder of a rickshaw coolie in Simla in 1925, by a drunken army officer who kicked him to death. Kanwar, *Imperial Simla*, pp. 173–6.

142　See Trevelyan, *The Competition Wallah*, p. 26, Chapman Collection (OIOC), /185, 1 January, 1846.

143　Satow and Ray, *Railways*, p. 36. See also Stokes Papers (CSAS), Box 3, 29 December 1921.

144　Cox, *My Thirty Years*, p. 11. 'All Europeans, excepting soldiers, artisans, etc., are expected to travel first-class.' Hull and Mair, *The European*, p. 141.

145 'The Serampore trains', *The Englishman*, 12 March 1870, p. 2. In 1865 a correspondent complained that ladies had to 'endure the impudent stare of the perspiring coolies who thronged upon us'. *The Englishman*, 11 February 1865. A couple of days later another correspondent complained of passengers on the ferry with smallpox. *The Englishman*, 13 February 1865.

146 *The Englishman*, 5 March 1920, p. 12. See also MacNabb Collection (Rawdon) (OIOC), /180, 10 December 1902.

147 Morris, *Hired to Kill*, p. 205. See also *The Englishman*, 31 March 1920.

148 Cited by Allen, *Raj*, p. 21.

149 Hull and Mair, *The European*, p. 143.

150 Trevelyan, *The Competition Wallah*, p. 28.

151 Cited by Parry, *Delusions and Discoveries*, p. 133.

152 P. Mason, *A Shaft of Sunlight*, p. 67.

153 Webb, *English Etiquette*, pp. 83–4.

154 Khilnani, 'A bodily drama', p. 6.

155 MacDonald Collection (OIOC), /13, 16 January 1939.

156 Cited by Allen, *Plain Tales*, pp. 247–8.

157 James, *Raj*, pp. 473–4.

Chapter 5 The Social Body

1 In 1880 there were 66,000 British troops in the Indian army. Brown, *Modern India*, p. 95. Renford gives the figure of 2,150 non-official Europeans in British India in 1830, which had grown to just over 10,000 by the 1850s. Renford, *The Non-Official British*, p. 15.

2 Beames, *Memoirs*, p. 132.

3 Trevelyan, *The Competition Wallah*, p. 25.

4 A weekly programme of events in Naini Tal in 1929 includes polo, golf, a regatta and dances, and, apart from the golf, is typical of such 'weeks' throughout the last half of the nineteenth century. Hume Papers (CSAS), Box 10.

5 Wiener, *English Culture*, pp. 50–6.

6 See Girouard, *The Victorian Country-House*.

7 Cannadine, *The Decline and Fall*, pp. 341–70.

8 Hobsbawm, *The Age of Empire*, p. 176.

9 See F. M. L. Thompson, *The Rise of Respectable Society*, pp. 267–70.

10 See also Hanmer Collection, pl. 15; Photographs of India and Southern Rhodesia, pl. 5; D'Arcy Waters Papers (CSAS), 'Photograph album 1914, 1915, 1916, 1917, Kistna district, Narsapur'.

11 Morris, *Hired to Kill*, p. 192. See also Baden-Powell, *Indian Memories*, p. 36. Rivett-Carnac described India as 'that country, so specially well adapted to the necessities of cadets of old families, like my own, whose progeny was numerous, and whose pedigrees are much longer than their purses.' Rivett-Carnac, *Many Memories*, p. 377.

12 A. B., *A Romance*, p. 9.
13 Mendilow, 'Merrie England', p. 54. Mendilow discusses the way in which writers on imperialism used the notion of empire to reconcile the myth of rural England with the brave new world brought about by the Industrial Revolution, not only in the space of the colonies but within England itself.
14 See E. P. Thompson, *English Landed Society*, p. 34; H. Cunningham, 'Leisure and culture', pp. 298–9.
15 B. Anderson, *Imagined Communities*, p. 150.
16 Cannadine, *Class in Britain*, p. 126.
17 Hunt and Harrison, *The District Officer*, p. 129. See also Westmacott Papers (OIOC), p. 154; Mrs Viola Bayley, p. 3; Allen, *Plain Tales*, p. 77.
18 Westmacott Papers (OIOC), p. 303. See also Hall Papers (CSAS), I, p. 8; Orwell, *Burmese Days*, p. 98.
19 A bearer, a *khidmutgar*, an *ayah*, a dressing-boy, a cook, a sweeper, a *dhobi*, a *dhirzee*, a *syce*, and a grasscutter, a *bhistee*, a *mali* and possibly a man to look after cows or goats.
20 Taylor, *English History*, p. 177.
21 Barr and Ray, *Simla*, p. 31.
22 'To the tolerant Hindu "we, the Sahib log, were just another caste".' Hunt and Harrison, *The District Officer*, p. 127; Allen, *Plain Tales*, pp. 96–7; Mr E. A. Jenkins, cassette 1, side 1.
23 Wakefield, *Past Imperative*, p. 3.
24 Hunt and Harrison, *The District Officer*, p. 127.
25 In Assam, for example, the weight of numbers meant that officials mixed socially with planters. Westmacott Papers (OIOC), pp. 202–3; Barr, *The Dust*, p. 125.
26 Gordon, *Work and Play*, p. 160.
27 See for example Mrs Winifred Brown, cassette 1, side 1; Mr J. Leonard, cassette 1, side 1.
28 Morris, *Hired to Kill*, p. 79. See also Ross, *Both Ends of the Candle*, pp. 122–3; Wakefield, *Past Imperative*, p. 3; Mrs Viola Bayley, p. 29. This was a characteristic of most colonial societies. 'Dorothea Irwin, a newly arrived American woman on the copperbelt in the late 1920s, noticed the white colonists, "were very long on ritual and precedence, calling, entertainment etc., in strict order of rank."' Hansen, *Distant Companions*, pp. 57–8.
29 Beames, *Memoirs*, p. 197.
30 See J. Burnett, *Plenty and Want*, p. 55; J. Burnett, *Liquid Pleasures*, p. 59.
31 From Mrs Amina Ismail's Recipe Book.
32 '*Culinary Jottings for Madras* by Wyvern. 1878', *The Calcutta Review*, 68 (1879), pp. xiii–xiv. The development of tea-time with English cakes and the banishment of Indian food from the dinner menu is borne out by the sample menus and recipes to be found in the numerous cookery books produced for the Anglo-Indian market. See for example Burke, *Every-day Menus*; Carne, *Simple Menus*; Chota Sahib, *Camp Recipes*;

Franklin, *The Wife's Cookery Book*; Gordon, *Anglo-Indian Cuisine*; *What to Tell the Cook*; Wyvern, *Culinary Jottings*.

33 'Culinary Jottings for Madras by Wyvern. 1878', *The Calcutta Review*, 68 (1879), p. xiii.

34 The book was written for middle- and lower-middle-class households which could not afford the extravagance of the recipes suggested in better-known standard books such as Eliza Acton's *Modern Cookery* and Mrs Beeton, both of whom tended to call for economy while concentrating mainly on extravagant recipes. See J. Burnett, *Plenty and Want*, p. 184–5.

35 Bruce Papers (CSAS), Vol. I, 1894, p. 23.

36 J. Burnett, *Plenty and Want*, p. 186, John William Laing, 'Diaries', pp. 43, 161.

37 Ouwekerk Collection (OIOC), /60, 18 August 1929. See also Stewart Papers (CSAS), p. 33. Interview with Mrs Wright, 1995.

38 See Blanchard, *Yesterday and Today*, p. 45; Dutton, *Life in India*, pp. 100–1; Hull and Mair, *The European*, p. 93.

39 Wonnacott Collection (OIOC), /3, 15 July 1871, p. 33.

40 Mrs Edwards' son, whom she visited in India in 1883, had a vegetable garden 'with Carter's seeds from England', while his neighbour, Mr Buff, was very proud of his own green peas at dinner one evening. Diaries of Mrs Louisa Edwards, III, pp. 27, 37.

41 Chapman Papers (CSAS), p. 25.

42 Campbell-Martin, *Out in the Midday Sun*, p. 19. See also Mrs Winifred Brown, cassette 1, side 2; Masters, *Bugles*, p. 157.

43 Steel, *The Garden*, p. 163.

44 [Bell], *Sahib-Log*, p. 155.

45 Hull and Mair, *The European*, p. 178.

46 Montgomery Papers (CSAS), 18 October 1927.

47 Westmacott Papers (OIOC), p. 174.

48 Allen, *Plain Tales*, p. 112.

49 Mrs Viola Bayley, pp. 107–8. Not everyone conformed. At home Philip Ray, a police officer during the Second World War, only wore trousers to ward off the mosquitoes. Interview with Philip Ray, 1998.

50 Dench Papers (CSAS), p. 24. See also Hall Papers (CSAS), p. 19; Ouwekerk Collection (OIOC), /60, 19 June 1929; Interview with Mrs Randhawa, 1995.

51 See comments of Kenneth Warren, tea planter, cited by Allen, *Plain Tales*, p. 79.

52 Orwell, *Burmese Days*, p. 199.

53 Wuthnow et al., *Cultural Analysis*, pp. 105, 115.

54 For the habitus as a force for continuity see Hans-Ulrich Wehler, 'Pierre Bourdieu', paper delivered at the University of Bielefeld, 23 December 1995.

55 Orwell, *Burmese Days*, p. 69.

56 Forster, *A Passage to India*, pp. 43, 55. See also Savory, *A Sportswoman*, p. 339–40; Allen, *Plain Tales*, p. 214. What E. M. Forster

observed as the dead weight of conformity pressing down on the individual can be explained as the result of the tendency of the habitus to form schemas of dispositions within individuals which predispose them to accept the limits of their social circumstances. J. B. Thompson, *Studies*, p. 53; Miller, 'Systematisch verzerrte Legitimationsdiskurse', p. 192.

57 Forster, *A Passage to India*, p. 61.
58 Allen, *Plain Tales*, p. 213.
59 Hunt and Harrison, *The District Officer*, p. 123. See also Lady Olive Crofton (CSAS), p. 38; Maconochie, *Life*, p. 22.
60 Barr, *The Dust*, p. 59.
61 See Scott Papers (CSAS), pp. 34, 62.
62 Christopherson, 'The motive'.
63 Hyde Papers (CSAS), p. 42.
64 Scott Papers (CSAS), pp. 34, 62; Mrs Viola Bayley, p. 108.
65 Mrs Viola Bayley, p. 28; Interview with Mrs Randhawa, 1995; West-macott Papers (OIOC), p. 60.
66 Mrs Viola Bayley, p. 108; Interview with Mrs Randhawa, 1995.
67 See King, *Colonial Urban Development*, pp. 38–9.
68 Anxiety about the high death rate of British soldiers in the Indian army was partly a result of the Mutiny and the consequent need to rely more on British rather than Indian troops. Arnold, *Colonizing the Body*, pp. 61–73.
69 Cole, *Notes*, p. 3.
70 Chandavarkar, 'Plague, panic and epidemic politics', p. 211.
71 Ibid., p. 11. For an example of British attempts to improve sanitation in Indian towns see Harrison, 'Allahabad'. The seminal work on sanitation in the army was Parkes, *A Manual of Practical Hygiene*, which was reissued as Notter and Firth, *The Theory and Practice of Hygiene*. Another important and influential work on hygiene in the Indian army was Clark, *Practical Observations*.
72 King, *Colonial Urban Development*, p. 143.
73 Moore, *A Manual of Family Medicine*, 4th edn, p. 682.
74 Moore, *Health in the Tropics*; Balfour, 'Personal hygiene'; Jones, *A Manual of Hygiene*; Lucas, *The Elements of Indian Hygiene*; McNally, *A Sanitary Handbook*; Simpson, *The Maintenance of Health*.
75 Hunt and Kenny, *Tropical Trials*, p. 176.
76 A Bombay Army Surgeon, *Medical Hints*, pp. 132–42; Brigg, *The Anglo-Indian's Health*, pp. 4–15; Adams, *The Western Rajputana States*, pp. 197, 221–2; Bishop, *Medical Hints*, pp. 63, 117; Notter, 'Hygiene'; *The Englishman*, 30 July 1870, p. 2.
77 The openness of the bungalow was characteristic of many colonial homes in which the colonizer was constantly on display. See Hansen, *Distant Companions*, p. 69.
78 [Bell], *Sahib-Log*, p. 163.
79 J. E. Dawson, 'Woman in India', *The Calcutta Review*, 83 (1886), p. 362.

80   Steel and Gardiner, *The Complete Indian Housekeeper*, p. 5.
81   The only significant difference between British and Indian manuals was that the role of the housewife was more supervisory in India and the number of servants greater. Davidson, *The Book of the Home*, V, pp. 36–8; Attar, *A Bibliography*, pp. 30–1. The daily routine advocated in other colonies was very similar. Hansen, *Distant Companions*, pp. 57, 61.
82   Campbell-Martin, *Out in the Midday Sun*, p. 76.
83   Steel and Gardiner, *The Complete Indian Housekeeper*, pp. 1–10; Dawe, *The Wife's Help*, p. 7; Lang, *Hints*, p. 3; Wilson, *Hints*, pp. 55–9. Bachelors were also reminded of the necessity of regular inspection tours of the kitchen, storeroom and so on by Shadwell, *Notes*, pp. 23–38.
84   Berners Papers (CSAS), 26 January 1854, p. 25; Massy Collection (OIOC), /10, 9 May 1875; Dr Mildred Archer, cassette 1, side 2; Taylor Papers (CSAS), p. 30; Dench Papers (CSAS), p. 18; Chapman Papers (CSAS), p. 15; Masters, *Bugles*, p. 161; Stoler, 'Carnal knowledge', p. 52.
85   Hansen, *Distant Companions*, p. 65.
86   Beverly Gartrell finds the same pressures operating in colonial Uganda. See Gartrell, 'Colonial wives'.
87   King, *Colonial Urban Development*, p. 90.
88   Scott Papers (CSAS), p. 110; Diver, *Ships of Youth*, p. 75.
89   Allen, *Plain Tales*, p. 88.
90   King, *Colonial Urban Development*, p. 90.
91   Savory, *A Sportswoman*, p. 337. See also Fleming, *A Pinchbeck Goddess*, p. 33.
92   King, *Colonial Urban Development*, p. 153.
93   Cited by ibid., p. 120.
94   Godden, *Two*, p. 23.
95   Bourne Papers (CSAS), p. 32.
96   M. Roberts, 'Noise as cultural struggle', pp. 241–7.
97   Hall Papers (CSAS), X, p. 4.
98   Mrs Monica Clough, cassette 1, side 1.
99   Stuart Papers (CSAS), 3 October 1855. See also Hibbert, *The Great Mutiny*, p. 27.
100 Medical advances were finally fully acknowledged in the layout of textbooks of tropical medicine published after the First World War which no longer categorized tropical diseases according to, for example, types of fever, but according to the type of microbe causing the disease. See for example Byam and Archibald, *The Practice of Medicine*, II, the contents of which were ordered under the headings, 'Bacterial diseases', 'Spirochaetal diseases', 'Protozoal diseases'; Masters, *Essentials of Tropical Medicine*, which assigned separate chapters to diseases caused by protozoa, bacteria, helminths, etc.
101 Vigarello, *Concepts of Cleanliness*, p. 202.
102 Balfour, 'Personal hygiene', p. 35.

103   Vigarello, *Concepts of Cleanliness*, p. 205.
104   Hall Papers (CSAS), X, p. 48.
105   Godden, *A Time to Dance*, p. 124. Major Shadwell even went so far as to suggest that a 'hamal' should be employed to sweep inside the house so that the pollution of the sweeper would be confined to the bathroom. In addition he advocated a separate room for the 'water-closet' so that the 'sweeper is then restricted to one room, only the *bhisti* and the bearer having access to the bath-room'. Shadwell, *Notes*, pp. 51–2.
106   Mrs Coralie Taylor, cassette 1, side 1.
107   Briggs, *Letters*, p. 58; [Bell], *Sahib-Log*, p. 95; Duncan, *The Simple Adventures*, p. 79.
108   Cited by Masani, *Indian Tales*, p. 56.
109   Douglas, *Purity and Danger*, pp. 1–40.
110   Mrs Monica Clough, cassette 1, side 2.
111   See Kennedy, *Islands of White*, p. 127; Kennedy, 'The perils of the mid-day sun', p. 131; Kennedy, 'Climatic theories', p. 50.
112   Dawson, 'Woman in India', pp. 364–5.
113   [Bell], *Sahib-Log*, p. 66.
114   Kennedy, *Islands of White*, p. 154.
115   This was an autobiographical novel based on her own experience of the effects of India on the Englishwoman. Fowler, *Redney*, pp. 170–96.
116   Duncan, *The Simple Adventures*, p. 308.
117   See also Diver, *The Englishwoman*, pp. 7–8.
118   Hall Papers (CSAS), XII, pp. 2–3.
119   A. E. Grant, *The Indian Manual*, I, p. xxiv.
120   A reference to Lawrence Stone by V. Smith, 'Cleanliness', p. 30.
121   Vigarello, *Concepts of Cleanliness*, pp. 216, 231.
122   Hunter, *A New and Complete Domestic Medicine*, p. 199.
123   Godden, *Two*, p. 13.
124   Lambert, *Unquiet Souls*, p. 146.
125   *The Englishman*, 14 February 1870, p. 1; Gilmour, *Curzon*, p. 146.
126   For sanitation and conservancy in Simla see Kanwar, *Imperial Simla*, pp. 65–9; Mrs Viola Bayley, p. 41.
127   Masters, *Bugles*, pp. 84–5.
128   Hart, *Everyday Life*, p. 72.
129   Battye, *Costumes*, p. 52.
130   Lawrence, *Indian Embers*, p. 48.
131   Cited by Allen, *Plain Tales*, p. 75.
132   Cited by ibid. p. 90.
133   Morris, *Hired to Kill*, p. 84.
134   Davidoff and Hall, *Family Fortunes*, pp. 382–6.
135   George Latham Papers (OIOC), p. 148; Ouwekerk Collection (OIOC), /60, 28 June, 1929, p. 13.
136   Moore, *A Manual of Family Medicine*, p. 650; Hull and Mair, *The European*, p. 61.

137 Hunter, *A New and Complete Domestic Medicine*, p. 207.
138 Cullimore, *The Book of Climates*, p. 5; Jeffreys, *The British Army*, p. 49; Hunter, *Health in India*, p. 10.
139 Examples can be found in *The Friend of India*, 9 and 23 April 1846, *The Civil and Military Gazette*, 31 May, 3 and 10 June 1876, *The Englishman*, 2 May 1870.
140 Coetzee, *White Writing*, pp. 138–47.
141 Cullimore, *The Book of Climates*, p. 8.
142 Allan Papers (CSAS), 2 January 1880, p. 49.
143 Jeffreys, *The British Army*, p. 42. See also *The Englishman*, 12 July 1870, p. 2, 21 July 1871, p. 2.
144 'The Indian Civil Service as a career for University men', *The Oxford and Cambridge Undergraduate's Journal*, 30 November 1882, p. 133.
145 Moore, *The Constitutional Requirement*, p. 53; Hunter, *Health in India*, pp. 11–12; Birch, 'Influence of warm climates'.
146 Hunter, *Health in India*, pp. 13–14.
147 Maxwell Papers (CSAS), Box XVII, 10 February 1924.
148 Hull and Mair, *The European*, p. 215. Green and Green-Armytage, *Birch's Management*, pp. 9, 11.
149 Fayrer, *European Child-life*, pp. 13, 30–1.
150 See Searle, *Eugenics and Politics*, pp. 25–6.
151 Pick, *Faces of Degeneration*, pp. 195, 212.
152 Kennedy, 'The perils of the midday sun', p. 131.
153 Hunt and Kenny, *Tropical Trials*, pp. 116, 119, 180.
154 Diver, *The Englishwoman*, pp. 14–15.
155 Lyall Collection (OIOC), /10A , 30 October 1883.
156 Kipling, *Plain Tales*; Cunningham, *Chronicles of Dustypore*, I, p. 128.
157 Lutyens, *The Lyttons*, pp. 45, 96–100, 139, 155.
158 Hall Papers (CSAS), VIII 4; Ouwekerk Collection (OIOC), /62, 3 November 1929, 15 January 1939; Westmacott Papers (OIOC), p. 138; Skrine Collection (OIOC), /6, 14 September 1920; Bowman Collection (OIOC), /1, 3 May 1942; Interview with Philip Ray.
159 Barr, *The Dust*, p. 108; *The Englishman*, 14 January 1920.
160 This did not prevent one civil servant from conducting a long-standing affair without showing any concern about hiding it from the servants. However he was certainly wary of the 'Mrs Grundys', and in an attempt to disguise the affair his wife would go out in public with the mistress when she came on a visit so that anyone's suspicions would be allayed by seeing the two women friendly together. Skrine Collection (OIOC), /21, 29 March 1935, 26 April 1935, 28 June 1935; /22, 5 April 1937, 11 May 1937, 21 May 1937.
161 Weeks, *Sex*, p. 86. See Mason, *Victorian Sexuality*, pp. 112–13; Mosse, *Nationalism and Sexuality*, p. 5.
162 Hunt and Kenny, *Tropical Trials*, p. 215.
163 Trevelyan, *The Competition Wallah*, p. 238. A similar process of distancing themselves from the old-style dissipated and indolent colonials and defining themselves as a new energetic breed of colonials

went on in French colonies, although on a shorter and later time-scale. See Stoler, 'Carnal knowledge', p. 77.

164 *The Englishman*, 12 July 1870, p. 2.
165 Ibid., 21 July 1871, p. 2.
166 Weeks, *Sex*, p. 92.
167 Mason, *Victorian Sexual Attitudes*, p. 60.
168 See Butler, *The Eldest Brother*, p. 152; Bruce, *The Native Wife*, pp. 37, 131; Papers of Marie Carmichael Stopes, Box 3, letter A21.
169 Dubois, *Description*, p. 191; MacMunn, *The Underworld*, pp. 204–7; Hyam, *Empire and Sexuality*, pp. 127–33; Parry, *Delusions and Discoveries*, p. 98.
170 Cullimore, *The Book of Climates*, p. 7; Balfour, 'Personal hygiene', p. 5. Letters addressed to Marie Stopes by Anglo-Indians indicate that the climate was held responsible for male impotence. See Papers of Marie Carmichael Stopes, Box 11, letter A74; Box 6, letter A42.
171 *The Englishman*, 8 March 1920, p. 12.
172 Ballhatchet, *Race*, pp. 137–40.
173 Ibid., pp. 116–17.
174 Paxton, 'Mobilising chivalry'; Sharpe, *Allegories of Empire*, pp. 62–81; Sinha, *Colonial Masculinity*, pp. 52–4.
175 Bruce, *The Native Wife*, p. 200.
176 Butcher, *The British in Malaya*, pp. 206–7.
177 See Taylor, *Seeta*; Steel, *On the Face*; Masani, *Indian Tales*, p. 54. As the British seem to have known so much about affairs between themselves it seems likely that if the practice of keeping native mistresses had survived into this period others would have known about it and more comments on this practice would be found in the sources.
178 Interview with Douglas Stanton-Ife, ICS Behar 1930s, in *Ruling Passions*, broadcast 20 March 1996, BBC2.
179 Hunt and Harrison, *The District Officer*, p. 120.
180 See Bristow, *Vice and Vigilance*; Walkowitz, *Prostitution*.
181 Ballhatchet, *Race*, pp. 68–95; Hyam, *Empire and Sexuality*, pp. 121–7.
182 Tosh, 'Imperial masculinity'.
183 Maud Diver, cited by Parry, *Delusions and Discoveries*, p. 88.
184 Hyam, *Empire and Sexuality*, pp. 127–33.
185 Interview with Mrs Randhawa, 1995; Mrs Monica Clough, cassette 1, side1; Masani, *Indian Tales*, p. 53.
186 Woolf, *An Autobiography*, p. 172.
187 Bowman Collection (OIOC), /1, 25 November 1942, 31 December 1942.
188 Stewart Papers (CSAS), Box III, p. 57.
189 Allen, *Plain Tales*, p. 147; Godden, *A Time to Dance*, p. 89; Interview with Mrs Randhawa, 1995.
190 Hobhouse, *Report*, I, p. 230, II, pp. 103, 115, 250, III, pp. 84–5, IV, pp. 149, 153, VI, pp. 39, 67, VII, p. 48. See also *Manual on Indian Etiquette*; *The Indian Civil Service Manual*.

191 Hobhouse, *Report*, VII, p. 70.
192 Ibid., VI, p. 39.
193 Chaudhary, *Imperial Honeymoon*, p. 435.
194 Maxwell Papers (CSAS), Box XVII, 11 November 1925.
195 Sir Spencer Harcourt Butler Collection (OIOC), /2, 20 May 1891.
196 Maxwell Papers (CSAS), Box XVII, 23 February 1924. See also Sir Walter Roper Lawrence Collection (OIOC), /10, Deputy Commissioner's Camp, Kasur, 1880.
197 Fraser, *Among Indian Rajahs*, pp. 92–3.
198 E. P. Thompson, *Customs in Common*, p. 22.
199 Newby, *The Deferential Worker*, p. 425.
200 See Braddon, *Thirty Years of Shikar*, pp. 251–8; Mrs Viola Bayley p. 6; Massy Collection (OIOC), October 1895; Stewart Papers (CSAS), p. 131.
201 M. Misra, *Business, Race and Politics*, pp. 4, 123–4.
202 Ibid., p. 9.
203 Ibid., p. 181.
204 Barr, *The Dust*, p. 141.
205 Interview with Philip Ray.
206 'Q' Telegram, 16 August 1937, Brabourne Collection (OIOC)/8A, File No. 4, p. 98.
207 Lawrence, *Indian Embers*, p. 42.
208 Maxwell Papers (CSAS), Boxes XI and XII/2, 11 February 1926.
209 Ibid.
210 Mrs Mildred Archer, cassette 1, sides 1 and 2.
211 Godden, *Two* p. 80.
212 Maxwell Papers (CSAS), Boxes XI and XII/2, 11 February 1926.
213 Ibid., 16 March 1926.
214 Ray Collection (OIOC), /8, Diary 1945, p. 33.
215 Maxwell Papers (CSAS), Box XVII, 14 September 1926. See also 28 November 1935.
216 Raychaudhuri, *Europe Reconsidered*, p. 62.
217 Interview with Philip Ray. See also E. Fraser, *A Home*, p. 110.
218 Cited by Masani, *Indian Tales*, p. 52.
219 See Barr, *The Dust*, p. 142.
220 Skrine Collection (OIOC), /22, 28 August 1937.
221 Ouwekerk Collection (OIOC), /61, 2 July 1938.
222 Skrine Collection (OIOC), /6, 4 November 1919.
223 Chapman Papers (CSAS), pp. 28–9.
224 Masani, *Indian Tales*, pp. 116–17.
225 Ibid, p. 16.
226 W. H. S. Smith, *A Young Man's Country*, p. 12.
227 Interview with Philip Ray.
228 Horne, *Work and Sport*, p. 22.
229 Dr Mildred Archer, cassette 1, side 1.
230 Wakefield, *Past Imperative*, p. 4. See also Ouwekerk Collection (OIOC), /60, 30 March 1930.

231   Dewey, *Anglo-Indian Attitudes*, pp. 166, 196–8.
232   Interview with Philip Ray.
233   Stewart Papers (CSAS), p. 68.

Epilogue: The Dissolution of the Anglo-Indian Body, 1939–1947

 1   P. Mason, *A Shaft of Sunlight*, p. 151.
 2   Gray Papers (OIOC), /9, 3 April 1940. See also Hall Papers (CSAS), I, p. 5.
 3   Damodaran, *Broken Promises*, p. 214, Pearce, *Indian Copper*, pp. 102–3.
 4   Damodaran, *Broken Promises*, p. 214.
 5   See French, *Liberty*, p. 135; Royle, *The Last Days*, pp. 76–7.
 6   Griffiths Collection (OIOC), /11, 2 June 1942.
 7   Moon Collection (OIOC), /17, 14 June 1942.
 8   Bowman Collection (OIOC), /1, 2 November 1942.
 9   S. Bhattacharya, 'Wartime policies', pp. 160, 164.
10   Moon Collection (OIOC), /17, 21 April 1942.
11   Damodaran, *Broken Promises*, p. 189.
12   Ibid., pp. 229–30.
13   French, *Liberty*, pp. 141, 159–60.
14   Damodaran, *Broken Promises*, p. 242.
15   S. Bhattacharya, 'An unjustly forgotten facet', p. 15.
16   French, *Liberty*, p. 183.
17   Ray Collection (OIOC), Diary 1945 /8, p. 17.
18   S. Bhattacharya, 'An unjustly forgotten facet', p. 15.
19   E. Fraser, *A Home*, pp. 120–1, 147.
20   Mrs Rhoda Gandhi of Allahabad, cited by Chris Bayly in conversation with the author.
21   E. Fraser, *A Home*, p. 147.
22   Royle, *The Last Days*, pp. 66–7. See also C. A. Bayly, 'Eric Thomas Stokes', p. 469.
23   Cited by Royle, *The Last Days*, p. 101.
24   Cited by Mansergh, *The Transfer*, II, p. 112.
25   Cited by Masani, *Indian Tales*, p. 68.
26   Voigt, *India in the Second World War*, p. 16.
27   Masters, *The Road Past Mandalay*, pp. 19–20.
28   Ibid.
29   Walter Monckton, cited by Ziegler, *Mountbatten*, p. 364.
30   Ibid., p. 375.
31   E. Fraser, *A Home*, p. 149.
32   C. A. Bayly, 'Eric Thomas Stokes', p. 470.
33   Mrs Winifred Brown, cassette 1, side 1; Mrs Viola Bayley, pp. 30–1.
34   Colesworthy Grant reported that 'Calcutta now possesses as many as twenty-five Wine Merchants, dealers in Italian and Oilman's Stores, Confectionery &c., . . . eleven Provisioners and Bakers, . . . five Chemists and Druggists . . . five Cabinet Makers, eight Carvers, Gilders, House

Painters and Decorators, one General Hardware Man, eight Tailors and Habit Makers, and four Hairdressers and Perfumers, all these being independent of about twenty-one *Native* shopkeepers resident in the old and new China Bazars.' C. Grant, *Anglo-Indian Domestic Life*, p. 39. Mrs Randhawa commented on the fact that when the British left India in 1947 this hybrid colonial economy died away. Interview with Mrs Randhawa.

35 Porter, 'Bodies of thought', p. 99.
36 A. Burton, *Burdens of History*, pp. 37–40.
37 Marshall, 'Imperial Britain', p. 321.
38 Dutton, *Life in India*, p. 43; 'Anglo-Indians at home – the popularity of Eastbourne', *The Englishman*, 7 January 1920, p. 8.
39 Hunter, *Health in India*, p. 90.
40 See Hervey, *Anglo-Indian Cookery at Home*; Sir William Hawthorne Lewis Papers (OIOC), /38 Photograph album.

Bibliography

I Primary sources

A Private papers

Bodleian Library, Oxford

Papers of Brian Houghton Hodgson and his wife, MSS Hodgson 9–17

University Library, Cambridge

Edmonstone Papers, Add. 7616

Royal Commonwealth Society Collection, University Library, Cambridge

Burke, Norah, 'The Raj: India 1890–1920. A story in photographs'
Photographs of India and Southern Rhodesia 1890s–1930s. By S. H. Dagg, Thomas A. Rust and others unknown, Y3022HH
H. H. Davies Collection on India, Y3022Q
Hanmer Collection, Y3022MM-PP
Laing, John William, 'Diaries in India and Europe 1873–1875'
Millar, William Robert, 'Indian letters, 1874–75'

British Library Manuscripts, London

Journal of R. N. Cust, Add. MSS 45,390
Diaries of Mrs Louisa Edwards, Add. MSS 43,809–13
Letters and Papers Relating to the Indian Mutiny, Add. MSS.41,488

Wellcome Institute Library, London

Marie Carmichael Stopes (1880–1958), PP/MCS

Centre for South Asian Studies, Cambridge (CSAS)

Allan Papers
Bagnall Papers
Mrs Viola Bayley, Microfilm Box 7, No. 57
Berners Papers, Microfilm Box 7, No. 55
Bourne Papers
Bruce Papers
Chapman Papers
Lady Olive Crofton, Microfilm Box 1, No. 8
D'Arcy Waters Papers
Dench Papers
Hall Papers
Hume Papers
Hyde Papers
Knight Papers
Maxwell Papers
Montgomery Papers, Microfilm Box 54
Scott Papers
Stewart Papers
Stock Papers
Stokes Papers
Stuart Papers, Microfilm Box 2, No. 17B
Taylor Papers, Microfilm Box 6, No. 48

Oriental and India Office Collections, London (OIOC)

Bowman Collection, MSS Eur. F229
Brabourne Collection, MSS Eur. F97
Sir Spencer Harcourt Butler Collection, MSS Eur. F116
Chapman Collection, MSS Eur. F234
Journal of James Fenn Clark, MSS Eur. A185
Fowke Manuscripts, MSS Eur. F3
The Story of Mrs Goldney's Escape, MSS Eur. Photo. Eur. 187
Gray Papers, MSS Eur. D1037
Griffiths Collection, MSS Eur. D1111
Kirkpatrick Collection, MSS Eur. F228
George Latham Papers, MSS Eur. A120
La Touche Collection, MSS Eur. C258
Sir Walter Roper Lawrence Collection, MSS Eur. F143
Sir William Hawthorne Lewis Papers, MSS Eur. G111
Lyall Collection, MSS Eur. F132
Lytton Collection, MSS Eur. E218

MacDonald Collection, MSS Eur. E360
MacFarlan Collection, MSS Eur. C315
MacNabb Collection, MSS Eur. F206
Massy Collection, MSS Eur. B181
Maynard Collection, MSS Eur. F224
Moon Collection, MSS Eur. F230
Ouwekerk Collection, MSS Eur. F233
Edward Ward Walter Raleigh Papers, MSS Eur. D786
Ray Collection, MSS Eur. F256
Frederick John Shore Collection, MSS Eur. E307
Skrine Collection, MSS Eur. F154
Spilsbury Collection, MSS Eur. D909
Thornhill Collection, MSS Eur. B298
Lt.-Col. Tredway-Clarke Papers, Photo. Eur. 219
Watson Collection, MSS Eur. F244
Westmacott Papers, MSS Eur. C349
Wonnacott Collection, MSS Eur. C376

Oral Archives, Oriental and India Office Collections, London

Dr Mildred Archer, MSS Eur. R146
Mrs Winifred Brown, MSS Eur. R138
Mrs Monica Clough, MSS Eur. R148
Mr E. A. Jenkins, MSS Eur. R140
Mr J. Leonard, MSS Eur. R147
Mrs Coralie Taylor, MSS Eur. R142
Sir Ronald Evelyn Leslie Wingate, MSS Eur. R180

Oral interviews with the author

Mr Philip Ray, Cambridge, 1998
Mrs Celia Randhawa, Calcutta, 1995
Mrs Anne Wright, Calcutta, 1995

Private collections

Mrs Amina Ismail's Recipe Book

B   Newspapers and periodicals

The Calcutta Review, 1844–90
The Civil and Military Gazette, 1876
The Englishman, 1830–5, 1860–5, 1870–5, 1920
The Fortnightly Review, 1887
The Friend of India, 1846
The Humane Review, 1906, 1908

The Indian Charivari, 1872–7
The Leader, 1920–2
The Meerut Universal Magazine, 1835–7
The Oxford and Cambridge Undergraduate's Journal, 1882
Punch, 1882
The Times of India, 1920–2

C   Unpublished government records

Oriental and India Office Collections, London

Board's Collections, 1796–1858
Home Miscellaneous Series, c.1600–c.1900
Political and Judicial Department papers, 1880–1930
The Records, East India College, Haileybury, 1807–53
Wills, Probates, Inventories and Administrations, 1774–1943

D   Published government records

Hobhouse, C. E. H., *Report of the Royal Commission upon Decentralisation in India* (7 vols, London, 1909)
Indian Civil Service Manual (Madras), The (Madras, 1931)
Malcolm, John, 'Memorandum on the subject of social and official intercourse between European officers and Indian gentlemen', in *Manual on Indian Etiquette. For the use of European officers coming to India* (Allahabad, 1910)
Muir, William, *Records of the Intelligence Department of the North-West Provinces of India during the Mutiny of 1857* (2 vols, Edinburgh, 1902)
Papers Relating to the Selection and Training of Candidates for the Indian Civil Service (Calcutta, 1876)

E   Contemporary works

All books published in London unless otherwise stated.

A. B., *A Romance of Bureaucracy* (Allahabad, 1893).
Adams, Archibald, *The Western Rajputana States. A Medico-Topographical and General Account of Marwar, Siroki, Jaisalmir* (1899).
Ainslie, Whitelaw, *Medical, Geographical, and Agricultural Report of the Committee Appointed by the Madras Government to Inquire into the Causes of the Epidemic Fever which Prevailed in the Provinces of Coimbatore, Madras, Dindigul and Trinnivelly, during the Years 1809, 1810 and 1811* (1816).

Anon., *Hartly House, Calcutta. A Novel of the Days of Warren Hastings* (1st pub. 1789), (1989).

Arnold, W. D. (pseud. Punjabee), *Oakfield, or Fellowship in the East* (2 vols, 1853).

Atkinson, George Franklin, *Curry and Rice on Forty Plates; or the Ingredients of Social Life at 'Our Station' in India*, 2nd edn (1859).

——, *Indian Spices for English Tables. Rare relish of fun for the Far East. Being the adventures of our special correspondent* (1860).

Autobiography of an Indian Army Surgeon; or leaves turned down from a journal (1854).

Baden-Powell, Robert, *Pigsticking or Hoghunting. A Complete Account for Sportsmen and Others* (1889).

——, *Indian Memories. Recollections of Soldiering, Sport etc.* (1915).

Balfour, Andrew, 'Personal hygiene', in *The Practice of Medicine in the Tropics. By Many Authorities*, eds W. Byam and R. G. Archibald (3 vols, 1921), pp. 2–222.

Beames, John, *Memoirs of a Bengal Civilian* (1961).

Becher, Augusta Emily, *Personal Reminiscences in India and Europe 1830–1888*, ed. H. G. Rawlinson (1930).

Beddoe, John, 'On the stature and bulk of man in the British Isles', in *Memoirs of the Anthropological Society of London*, vol. III (1867-8-9), pp. 384–573.

[Bell, Eva Mary] (pseud. John Travers), *Sahib-Log* (1910).

Bellew, Captain, *Memoirs of a Griffin, or a Cadet's First Year in India* (2 vols, 1843).

Birch, Edward Alfred, *The Management and Medical Treatment of Children in India* 2nd edn (Calcutta, 1886).

——, 'The influence of warm climates on the constitution', in *Hygiene and Diseases of Warm Climates*, ed. Andrew Davidson (1893).

Birdwood, George C. M., *Competition and the Indian Civil Service. A paper read before the East India Association, Tuesday, May 21, 1872* (1872).

Bishop, S. O., *Medical Hints for the Hills* (Darjeeling, 1888).

Blanchard, Sidney, *Yesterday and Today in India* (1867).

Blomfield, David (ed.), *Lahore to Lucknow. The Indian Mutiny Journal of Arthur Moffatt Lang* (1992).

Boileau, A. H. E., *Personal Narrative of a Tour through the Western States of Rajwara in 1835* (Calcutta, 1837).

Bombay Army Surgeon, A, *Medical Hints for the Districts and Companion to the District Medicine Chest* (Bombay, 1872).

Braddon, Edward, *Thirty Years of Shikar* (1895).

Brigg, George Kilworth Sherman, *The Anglo-Indian's Health Abroad and at Home* (1887).

Briggs, John, *Letters Addressed to a Young Person in India; calculated to afford instruction for his conduct in general, and more especially in his intercourse with the natives* (1828).

Brown, J. Moray, *Shikar Sketches with Notes on Indian Field Sports* (1887).

Bruce, Henry, *The Native Wife; or Indian Love and Anarchism. A Novel* (1909).

Burke, W. S., *Every-day Menus*, 3rd edn (Calcutta, 1909).

Burnett, Frances Hodgson, *The Secret Garden* (1st pub. 1909), (1974).

Byam, W. and R. G. Archibald (eds), *The Practice of Medicine in the Tropics. By Many Authorities* (3 vols, 1921).

Campbell, James, *Excursions, Adventures, and Field Sports in Ceylon* (2 vols, 1843).

Campbell-Martin, Monica, *Out in the Midday Sun* (1951).

Carey, William, *Dialogues, Intended to Facilitate the Acquiring of the Bengalee Language* (Serampore, 1801).

Carne, Lucy, *Simple Menus and Recipes for Camp, Home and Nursery*, 2nd edn (Calcutta, 1919).

Carpenter, Percy, *Hog Hunting in Lower Bengal* (1861).

Case, Mrs, *Day By Day at Lucknow. A Journal of the Siege of Lucknow* (1858).

Cassidy, James, *Social Intercourse between Indians and Anglo-Indians* (Bombay, 1906).

Chapman, Priscilla, *Hindoo Female Education* (1839).

Chota Sahib, *Camp Recipes for Camp People* (Madras, 1890).

Christopherson, J. B., 'The motive in women's dress in the tropics', *The Journal of Tropical Medicine and Hygiene*, 33 14 (1930), pp. 201–7.

Clark, Stewart, *Practical Observations on the Hygiene of the Army in India: including remarks on the ventilation and conservancy of Indian prisons; with a chapter on prison management* (1864).

Cole, J., *Notes on Hygiene with Hints on Self-discipline for Young Soldiers in India* (Sanawar, 1882).

Cordiner, James, *A Voyage to India* (1820).

Cox, Edmund C., *My Thirty Years in India* (1909).

[Crosthwaite, Peter] (pseud. A Friendly Traveller), *The Ensign of Peace* (1775).

Cullimore, D. H., *The Book of Climates: Acclimatisation; Climatic Disease; Health Resorts and Mineral Springs; Sea Sickness; and Sea Bathing* (1890).

Cunningham, H. S., *Chronicles of Dustypore. A tale of modern Anglo-Indian society* (2 vols, 1875).

Danvers, Frederick Charles et al. (eds), *Memorials of Old Haileybury College* (1894).

Darton, F. J. (ed.), *The Life and Times of Mrs Sherwood (1775–1851). From the diaries of Captain and Mrs Sherwood* (1910).

Davidson, H. C. (ed.), *The Book of the Home. A practical guide to household management* (8 vols, 1900).

Dawe, W. H., *The Wife's Help to Indian Cookery: being a practical manual for housekeepers* (1888).

Day, Charles W., *Hints on Etiquette and the Usages of Society: with a glance at bad habits*, 2nd edn (1836).

Diver, Maud, *The Englishwoman in India* (1909).

——, *Ships of Youth: A Study of Marriage in Modern India* (n.d).

D'Oyly, Charles, *The Europeans in India* (1813).

——, *Indian Sports* (Behar, 1829).

Drewitt, Dawtrey F., *Bombay in the Days of George IV. Memoirs of Sir Edward West*, 2nd edn (1935).

Dubois, J. A., *Description of the Character, Manners and Customs of the People of India and of their Institutions, Religious and Civil* (1817).

Duncan, Sara Jeanette, *The Simple Adventures of a Memsahib* (1893).

Dunlop, R. H. W., *Hunting in the Himalaya, with Notices of Customs and Countries from the Elephant Haunts of the Dehra Doon, to the Bunchowr Tracks in Eternal Snow* (1860).

Dutton, C., *Life in India* (1882).

Eastwick, Edward B. (ed.), *Autobiography of Lutfulah, a Mohamedan Gentleman; and his transactions with his fellow creatures: interspersed with remarks on the habits, customs and character of the people with whom he had to deal* (1857).

Eden, Emily, *Up the Country. Letters from India* (1st pub. 1866), (1983).

Elsmie, G. R., *Thirty-five Years in the Punjab 1858–1893* (Edinburgh, 1907).

Elwood, Anne Katherine, *Narrative of a Journey Overland from England by the Continent of Europe, Egypt, and the Red Sea, to India; including a residence there, and a voyage home in the years 1825, 1826, 1827 and 1828* (2 vols, 1830).

English Homes in India (2 vols, 1869).

Ex-Civilian, An, *Life in the Mofussil; or, the Civilian in Lower Bengal* (2 vols, 1878).

Fane, Henry Edward, *Five Years in India* (2 vols, 1842).

Fayrer, J., *European Child-life in Bengal* (1873).

Fenton, Elizabeth Sinclair, *The Journal of Mrs. Fenton. A narrative of her life in India, the Isle of France, and Tasmania during the years 1826–1830*, ed. Henry Lawrence (1901).

Fleming, Mrs J. M., *A Pinchbeck Goddess* (1897).

Forbes East India and Colonial Guide (1841).

Forster, E. M., *A Passage to India* (1st pub. 1924), Harmondsworth, (1985).

Franklin, E. A. M., *The Wife's Cookery Book, being recipes and hints on Indian cookery* (Madras, 1906).

Fraser, Andrew, H. L., *Among Indian Rajahs and Ryots. A civil servant's recollections and impressions of thirty-seven years of work and sport in the Central Provinces and Bengal* (1912).

Fraser, Eugenie, *A Home by the Hooghly*, 3rd edn (Edinburgh, 1993).

Gilchrist, John Borthwick, *A Dictionary, English and Hindoostanee* (Calcutta, 1787).

——, *Dialogues; English and Hindoostanee* (1820).

——, *The General East India Guide and Vade Mecum... Being a Digest of the Work of the Late Captain Williamson with Many Improvements and Additions* (1825).

Godden, Rumer, *A Time to Dance, No Time to Weep* (1987).

—— and Jon Godden, *Two Under the Indian Sun* (New York, 1966).

Goodeve, Henry Hurray, 'A sketch of the progress of European medicine in the East', *Quarterly Journal of the Calcutta Medical and Physical Society* 2 (1837), pp. 124–56.

——, *Hints for the General Management of Children in India in the Absence of Professional Advice*, 3rd edn (Bombay, 1852).

Gordon, Constance E., *Anglo-Indian Cuisine (Khána Kitâb) and Domestic Economy*, 2nd edn (Calcutta, 1913).

Gordon, J. D., *Work and Play in India and Kashmir* (1893).

Graham, Maria, *Journal of a Residence in India*, 2nd edn (1813).

Grant, A. E., *The Indian Manual of Hygiene, being King's Madras Manual of Hygiene Revised, Rearranged and in Great Part Rewritten* (2 vols, Madras, 1894).

Grant, Colesworthy, *Anglo-Indian Domestic Life. A letter from an artist in India to his mother in England*, 2nd edn (Calcutta, 1862).

Green, C. R. M. and V. B. Green-Armytage, *Birch's Management and Medical Treatment of Children in India*, 5th edn (Calcutta, 1915).

Hart, William H., *Everyday Life in Bengal and Other Indian Sketches* (1906).

Heber, Reginald, *Narrative of a Journey Through the Upper Provinces of India, from Calcutta to Bombay, 1824–1825* (2 vols, 1828).

[Henderson, H. B.], *The Bengalee; or Sketches of Society and Manners in the East* (1829).

Hervey, Henrietta A., *Anglo-Indian Cookery at Home; a short treatise for returned exiles. By the Wife of a Retired Indian Officer* (1895).

Hockley, W. B., *The English in India* (3 vols, 1828).

Hoey, W., *'Going East'. Advice Regarding Outfit, the Voyage and Procedure on Arrival* (Oxford, 1913).

Hogg, Francis R., *Practical Remarks Chiefly Concerning the Health and Ailments of European Families in India, with Special Reference to Maternal Management and Domestic Economy* (Benares, 1877).

Horne, W. O., *Work and Sport in the Old I.C.S.* (1928).

Huggins, William, *Sketches in India* (1824).

Hull, Edmund C. P. and R. S. Mair, *The European in India; or Anglo-Indian's Vade Mecum* (1871).

Hunt, S. Leigh and Alexander S. Kenny, *Tropical Trials: a handbook for women in the tropics* (1883).

Hunter, George Yeates, *Health in India: Medical Hints as to who should go there: and how to retain health* (Calcutta, 1873).

——, *A New and Complete Domestic Medicine for Home and Abroad, containing practical hints on hygiene together with a list of drugs for the medicine chest, with plain directions for their use* (1879).

Irvine, R. H., *Some Account of the Medical Topography of Ajmere* (Calcutta, 1841).

Jacquemont, Victor, *Letters from India; describing a journey in the British Dominions of India, Tibet, Lahore and Cashmere, during the years 1828, 1829, 1830, 1831* (2 vols, 1834).

Jeffreys, Julius, *The British Army in India: its preservation by an appropriate clothing, housing, locating, recreative employment, and hopeful encouragement of the troops* (1858).

Johnson, G. W., *The Stranger in India, or three years in Calcutta* (2 vols, 1843).

Johnson, James, *The Influence of Tropical Climates, More Especially the Climate of India, on European Constitutions* (1813).

Jones, J. A., *A Manual of Hygiene, Sanitation and Sanitary Engineering; with special references to Indian conditions* (Madras, 1896).

Julius, S. de V., *Notes on Striking Natives and Corollaries for the British Officers and Soldiers* (Allahabad, 1903).

Kaye, John, *Peregrine Pultuney; or life in India* (3 vols, 1844).

Keene, H. G., *A Servant of 'John Company'. Being the recollections of an Indian official* (1897).

Kerr, Henry, *A Few Words of Advice to Cadets, and Other Young Persons Proceeding to India*, 2nd edn (1842).

Kipling, Rudyard, *Plain Tales from the Hills* (1st pub. 1888), (1994).

Knighton, William, *Tropical Sketches; or reminiscences of an Indian journalist* (2 vols, 1855).

Lady Resident, A., *The Englishwoman in India: containing information for the use of ladies proceeding to, or residing in, the East Indies, on the subject of their Outfit, Furniture, Housekeeping the rearing of children, duties and wages of servants, management of the stables and arrangements for travelling to which are added Receipts for Indian Cookery* (1864).

Lang, C., *Hints to the English Bride on Indian Housekeeping by Chota Mem.* (Madras, 1904).

Lawrence, Rosamund, *Indian Embers* (Oxford, n.d.).

Lind, James, *An Essay on Diseases Incidental to Europeans in Hot Climates*, 6th edn (1808).

Lodwick, R. W., *John Bolt, Indian Civil Servant. A tale of old Haileybury and India* (2 vols, 1891).

Lucas, John Cathick, *The Elements of Indian Hygiene* (1880).

Lunt, James (ed.), *From Sepoy to Subedar: being the life and adventures of Subedar Sita Ram, a native officer of the Bengal army* (1970).

Lyttleton, Mrs Neville, *How to Pack, How to Dress, How to Keep Well on a Winter Tour in India* (1892).

McCosh, John, *Medical Advice to the Indian Stranger* (1841).

MacMunn, George, *The Underworld of India* (1933).

McNally, C. J., *A Sanitary Handbook for India* (Madras, 1911).

Maconochie, Evan, *Life in the Indian Civil Service* (1926).

Mahomed, S. D., *Shampooing; or benefits arising from the use of the Indian medicated vapour bath* (Brighton, 1822).

Manual on Indian Etiquette. For the use of European officers coming to India (Allahabad, 1910).

Marryat, Florence, '*Gup*'. *Sketches of Anglo-Indian Life and Character* (1868).

Martin, James Ranald, *The Influence of Tropical Climates on European Constitutions* (1856).

Mason, Philip, *A Shaft of Sunlight. Memories of a Varied Life* (1978).

Masters, John, *Bugles and a Tiger. A personal adventure* (1956).

——, *The Road Past Mandalay. A Personal Narrative* (1961).

Medical Practitioner of Several Years Experience in India, A, *A Domestic Guide to Mothers in India*, 2nd edn revd (Bombay, 1848).

Medwin, Thomas, *The Angler in Wales, or days and nights of sports-men* (2 vols, 1834).

Mitchell, Mrs Murray, *In India. Sketches of Indian life and travel from letters and journals* (1876).

[Monkland Mrs], *Life in India; or the English at Calcutta* (3 vols, 1828).

——, *The Nabob at Home; or the return to England* (3 vols, 1842).

Moore, William James, *Health in the Tropics; or, sanitary art as applied to Europeans in India* (1862).

——, *A Manual of Family Medicine for India*, 4th edn (1883).

——, *The Constitutional Requirement for Tropical Climates* (1890).

Morris, John, *Hired to Kill. Some chapters of autobiography* (1960).

Newall, J. T., *Scottish Moors and Indian Jungles. Scenes of sport in the Lews and India* (1889).

Notter, J. Lane, 'Hygiene of the tropics', in *Hygiene and Diseases of Warm Climates*, ed. Andrew Davidson (1893), pp. 25–80.

—— and R. H. Firth, *The Theory and Practice of Hygiene* (1896).

Orwell, George, *Burmese Days* (1st pub. 1934), (1989).

Parbury, George, *Handbook for India and Egypt. Comprising the narrative of a journey from Calcutta to England*, 2nd edn (1842).

Parkes, E. A., *A Manual of Practical Hygiene*, 8th edn (1891).

Parks, Fanny, *Wanderings of a Pilgrim in Search of the Picturesque, during four-and-twenty years in the East* (2 vols, 1850).

Pearce, Bill Chaning, *Indian Copper. Adventures of an Indian Police-man* (Lewes, 1990).

Perrin, Alice, *The Anglo-Indians* (London, 1912).

Pike, L. Owen, 'On the physical characteristics of the English peo-ple', in *Memoirs of the Anthropological Society of London*, vol. II (1865–6), pp. 153–88.

Postans, T., *Hints to Cadets, with a few observations on the military service of the Honourable East India Company* (1842).

Quennell, Peter (ed.), *Memoirs of William Hickey* (1960).

Rankine, Robert, *Notes on the Medical Topography of the District of Sarun* (Calcutta, 1839).

Reece, Richard, *The Medical Companion for Visitors to the East and West Indies, the Coast of Africa, and Different Countries on the Continent* (1817).

——, *The Medical Guide, for the use of the Clergy, heads of families, and seminaries, and junior practitioners in medicine*, 15th edn (1828).

Rees, L. E. Ruutz, *A Personal Narrative of the Siege of Lucknow from its Commencement to its Relief by Sir Colin Campbell* (1858).

Rivett-Carnac, J. H., *Many Memories of Life in India, at Home and Abroad* (1910).

Roberts, Emma, *Scenes and Characteristics of Hindoostan, with sketches of Anglo-Indian society*, 2nd edn (2 vols, 1837).

——, *The East India Voyager, or, the outward bound* (1845).

Ross, Sir E. Denison, *Both Ends of the Candle. The autobiography of Sir E. Denison Ross* (n.d.).

Sanyal, Ram Gopal (ed.), *Record of Criminal Cases as Between Europeans and Natives for the Last Sixty Years* (Calcutta, 1893).

Savory, Isabel, *A Sportswoman in India. Personal adventures and experiences of travel in known and unknown India* (1900).

Scott, Paul, *The Raj Quartet* (1st pub. 1966–75), (1997).

Shadwell, L. J., *Notes on the Internal Economy of Chummery, Home, Mess and Club* (Bombay, 1904).

Sherwood, Mary Martha, *The History of Little Henry and his Bearer*, 2nd edn (1815).

——, *The History of Little Lucy and her Dhaye*, 2nd edn (1825).

Shore, Frederick John, *Notes on Indian Affairs* (2 vols, 1837).

Simpson, W. J., *The Maintenance of Health in the Tropics* (1905).

Sketches and Scenes in India (Calcutta, 1851).

Sleeman, W. H., *Rambles and Recollections of an Indian Official*, 2nd edn (2 vols, 1863).

Smith, W. H. Samurez, *A Young Man's Country. Letters of a Subdivisional Officer of the Indian Civil Service 1936–1937* (1977).

Solomon, Alexander, *The Indian Family Doctor* (Calcutta, 1878).

Spry, Henry H., *Modern India* (2 vols, 1837).

Steel, Flora Annie, *On the Face of the Waters* (8 vols, 1897).

——, *The Garden of Fidelity, being the autobiography of Flora Annie Steel, 1847–1929* (1929).

—— and G. Gardiner, *The Complete Indian Housekeeper and Cook* (3rd edn, 1898).

Stocqueler, J. H., *The Hand-book of India, a guide to the stranger and the traveller, and a companion to the resident* (1844).

[Stuart, Charles], *The Ladies' Monitor, being a series of letters first published in Bengal on the subject of female apparel, tending to favour a regulated adoption of Indian costume; and a rejection of superfluous vesture by the ladies of this country* (1809).

Tayler, William, *Sketches Illustrating the Manners and Customs of the Indians and Anglo-Indians* (1842).

Taylor, Meadows, *Seeta* (3 vols, 1872).

Tennant, William, *Indian Recreations*, 2nd edn (2 vols, 1804).

Thackeray, William M., *Vanity Fair* (1st pub. 1847), (1992).

——, *The Newcomes* (1st pub. 1853–5), (1996).

Thornhill, Mark, *The Personal Adventures and Experiences of a Magistrate during the rise, progress and suppression of the Indian Mutiny* (1884).

Trevelyan, G. O., *The Competition Wallah* (1864).

Tyacke, Mrs R. T., *How I Shot My Bears; or, two years' tent life in Kullu and Lahoul* (1893).

Tytler, Harriet, *An Englishwoman in India. The memoirs of Harriet Tytler, 1828–1858*, ed. Anthony Sattin (Oxford, 1986).

Valentia, Viscount George, *Voyages and Travels to India, Ceylon, the Red Sea and Egypt, in the Years 1802, 1803, 1804, 1805 and 1806* (3 vols, 1809).

Vansittart, Jane, *From Minnie with Love. The letters of a Victorian lady, 1849–1861* (1974).

Vogt, Carl, *Lectures on Man: his place in creation, and in the history of the earth* (1864).

Wakefield, Edward, *Past Imperative. My Life in India 1927–47* (1966).

Wallace, James, *A Voyage to India* (1824).

Webb, W. T., *English Etiquette for Indian Gentlemen*, 5th edn (Calcutta, 1915).

What to Tell the Cook; or the Native Cook's Assistant; being a choice collection of receipts for Indian cookery, 2nd edn (Madras, 1875).

Williamson, Thomas, *The East India Vade-Mecum; or complete guide to gentlemen intended for the Civil, Military or Naval Service of the Honourable East India Company* (2 vols, 1810).

Wilson, Anne C., *After Five Years in India or; life and work in a Punjaub district* (1895).

——, *Hints for the First Years of Residence in India* (Oxford, 1904).

Woolf, Leonard, *An Autobiography* (1st pub. 1960), (Oxford, 1980).

Wyvern, (pseud.), *Culinary Jottings. A treatise on reformed cookery for Anglo-Indian exiles*, 5th edn (Madras, 1885).

Yule, Henry and A. C. Burnell, *Hobson-Jobson. A glossary of colloquial Anglo-Indian words and phrases, and of kindred terms, etymological, historical, geographical and discursive* (1903).

II   Secondary sources

All books published in London unless otherwise stated.

Allen, Charles, *Raj: A Scrapbook of British India 1877–1947* (Harmondsworth, 1979).

——, *Plain Tales from the Raj: Images of British India in the twentieth century* (1994).

Anderson, Benedict, *Imagined Communities. Reflections on the origin and spread of nationalism*, rev. edn (1991).

Anderson, David and Richard Grove (eds), *Conservation in Africa, People, Policies and Practice* (Cambridge, 1987).

Anderson, Warwick, 'Climates of opinion: acclimatisation in nineteenth-century France and England', *Victorian Studies*, 35, 2 (1992), pp. 135–58.

Archer, Mildred, *India and British Portraiture, 1770–1825* (1979).

——, *Company Paintings. Indian paintings of the British period* (1992).

—— and Toby Falk, *India Revealed. The art and adventures of James and William Fraser 1801–35* (1989).

Arnold, David, *Colonizing the Body. State medicine and epidemic disease in nineteenth-century India* (1993).

——, 'European orphans and vagrants in India in the nineteenth century', *The Journal of Imperial and Commonwealth History*, 7, 2 (1979), pp. 104–27.

Attar, Dena, *A Bibliography of Household Books Published in Britain 1800–1914* (1987).

Backscheider, Paula R. and Douglas Howard (eds), *The Plays of Samuel Foote* (3 vols, New York, 1983).

Ballhatchet, K., *Race, Sex and Class Under the Raj: Imperial attitudes and policies and their critics, 1793–1905* (1980).

Barley, M. W., *The House and Home* (1963).

Barr, Pat, *The Dust in the Balance. British Women in India 1905–1945* (1989).

—— and Desmond Ray, *Simla, a Hill Station in British India* (1978).

Barrell, John, *The Infection of Thomas De Quincey: A psychopathology of imperialism* (New Haven, 1991).

Barthes, R., 'Toward a psychology of contemporary food consumption', in *Food and Drink in History: Selections from the Annales, Economies and Sociétés, Civilisations*, eds Robert Forster and Orest Ranum (Baltimore, 1979), pp. 166–73.

Bates, Crispin, 'Race, caste and tribe in central India: the early origins of Indian anthropometry', in *The Concept of Race in South Asia*, ed. Peter Robb (Delhi, 1995), pp. 219–59.

Battye, Evelyn, *Costumes and Characters of the British Raj* (Exeter, 1982).

Bayly, C. A., *The Local Roots of Indian Politics. Allahabad 1880–1920* (Oxford, 1975).

——, 'The origins of swadeshi (home industry): cloth and Indian society, 1700–1930', in *The Social Life of Things. Commodities in cultural perspective*, ed. A. Appadurai (Cambridge, 1986), pp. 285–321.

——, *Indian Society and the Making of the British Empire* (Cambridge, 1990).

——, (ed.), *The Raj. India and the British 1600–1947* (1990).

——, 'Eric Thomas Stokes 1924–1981', *Proceedings of the British Academy* (1997), pp. 467–98.

Bayly, Susan, 'Caste and "race" in the colonial ethnography of India', in *The Concept of Race in South Asia*, ed. Peter Robb (Delhi, 1995), pp. 165–218.

Bell, Catherine, *Ritual Theory, Ritual Practice* (Oxford, 1992).

Bennett, Scott, 'Shikar and the Raj', *South Asia*, 7, 2 (1984), pp. 72–88.

Benthal, J. and Ted Polhemus (eds), *The Body as a Medium of Expression* (1975).

Berg, Maxine, 'Manufacturing the Orient: Asian commodities and European industry 1500–1800', *Istituto Internazionale di Storia Economica 'F. Datini'*, 29 (1997), pp. 385–419.

Berridge, Virginia and Griffith Edwards, *Opium and the People: opiate use in nineteenth century England* (1981).

Berthelot, J., 'Sociological discourse and the body', *Theory, Culture and Society*, 3, 3 (1986), pp. 155–64.

Bhabha, Homi K., *The Location of Culture* (1994).

Bhattacharya, Nandini, *Reading the Splendid Body. Gender and consumerism in eighteenth-century British writing on India* (1998).

Bhattacharya, Sanjoy, 'An unjustly forgotten facet of the Second World War? The Allied army in India', *International Institute for Asian Studies Newsletter*, 11 (1997), p. 15.

——, 'Wartime policies of state censorship and the civilian population: Eastern India, 1939–45', *South Asia Research*, 17, 2 (1997), pp. 140–77.

Bitting, A. W., *Appertizing; or the art of canning; its history and development* (San Francisco, 1937).

Blacking, John (ed.), *The Anthropology of the Body* (1977).

Bogner, Artur, 'The structure of social processes. A commentary on the sociology of Norbert Elias', *Sociology*, 20 (1986), pp. 387–411.

Bourdieu, Pierre, 'Sport and social class', *Social Science Information*, 17, 6 (1978), pp. 819–40.

——, *The Logic of Practice* (1st pub. 1980), (Cambridge, 1990).

Bradley, Ian, *The Call to Seriousness. The evangelical impact on the Victorians* (1976).

Bristow, Edward J., *Vice and Vigilance. Purity movements in Britain since 1700* (1977).

Brodie, Fawn M., *The Devil Drives. A life of Sir Richard Burton* (1967).

Brown, Judith M., *Modern India. The origins of Asian democracy*, The Short Oxford History of the Modern World, 3rd edn (Oxford, 1988).

Budd, Michael Anton, *The Sculpture Machine. Physical culture and body politics in the age of empire* (1997).

Burke, Peter (ed.), *Critical Essays on Michel Foucault* (Aldershot, 1992).

Burnett, J., *Plenty and Want: A social history of diet in England from 1815 to the present day* (1966).

——, *A Social History of Housing 1815–1970* (1978).

——, *Liquid Pleasures. A social history of drinks in modern Britain* (1999).

Burton, Antoinette, *Burdens of History. British Feminists, Indian Women, and Imperial Culture, 1865–1915* (1994).

Burton, David, *The Raj at Table. A culinary history of the British in India* (1993).

Bush, M. L. (ed.), *Social Outlook and Social Classes in Europe since 1500. Studies in social stratification* (1992).

Bushman, Richard L. and Claudia L. Bushman, 'The early history of cleanliness in America', *The Journal of American History*, 74, 4 (1988), pp. 1213–38.

Butcher, John G., *The British in Malaya 1880–1941. The social history of a European community in colonial South-East Asia* (Oxford, 1979).

Butler, Iris, *The Eldest Brother. The Marquess of Wellesley, the Duke of Wellington's eldest brother* (1973).

Bynum, W. F. and Roy Porter (eds), *Fringe and Medical Orthodoxy, 1750–1850* (1987).

Byrde, Penelope, *The Male Image. Men's fashion in Britain 1300–1970* (1979).

Cannadine, David, *The Decline and Fall of the British Aristocracy* (1990).

——, *Aspects of Aristocracy: Grandeur and decline in modern Britain* (1994).

——, 'The context, performance and meaning of ritual: the British monarchy and the "invention of tradition", c.1820–1977', in *The Invention of Tradition*, eds Eric Hobsbawm and Terence Ranger, 2nd edn (Cambridge, 1996), pp. 101–64.

——, *Class in Britain* (1998).

Castle, Terry, *Masquerade and Civilisation. The carnivalesque in eighteenth-century English culture and fiction* (1986).

Chandavakar, Rajnarayan, 'Plague, panic and epidemic politics in India, 1896–1914', in *Epidemics and Ideas. Essays on the historical perception of pestilence*, eds Terence Ranger and Paul Slack (Cambridge, 1992), pp. 203–40.

Chatterjee, Indrani, *Gender, Slavery and Law in Colonial India* (New Delhi, 1999).

Chaudhary, V. C. P., *Imperial Honeymoon with Indian Aristocracy* (Patna, 1980).

Chaudhuri, Nupur, 'Memsahibs and motherhood in nineteenth-century colonial India', *Victorian Studies*, 31, 4 (1988), pp. 517–36.

Codell, Julie F. and Dianne Sachko Macleod (eds), *Orientalism Transposed. The impact of the colonies on British culture* (Aldershot, 1998).

Coetzee, J. M., *White Writing. On the culture of letters in South Africa* (1988).

Cohn, B. S, 'The British in Benares: a nineteenth-century colonial society', *Comparative Studies in Society and History*, 4 (1962), pp. 169–208.

——, 'Recruitment and training of British civil servants in India, 1600–1800', in *Asian Bureaucratic Systems Emergent from the British Imperial Tradition*, ed. R. Braibanti (Durham, NC, 1966), pp. 87–140.

——, 'The command of language and the language of command', in *Subaltern Studies IV. Writings on South Asian history and society*, ed. R. Guha (Oxford, 1985), pp. 276–329.

——, 'Cloth, clothes and colonialism: India in the nineteenth century', in *Cloth and Human Experience*, eds A. Weiner and J. Schneider (Washington, DC, 1989), pp. 303–53.

——, 'Representing authority in Victorian India', in *The Invention of Tradition*, eds Eric Hobsbawm and Terence Ranger, 2nd edn (Cambridge 1996), pp. 165–210.

Colley, Linda, *Britons. Forging the nation 1707–1837* (1994).

Compton, J. M., 'Open competition and the ICS, 1854–1876', *English Historical Review*, 83 (1968), pp. 265–84.

Cooter, Roger, 'The power of the body: the early nineteenth-century', in *Natural Order. Historical studies of scientific culture*, eds Barry Barnes and Steven Shapin (1979).

Corbin, Alain, *The Foul and the Fragrant. Odour and the French social imagination* (Leamington Spa, 1986).

Cotton, Julian James, 'George Beechey and his Indian wife', *Bengal Past and Present*, 24, 1 (1922), pp. 49–52.

Cowling, Mary, *The Artist as Anthropologist. The representation of type and character in Victorian art* (Cambridge, 1989).

Crawford, D. G., *A History of the Indian Medical Service 1600–1913* (2 vols, 1914).

Cunningham, H., 'Leisure and culture', in *The Cambridge Social History of Britain 1750–1950. Vol. 2. People and their environment*, ed. F. M. L. Thompson (Cambridge, 1990), pp. 279–339.

Curtin, Philip D., *Death by Migration: Europe's encounter with the tropical world in the nineteenth century* (Cambridge, 1989).

Damodaran, *Broken Promises. Popular protest, Indian nationalism and the Congress Party in Bihar, 1935–1946* (Delhi, 1992).

Darnton, Robert, *The Great Cat Massacre and Other Episodes in French Cultural History* (1984).

Davidoff, Leonore and Catherine Hall, 'The architecture of public and private life. English middle-class society in a provincial town 1780 to 1850', in *The Pursuit of Urban History*, eds Derek Fraser and Anthony Sutcliffe (1983), pp. 326–45.

——, *Family Fortunes. Men and women of the English middle class 1780–1850* (1988).

Dawson, Graham, 'The imperial adventure hero and British masculinity: the imagining of Sir Henry Havelock', in *Gender and Colonialism*, eds Timothy Foley, Lionel Pilkington, Sean Ryder and Elizabeth Tilley (Galway, 1995), pp. 46–59.

Dewey, Clive, 'The Education of a Ruling Caste: the ICS in the era of the competitive examination', *English Historical Review*, 88 (1973), pp. 262–85.

——, *Anglo-Indian Attitudes. The mind of the Indian civil service* (1993).

Dilks, David, *Curzon in India* (2 vols, 1969).

Dirks, N. B., 'Castes of mind', *Representations*, 37 (1992), pp. 56–78.

Dixon, Roger and Stefan Muthesius, *Victorian Architecture* (1st pub. 1978), (1993).

Dodwell, Henry, *The Nabobs of Madras* (1926).

Douglas, Mary, 'Deciphering a meal', in *Implicit Meanings. Essays in anthropology*, Mary Douglas (1975), pp. 249–75.

——, 'Do dogs laugh? A cross-cultural approach to body symbolism', in *Implicit Meanings. Essays in anthropology*, Mary Douglas (1975), pp. 83–9.

——, *Purity and Danger: an analysis of the concepts of pollution and taboo* (1st pub. 1966), (1984).

——, *Natural Symbols. Explorations in cosmology*, 3rd edn (1996).

Duden, Barbara, *The Woman Beneath the Skin. A doctor's patients in eighteenth-century Germany* (1st pub. 1987), (1991).

Duerr, Hans Peter, *Der Mythos vom Zivilisationsprozeß* (2 vols, Frankfurt am Main, 1988).

Dyson, K. K., *A Various Universe. A study of the journals and memoirs of British men and women in the Indian subcontinent, 1765–1856* (Oxford, 1978).

Edwardes, Michael, *High Noon of Empire* (1965).

——, *Bound to Exile: The Victorians in India* (1970).

——, *Warren Hastings. King of the nabobs* (1976).

——, *The Nabobs at Home* (1991).

Elias, Norbert, *The Civilizing Process. The history of manners and state formation and civilisation* (1st pub. 1939), (Oxford, 1982).

Ernst, Waltraud, *Mad Tales from the Raj. The European insane in British India, 1800–1858*, The Wellcome Institute Series in the History of Medicine (1991).

Ewing, Elizabeth, *Dress and Undress. A history of women's underwear* (London, 1978).

Exotic Europeans, Exhibition Catalogue, South Bank Centre (1991).

Featherstone, Mike, 'The body in consumer culture', *Theory, Culture and Society*, 1, 2 (1982), pp. 12–34.

——, 'Norbert Elias and figurational sociology: some prefatory remarks', *Theory, Culture and Society*, 4 (1987), pp. 197–212.

Feiling, K., *Warren Hastings* (1954).

Fildes, Valerie A., *Breasts, Bottles and Babies. A history of infant feeding* (Edinburgh, 1986).

——, *Wet Nursing. A History from Antiquity to the present* (Oxford, 1988).

Finch, Casey, '"Hooked and buttoned together": Victorian underwear and representations of the female body', *Victorian Studies*, 34, 3 (1991), pp. 337–63.

Fisch, Jörg, 'A solitary vindicator of the Hindus: the life and writings of General Charles Stuart (1757/58–1828)', *Journal of the Royal Asiatic Society*, 4, 2–3 (1985), pp. 35–57.

Fisher, Michael H., 'The imperial coronation of 1819: Awadh, the British and the Mughals', *Modern Asian Studies*, 14, 2 (1985), pp. 239–77.

——, 'The Resident in court ritual, 1764–1858', *Modern Asian Studies*, 24, 3 (1990), pp. 419–58.

——, *The First Indian Author in English. Dean Mahomed (1759–1851) in India, Ireland and England* (Delhi, 1996).

Foley, Timothy, Lionel Pilkington, Sean Ryder and Elizabeth Tilley (eds), *Gender and Colonialism* (Galway, 1995).

Fontaine, Stanislas, 'The civilising process revisited: interview with Norbert Elias', *Theory and Society*, 5, 2 (1978), pp. 243–53.

Foucault, Michel, *Discipline and Punish. The birth of the prison* (Harmondsworth, 1977).

——, *The History of Sexuality* (3 vols, Harmondsworth, 1990).

Fowler, Marian, *Redney. A life of Sara Jeanette Duncan* (1983).

Frank, A. W., 'Bringing bodies back in: a decade review', *Theory Culture and Society*, 7, 1 (1990), pp. 131–62.

——, 'For a sociology of the body: an analytical review', in *The Body: social process and cultural theory*, eds Mike Featherstone, Mike Hepworth and Bryan S. Turner (1991).

Fraser, Derek and Anthony Sutcliffe, *The Pursuit of Urban History* (1983).

French, Patrick, *Liberty or Death. India's Journey to Independence and Division* (1997).

Frey, Manuel, *Der reinliche Bürger. Entstehung und Verbreitung bürgerlicher Tugenden in Deutschland, 1760–1860*, Kritische Studien zur Geschichtswissenschaft, Vol. 119 (Göttingen, 1997).

Gartrell, Beverley, 'Colonial wives: villains or victims?', in *The Incorporated Wife*, eds Hilary Callan and Shirley Ardener (1984), pp. 165–85.

Gatrell, V. A. C., 'The decline of theft and violence in Victorian and Edwardian England', in *Crime and the Law. The social history of crime in Western Europe since 1500*, eds V. A. C. Gatrell, Bruce Lenman and Geoffrey Parker, The Europa Social History of Human Experience (1980), pp. 238–338.

Gay, Peter, *The Cultivation of Hatred. The bourgeois experience: Victoria to Freud* (1995).

Gerard, Jessica, *Country House Life. Family and servants, 1815–1914* (Oxford, 1994).

Gilmour, David, *Curzon* (1994).

Girouard, Mark, *The Victorian Country House* (New Haven, 1979).

Goffman, Erving, *The Presentation of Self in Everyday Life* (Harmondsworth, 1969).

Goodman, Jordan, *Tobacco in History. The cultures of dependence* (1993).

Gowan, Peter, 'The origins of the administrative elite', *New Left Review* 162 (1987), pp. 4–34.

Greenberger, A., *The British Image of India. A study of the literature of imperialism 1880–1960* (1969).

Haley, Bruce, *The Healthy Body and Victorian Culture* (Cambridge, Mass., 1978).

Hansen, Karen Tranberg, *Distant Companions. Servants and employers in Zambia, 1900–1985* (1989).

Harkar, R., C. Mahar and C. Wilkes (eds), *An Introduction to the Work of Pierre Bourdieu: The practice of theory* (1990).

Harris, Jose, *Private Lives, Public Spirit: Britain 1870–1914* (1st pub. 1993), The Penguin Social History of Britain (Harmondsworth, 1994).

Harrison, J. B., 'Allahabad: a sanitary history', in *The City in South Asia. Pre-modern and modern*, eds K. Ballhatchet and John Harrison (1980), pp. 167–96.

Harrison, Mark, *Public Health in British India: Anglo-Indian preventive medicine 1859–1914* (Cambridge, 1994).

Harrison, Mark, *Climates and Constitutions. Health, race, environment and British Imperialism in India 1600–1850* (New Delhi, 1999).

Harvey, John, *Men in Black* (1995).

Hawes, Christopher J., *Poor Relations. The making of a Eurasian community in British India 1773–1833* (Richmond, 1996).

Haynes, Douglas, 'Imperial ritual in a local setting: the ceremonial order in Surat, 1890–1939', *Modern Asian Studies*, 24, 3 (1990), pp. 493–527.

——, *Rhetoric and Ritual in Colonial India. The shaping of a public culture in Surat City, 1852–1928* (Berkeley, Calif. 1991).

Headrick, Daniel R., *The Tools of Empire. Technology and European imperialism in the nineteenth century* (Oxford, 1981).

Hibbert, Christopher, *The Great Mutiny. India 1857* (Harmondsworth, 1980).

Hobsbawm, Eric, *The Age of Empire 1875–1914* (1987).

—— and Terence Ranger (eds), *The Invention of Tradition*, 2nd edn (Cambridge, 1996).

Hockings, Paul, 'British society in the Company, Crown and Congress Eras', in *Blue Mountains. The ethnography and biogeography of a South Indian region*, ed. Paul Hockings (New Delhi, 1989), pp. 360–76.

—— (ed.), *Blue Mountains. The ethnography and biogeography of a South Indian region* (New Delhi, 1989).

Honneth, Axel, Hermann Kocyba and Bernd Schwibs, 'The struggle for symbolic order. An interview with Pierre Bourdieu', *Theory, Culture and Society*, 3, 3 (1986), pp. 35–51.

Horn, Pamela, *The Rise and Fall of the Victorian Servant*, 2nd edn (Gloucester, 1986).

Humphrey, Caroline and James Laidlow, *The Archetypal Actions of Ritual. A theory of ritual illustrated by the Jain rite of worship* (Oxford, 1994).

Hunt, Lynn, 'French history in the last twenty years: the rise and fall of the Annales paradigm', *Journal of Contemporary History*, 21, 2 (1986), pp. 209–24.

Hunt, Roland and John Harrison, *The District Officer in India 1930–1947*, 2nd edn (1982).

Hutton, Patrick H., 'The history of mentalities: the new map of cultural history', *History and Theory* 20 (1981), pp. 237–57.

Hyam, Ronald, *Empire and Sexuality. The British experience*, 2nd edn (Manchester, 1992).

Inden, Ronald, *Imagining India* (Oxford, 1990).

Irschick, Eugene F., *Dialogue and History. Constructing South India, 1795–1895* (Berkeley, Calif., 1994).

Isaac, Rhys, *The Transformation of Virginia 1740–1790* (1982).

James, Lawrence, *Raj. The making and unmaking of British India* (1997).

Jones, Colin and Roy Porter (eds), *Reassessing Foucault. Power, medicine and the body* (1994).

Jones, Greta, *Social Darwinism and English Thought. The interaction between biological and social theory* (Brighton, 1980).

Kanwar, Pamela, *Imperial Simla. The political culture of the Raj* (Delhi, 1990).

Kennedy, Dane, 'Climatic theories and culture in colonial Kenya and Rhodesia', *The Journal of Imperial and Commonwealth History*, 10, 1 (1981), pp. 50–66.

——, *Islands of White. Settler society and culture in Kenya and Southern Rhodesia, 1890–1939* (Durham, NC, 1987).

——, 'The perils of the midday sun: climatic anxieties in the colonial tropics', in *Imperialism and the Natural World*, ed. John MacKenzie Studies in Imperialism (Manchester, 1990), pp. 115–40.

——, *The Magic Mountains. Hill stations and the British Raj* (1996).

Khilnani, Sunil, 'A bodily drama', *The Times Literary Supplement* (8 August 1997), p. 6.

Kidwell, Claudia Brush and Valerie Steel, *Men and Women: dressing the part* (Washington, DC, 1989).

King, A. D., *Colonial Urban Development. Culture, social power and environment* (1976).

Knapman, Claudia, *White Women in Fiji 1835–1930. The ruin of Empire?* (1986).

Krieken, van, Robert, 'Violence, self-discipline and modernity: beyond the "civilising process"', *Sociological Review*, 37, 2 (1989), pp. 193–218.

Kuzmics, Helmut, 'Civilization, state and bourgeois society: the theoretical contribution of Norbert Elias', *Theory, Culture and Society*, 4, 2–3 (1987), pp. 515–37.

Lambert, Angela, *Unquiet Souls. The Indian summer of the British aristocracy, 1880–1918* (1984).

Leask, Nigel, *British Romantic Writers and the East. Anxieties of empire* (Cambridge, 1992).

Leppert, R., *The Sight of Sound. Music, representation and the history of the body* (Berkeley, Calif., 1993).

Lewis, Judith Schneid, *In the Family Way. Childbearing in the British aristocracy, 1760–1860* (New Brunswick, NJ, 1986).

Livingstone, David N., 'Human acclimatisation: perspectives on a contested field of inquiry in science, medicine, and geography', *History of Science*, 25, 4 (1987), pp. 359–94.

Lock, Margaret, 'Cultivating the body: anthropology and epistemologies of bodily practice and knowledge', *Annual Review of Anthropology*, 22 (1993), pp. 133–55.

Long, James, 'A peep into the social life of Calcutta during the second half of the eighteenth century', in *British Social Life in Ancient Calcutta (1750–1850)*, ed. P. Thankappan Nair (Calcutta, 1983), pp. 12–43.

Lorimer, Douglas A., *Colour, Class and the Victorians. English attitudes to the Negro in the mid-nineteenth century* (1978).

Losty, J. P., *Calcutta. City of palaces. A survey of the city in the days of the East India Company, 1690–1858* (1990).

Low, D. A., *Lion Rampant. Essays in the study of British imperialism* (London, 1973).

Lutyens, Mary, *The Lyttons in India. An account of Lord Lytton's viceroyalty 1876–1880* (1979).

MacDougall, Hugh A., *Racial Myth in English History. Trojans, Teutons, and Anglo-Saxons* (1982).

MacKenzie, John, 'Chivalry, social Darwinism and ritualised killing: the hunting ethos in Central Africa up to 1914', in *Conservation in Africa, People, Policies and Practice*, eds David Anderson and Richard Grove (Cambridge, 1987), pp. 41–62.

——, *The Empire of Nature. Hunting conservation and British imperialism* (Manchester, 1988).

——,'Essay and reflection: on Scotland and the empire', *The International History Review*, 15, 4 (1993), pp. 714–39.

McKenzie, Ray, '"The laboratory of mankind": John McCosh and the beginning of photography in British India', *History of Photography*, 11, 2 (1987), pp. 109–18.

Macleod, Dianne Sachko, 'Cross-cultural cross-dressing: class, gender and modernist sexual identity', in *Orientalism Transposed. The impact of the colonies on British culture*, eds Julie F. Codell and Dianne Sachko Macleod (Aldershot, 1998), pp. 63–85.

McNay, Lois, *Foucault. A Critical Introduction* (Cambridge, 1994).

Mahar, Cheleen, Richard Harker and Chris Wilkes (eds), *An Introduction to the Work of Pierre Bourdieu. The practice of theory* (1990).

——, 'The basic theoretical position', in *An Introduction to the Work of Pierre Bourdieu. The practice of theory*, eds Cheleen Mahar, Richard Harker and Chris Wilkes (1990), pp. 1–25.

Majeed, Javeed, *Ungoverned Imaginings. James Mill's 'The History of British India' and orientalism* (Oxford, 1992).

Mangan, James A., *Athleticism in the Victorian and Edwardian Public School. The emergence and consolidation of an educational ideology* (Cambridge, 1981).

Mansergh, Nicholas (ed.), *The Transfer of Power 1942–7* (12 vols, 1977).

Marshall, P. J. (ed.), *The Writings and Speeches of Edmund Burke. Vol. VI. India: the launching of the Hastings impeachment, 1786–1788* (Oxford, 1991).

——, 'The private fortune of Marian Hastings', in *Trade and Conquest. Studies in the rise of British dominance in India*, Peter Marshall (Aldershot, 1993), pp. 245–53.

——, 'Imperial Britain', in *The Cambridge Illustrated History of the British Empire*, ed. P. J. Marshall (1996), pp. 318–37.

—— and Glyndwr Williams, *The Great Map of Mankind: British perceptions of the world in the Age of Enlightenment* (1982).

Masani, Zareer, *Indian Tales of the Raj* (1987).

Mason, Michael, *The Making of Victorian Sexuality* (Oxford, 1994).

——, *The Making of Victorian Sexual Attitudes* (Oxford, 1994).

Mauss, Marcel, 'Body techniques', in *Sociology and Psychology. Essays*, Marcel Mauss (1979), pp. 95–123.

Mayer, Peter, 'Inventing village tradition: the late nineteenth century origins of the jajmani system', *Modern Asian Studies*, 27, 2 (1993), pp. 357–95.

Maynard, Margaret, *Fashioned from Penury. Dress as cultural practice in colonial Australia* (Cambridge, 1994).

Mendilow, Jonathon, 'Merrie England and the brave new world: two myths of the idea of empire', *History of European Ideas*, 6, 1 (1985), pp. 41–58.

Metcalf, Thomas R., *The Aftermath of Revolt. India 1857–1870* (1965).

——, *Ideologies of the Raj*. The New Cambridge History of India, vol. III, no. 4 (Cambridge, 1994).

Miller, Max, 'Systematisch verzerrte Legitimationsdiskurse. Einige kritische Überlegungen zu Bourdieus Habitustheorie', in *Klas-*

senlage, Lebensstil und kulturelle Praxis. Beiträge zur Auseinandersetzung mit Pierre Bourdieus Klassentheorie, ed. Klaus Eder (Frankfurt am Main, 1989), pp. 191–219.

Milligan, Barry, *Pleasures and Pains. Opium and the orient in nineteenth-century British culture* (1995).

Misra, B. B., *The Bureaucracy in India. An historical analysis of development up to 1947* (Delhi, 1977).

Misra, Maria, *Business, Race and Politics in British India c.1850–1960* (Oxford, 1999).

Mollo, Boris, *The Indian Army* (Poole, 1981).

Morgan, Marjorie, *Manners, Morals and Class in England, 1774–1858* (1994).

Mosse, George L., *Nationalism and Sexuality. Respectability and abnormal sexuality in modern Europe* (New York, 1985).

Mukherjee, Rudrangsh, '"Satan let loose upon the Earth": the Kanpur massacres in India in the revolt of 1857', *Past and Present*, 128 (1990), pp. 92–116.

Naidis, Mark, 'Evolution of the sahib', *The Historian*, 19, 4 (1957), pp. 425–35.

Neill, Stephen, *A History of Christianity in India 1707–1858* (Cambridge, 1985).

Newby, Howard, *The Deferential Worker. A study of farm workers in East Anglia* (1977).

Nilsson, Sten, *European Architecture in India 1750–1850* (1968).

Nistroj, Brigitte H. E., 'Norbert Elias: a milestone in historical pyscho-sociology. The making of the social person', *Journal of Historical Sociology*, 2, 2 (1989), pp. 136–60.

Nuckolls, Charles W., 'The durbar incident', *Modern Asian Studies*, 24, 3 (1990), pp. 529–59.

O'Neill, John, *Five Bodies: The human shape of modern society* (Ithaca, NY, 1985).

Ortiz, Fernando, *Cuban Counterpoint: Tobacco and sugar* (New York, 1947).

Outram, Dorinda, *The Body in the French Revolution. Sex, class and political culture* (1989).

Pandian, M. S. S., 'Gendered negotiations: hunting and colonialism in the late nineteenth century Nilgiris', *Contributions to Indian Sociology*, 29, 1–2 (1995), pp. 239–63.

Parry, Benita, *Delusions and Discoveries: Studies on India in the British imagination 1880–1930* (1972).

Patterson, T. J. S., 'The medical practice of the East India Company', *The Society for the Social History of Medicine Bulletin*, 26 (1980), pp. 40–3.

Paxton, Nancy L., 'Mobilising chivalry: rape in British novels about the Indian uprising of 1857', *Victorian Studies*, 36, 1 (1992), pp. 5–30.

Peabody, Norbert, 'Tod's *Rajast'han* and the boundaries of imperial rule in nineteenth-century India', *Modern Asian Studies*, 30, 1 (1996), pp. 185–220.

Perrot, Phillippe, *Fashioning the Bourgeoisie. A history of clothing in the nineteenth century* (Princeton, NJ, 1994).

Pfeiffer, Carl J., *The Art and Practice of Western Medicine in the Early Nineteenth Century* (1985).

Philips, C. H. (ed.), *The Correspondence of Lord William Cavendish Bentinck. Governor-General of India 1828–1835* (2 vols, Oxford, 1977).

Pick, Daniel, *Faces of Degeneration. A European disorder, c.1848–1918* (Cambridge, 1989).

Pinney, Christopher, 'Colonial anthropology in the "laboratory of mankind"', in *The Raj. India and the British 1600–1947*, ed. C. A. Bayly (1991) pp. 252–63.

Porter, Roy, 'The History of the Body', in *New Perspectives on Historical Writing*, ed. Peter Burke (Oxford, 1991), pp. 206–32.

——, 'Bodies of thought: thoughts about the body in eighteenth-century England', in *Interpretation and Cultural History*, eds. Joan H. Pittock and Andrew Wear (1991), pp. 84–100.

Pott, Janet, *Old Bungalows in Bangalore, South India* (1977).

Prior, Katherine, Robin Haines and Lance Brennan, 'Bad language: the role of English, Persian and other esoteric tongues in the dismissal of Sir Edward Colebrooke as Resident of Delhi in 1829', *Modern Asian Studies* 35, 1 (2001), pp. 75–112.

Raychaudhuri, Tapan, *Europe Reconsidered. Perceptions of the West in nineteenth century Bengal* (Delhi, 1988).

Razzell, P. E., 'Social origins of officers in the Indian and British Home Army: 1758–1962', *The British Journal of Sociology*, 14, 3 (1963), pp. 248–60.

Renbourne, E. T, 'The history of the flannel binder and cholera belt', *Medical History*, 1 (1957), pp. 211–25.

——, 'Life and death of the solar topi. A chapter in the history of sunstroke', *The Journal of Tropical Medicine and Hygiene*, 45, 7 (1962), pp. 203–18.

Renford, Raymond K., *The Non-Official British in India to 1920* (Delhi, 1987).

Ribeiro, Aileen, *The Dress Worn at Masquerades in England, 1730 to 1790, and its Relation to Fancy Dress in Portraiture* (1984).

——, *Fashion in the French Revolution* (1988).

Rich, Paul, *Race and Empire in British Politics*, 2nd edn (Cambridge, 1990).

Robb, Peter, (ed.), *The Concept of Race in South Asia* (Delhi, 1995).

Robbins, Bruce, *The Servant's Hand. English fiction from below* (New York, 1986).

Roberts, Ann, 'Mothers and babies: the wet-nurse and her employer in mid-nineteenth century England', *Women's Studies*, 3, 3 (1976), pp. 279–93.

Roberts, Michael, 'Noise as cultural struggle: tom-tom beating, the British, and communal disturbances in Sri Lanka, 1880s–1930s', in *Mirrors of Violence. Communities, riots and survivors in South Asia*, ed. Veena Das (Delhi, 1990), pp. 240–85.

Robinson, Jane, *Angels of Albion. Women of the Indian Mutiny* (1997).

Roche, Daniel, *The Culture of Clothing. Dress and fashion in the 'ancien régime'* (1st pub. 1989), (Cambridge, 1994).

Ross, Robert, *Status and Respectability in the Cape Colony, 1750–1870. A tragedy of manners* (Cambridge, 1999).

Rosselli, John, 'The self-image of effeteness: physical education and nationalism in nineteenth-century Bengal', *Past and Present*, 86 (1980), pp. 121–48.

Royle, Trevor, *The Last Days of the Raj* (1989).

Rubinstein, W. D., *Elites and the Wealthy in Modern British History. Essays in social and economic history* (Brighton, 1987).

Satow, Michael and Ray Desmond, *Railways of the Raj* (1980).

Schivelbusch, Wolfgang, *Das Paradies, der Geschmack und die Vernunft. Eine Geschichte der Genußmittel* (1st pub. 1980), (Frankfurt am Main, 1990).

Schumpeter, Joseph A., *Imperialism and Social Classes* (Oxford, 1951).

Scott, James C., *Weapons of the Weak. Everyday forms of peasant resistance* (1985).

——, *Domination and the Arts of Resistance. Hidden transcripts* (1990).

Searle, G. R., *The Quest for National Efficiency. A study in British politics and political thought, 1899–1914* (Oxford, 1971).

——, *Eugenics and Politics in Britain 1900–1914* (Leyden, 1976).

——, 'Eugenics and class', in *Biology, Medicine and Society 1840–1940*, ed. Charles Webster (Cambridge, 1981), pp. 217–42.

Sennett, Richard, *The Fall of Public Man* (New York, 1977).

Sharpe, Jenny, *Allegories of Empire. The figure of woman in the colonial text* (Minneapolis, Minn., 1993).

Shilling, C., *The Body and Social Theory* (1993).

Shrimpton, Jayne, 'Dressing for a tropical climate: the role of native fabrics in fashionable dress in early colonial India', *Textile History*, 23, 1 (1992), pp. 55–70.

Shumway, David R., *Michel Foucault* (Boston, Mass., 1989).

Sinha, M., *Colonial Masculinity. The 'manly Englishman' and the 'effeminate Bengali' in the late nineteenth century* (Manchester, 1995).

Smith, F. B., 'Sexuality in Britain, 1800–1900', *The University of Newcastle Historical Journal*, 2, 3 (1974), pp. 19–32.

Smith, Virginia, 'Physical puritanism and sanitary science: material and immaterial beliefs in popular physiology, 1650–1840', in *Fringe and Medical Orthodoxy, 1750–1850*, eds W. F. Bynum and Roy Porter (1987), pp. 174–97.

Snell, K. D. M., 'Deferential bitterness: the social outlook of the rural proletariat in eighteenth- and nineteenth-century England and Wales', in *Social Outlook and Social Classes in Europe since 1500. Studies in social stratification*, ed. M. L. Bush (1992), pp. 158–84.

Spear, P., *Twilight of the Mughals. Studies in late Mughal Delhi* (Cambridge, 1951).

——, *The Nabobs. A study of the social life of the English in eighteenth-century India*. (1st pub. 1932), (1980).

Stanford, J. K. (ed.), *Ladies in the Sun. The memsahib's India, 1790–1860* (1962).

Stocking, George W., *Victorian Anthropology* (1987).

Stokes, E., *The English Utilitarians and India* (New Delhi, 1989).

Stoler, Ann, 'Carnal knowledge and imperial power. Gender, race and morality in colonial Asia', in *Gender at the Crossroads of Knowledge. Feminist Anthropology in the Postmodern Era*, ed. Micaela di Leonardo (Berkeley, Calif., 1991), pp. 51–88.

Synnott, Anthony, *The Body Social. Symbolism, self and society* (1993).

Szreter, Simon, *Fertility, Class and Gender in Britain, 1860–1940* (Cambridge, 1996).

Tarlo, Emma, *Clothing Matters: Dress and Identity in India* (1996).

Taylor, A. J. P., *English History 1914–1945. The Oxford History of England* (1st pub. 1965), (Oxford, 1992).

Teltscher, Kate, *India Inscribed. European and British writing on India 1600–1800* (New Delhi, 1995).

Tholfsen, T. R., *Working Class Radicalism in Mid-Victorian England* (1976).

Thomas, Nicholas, *Colonialism's Culture. Anthropology, travel and government*. (Cambridge, 1994).

Thompson, E. P, 'Patrician society, plebeian culture', *Journal of Social History*, 7, 4 (1974), pp. 382–405.
——, *Customs in Common* (1991).
Thompson, F. M. L., *English Landed Society in the Nineteenth Century* (1963).
——, *The Rise of Respectable Society. A Social History of Victorian Britain, 1830–1900* (1988).
——(ed.), *The Cambridge Social History of Britain 1750–1950. Vol. 2. People and their environment* (Cambridge, 1990).
Thompson, J. B., *Studies in the Theory of Ideology* (Cambridge, 1984).
Tosh, John, 'Imperial masculinity and the flight from domesticity in Britain 1880–1914', in *Gender and Colonialism*, eds Timothy Foley, Lionel Pilkington, Sean Ryder and Elizabeth Tilley (Galway, 1995), pp. 72–85.
——, *A Man's Place. Masculinity and the Middle-Class Home in Victorian England* (1999).
Trevithick, Alan, 'Some structural and sequential aspects of the British imperial assemblages at Delhi: 1877–1911', *Modern Asian Studies*, 24, 3 (1990), pp. 561–78.
Trousdale, William (ed.), *War in Afghanistan, 1879–80. The personal diary of Major General Sir Charles Metcalfe MacGregor* (Detroit, Mich., 1985).
Turner, B. S., *The Body and Society. Explorations in social theory* (Oxford, 1984).
Turner, Terence, 'Review of *The Body and Society. Explorations in Social Theory* by Bryan S. Turner', *American Journal of Sociology*, 92, 1 (1986), pp. 211–13.
Vigarello, Georges, *Concepts of Cleanliness. Changing attitudes in France since the Middle Ages* (1st pub. 1985), (Cambridge, 1988).
Voigt, Johannes H., *India in the Second World War* (New Delhi, 1987).
Walkowitz, J. R., *Prostitution and Victorian Society: Women, class and the state* (Cambridge, 1980).
Washbrook, David, 'Economic depression and the making of "traditional" society in colonial India 1820–1855', *Transactions of the Royal Historical Society*, 3 (1993), pp. 237–63.
Weeks, Jeffrey, *Sex, Politics and Society. The regulation of sexuality since 1800*, 2nd edn (1981).
Weiner, A. and J. Schneider (eds), *Cloth and Human Experience* (Washington, DC, 1989).
Weintraub, Stanley, *Albert. Uncrowned King* (1997).

Whorton, James C., *Crusaders for Fitness. The history of American health reformers* (Princeton, NJ, 1982).

Wiener, Martin, *English Culture and the Decline of the Industrial Spirit 1850–1980* (Cambridge, 1981).

Wood, Anthony, *Nineteenth Century Britain: 1815–1914*, 2nd edn (Harlow, 1982).

Wright, Lawrence, *Clean and Decent. The fascinating history of the bathroom and the water closet and of sundry habits, fashions and accessories of the toilet principally in Great Britain, France, and America* (1960).

Wurgaft, Lewis D., *The Imperial Imagination. Magic and myth in Kipling's India* (Middletown, Conn., 1983).

Wuthnow, R., James Davison, Hunter Albert Bergesen and Edith Kurwel, *Cultural Analysis. The work of Peter L. Berger, Mary Douglas, Michel Foucault and Jürgen Habermas* (1984).

Yalland, Zoë, *Traders and Nabobs. The British in Cawnpore, 1765–1857* (Salisbury, 1987).

——, *Boxwallahs. The British in Cawnpore, 1857–1901* (Norwich, 1994).

Young, Arlene, 'Virtue domesticated: Dickens and the lower middle class', *Victorian Studies*, 39, 4 (1996), pp. 483–511.

Young, Robert J. C., *Colonial Desire. Hybridity in theory, culture and race* (1995).

Zastoupil, Lynn, *John Stuart Mill and India* (Stanford, Calif., 1994).

Ziegler, Philip, *Mountbatten. The official biography* (1985).

—— (ed.), *The Diaries of Lord Louis Mountbatten 1920–1922. Tours with the Prince of Wales* (1987).

III   Ph.D. theses

Alavi, Seema, 'North Indian military culture in transition *c*.1770–1830', University of Cambridge, 1991.

Datta, Damayanti, 'The Europeans of Calcutta, 1858–1883', University of Cambridge, 1995.

Grant, Charlotte, 'The visual culture of sensibility. Optics, the sentimental and the picturesque 1712–1788', University of Cambridge, 1995.

Raven, James R., 'English popular literature and the image of business 1760–1790', University of Cambridge, 1985.

Smith, Virginia, 'Cleanliness: idea and practice in Britain 1770–1850', University of London, 1985.

Index